Lewis Appleton

**Memoirs of Henry Richard**

The Apostle of Peace

Lewis Appleton

**Memoirs of Henry Richard**
*The Apostle of Peace*

ISBN/EAN: 9783743407640

Manufactured in Europe, USA, Canada, Australia, Japa

Cover: Foto ©ninafisch / pixelio.de

Manufactured and distributed by brebook publishing software (www.brebook.com)

Lewis Appleton

**Memoirs of Henry Richard**

# MEMOIRS

OF

# HENRY RICHARD,

## The Apostle of Peace.

BY

## LEWIS APPLETON, F.R.H.S.,

HONORARY SECRETARY OF THE BRITISH AND FOREIGN ARBITRATION ASSOCIATION
AUTHOR OF REMINISCENCES OF THE FRANCO-GERMAN WAR; FIFTY YEARS OF
FOREIGN POLICY; MILITARY AND FINANCIAL CONDITION OF EUROPE,
ETC., ETC.

LONDON:

TRÜBNER & CO., LUDGATE HILL.

1889.

HENRY RICHARD.

To the Right Honorable

# WILLIAM EWART GLADSTONE, M.P.;

WHOSE ENLIGHTENED STATESMANSHIP,

DURING HIS PREMIERSHIP OF THE GOVERNMENT OF ENGLAND,

POWERFULLY CONTRIBUTED TO THE PEACEFUL SETTLEMENT OF

## International Differences;

AND WHOSE COMMANDING ELOQUENCE, AND BRILLIANT SERVICES,

THROUGHOUT HIS ILLUSTRIOUS CAREER,

HAVE CONSPICUOUSLY ADVANCED THE CAUSE

OF JUSTICE, OF FREEDOM, AND OF HUMANITY,

AMONGST THE NATIONS OF THE WORLD;

## This Memoir
## Is Inscribed,

WITH THE WARMEST SENTIMENTS

OF ESTEEM AND ADMIRATION,

## By The Author.

# PREFACE.

IN presenting to the reader of these pages, a brief record of the public life and labours of our honoured friend Henry Richard, over a period of upwards of half-a-century, in the great cause of International Peace, as well as of political, civil, and religious freedom, to both of which he consecrated his great gifts, and for the furtherance of which he indefatigably laboured, I am deeply sensible that this " frail memorial though sincere," with its many imperfections, inadequately sets forth the great labours and eminent services of his noble life.

> " For poor my eloquence *thy* worth to tell,
> And small the need,—embalmed in every heart
> Shall live thy memory."

The career and incidents of his early life and manhood are generally well-known, and though comparatively unimportant, a reference to them may possibly be of interest, for they were the preliminary discipline in training and qualifying him, under the guiding hand of an All-wise Power, to those wider spheres of public usefulness and splendid service for peace and freedom, in which he has justly won an enduring and an honourable fame.

He was the son of the Rev. Ebenezer Richard, a Minister in the front rank of the Calvinistic Methodist Church, a man of great energy and zeal for the spiritual welfare of his countrymen, and whose piety and eloquence are still treasured in the hearts of the Welsh people.

At the little hamlet of Tregaron, in Cardiganshire, Mr. Richard, in 1812, was born, and under the tuition and train- ing of so good a father, and the wise counsels of a devoted Christian mother, he was well equipped for the life of con- flict before him.

Of his boyhood and youth, few records are to be found, beyond the fact that he received his first education at Llangeitho Grammar School, where his ardent spirit was fired with that glowing love for freedom, based on justice, which were the marked features of his action throughout his remarkable career.

In 1830, then 18 years of age, full of high hopes, and stirred with a youthful ambition, he left the home of his fathers, and the land of his adoption, to fight the battle of life, and made his way to London, for the purpose of entering Highbury Independent College, to be trained for the Congregational Ministry; * and there, under the immediate training of Dr. Henderson, Dr. Halley, and others, and with the companionship of such excellent fellow-students as Mr. Stoughton and David Thomas, (subsequently Dr.

---

* In 1866, Mr. Richard, addressing a meeting in Wales, thus refers to his entrance into Highbury College, in 1830 :—It happened with me when I first became a student of theology, that I went up to London on a "wild-goose chase," hardly knowing what I should do, but I intended going into some English college to be educated for the ministry ; but after I had been in London for some days I went without a single letter of introduction to apply for admission into a college. I was introduced to a good man, Thomas Wilson, who, after making inquiries, told me when I called again that the committee of the college were going to meet that afternoon and I must come and preach before them. Well, the committee of the college consisted of the principal ministers of religion in London, and I was a young Welshman of eighteen years of age, who probably had not heard half-a-dozen English sermons in my life ; but as it is said that a coward if he is put in a corner must fight and will fight, so I managed to get through it.

Stoughton, and the Rev. David Thomas, of Bristol,) he remained for five years, until 1835, when he became Minister of Marlborough Chapel, in the Old Kent Road.

Mr. Richard was comparatively a young man (in his 23rd year) when he entered on the pastorate of Marlborough Chapel, its affairs were not flourishing, but the vigour of his preaching, and the youthful earnestness which he threw into the Church affairs, and all its surroundings, by the establishment of Sunday Schools for the children, and a literary institution for the adults, as well as by the power of his pulpit addresses, he soon infused restoration and life into, and around it.

From this period, 1835 to 1848, when Mr. Richard succeeded Dr. Jefferson in the Secretariat of the Peace Society, his ministerial career was marked by only two incidents, worthy of note, the one semi-political, in connection with what was known as the Rebecca riots; and the other semi-religious, in connexion with the work of training for teachers, and popular education generally.

The Rebecca riots of 1843 arose, chiefly from the turnpike system of Wales, which the local magnates, who had the administration of the turnpike trusts, erected in every direction, and caused serious obstacles to the tenant farmers, especially of Cardiganshire and Carmarthenshire.

Against this intolerable grievance they formed themselves into companies, under the guidance of a female leader named Rebecca, and pulled down the obnoxious gates, and this uprising was taken advantage of by evil-minded persons to attribute to other and more sinister purposes.

Mr. Richard manfully stood in the breach as the exponent of the real truth in regard to this rebellion of a portion of the

Welsh people, defended them from the grossly exaggerated charges, and helped, by securing a mitigation of unjustly severe sentences, and by a calm and comprehensive statement of the facts, to allay the excitement and animosity that was aroused.

On the subject of popular education, in 1844, he visited Wales, as a deputation of the Congregational Union, and he took an active part in founding the Normal School at Brecon, for the training of teachers, and subsequently in 1847, assisted by Edward Miall and Samuel Morley, he founded the Voluntary School Association, and, as its Honorary Secretary, he actively opposed the educational policy of the Government of the day, in making large grants from the national exchequer for the erection of Church schools throughout Wales, ostensibly for education, but in reality for the prosletyzing of the people in the doctrines of the Church Catechism, and the enforcement of attendance at Church services, both of which were repugnant to the Welsh mind and character.

In 1848, Mr. Richard resigned his useful ministerial post as Minister of Marlborough Chapel, in obedience, there can be no doubt whatever, to the call of duty, and especially at the solicitation of his friends, to occupy the responsible position as Secretary of the Peace Society, and the record of his remarkable and valuable services, throughout that memorable period of national and of international history of forty years, I have endeavoured faithfully and fully to describe, in the accompanying memoir.

In the execution of this task, I have not been fortunate in having access to his wide and extensive correspondence, (for that has been entrusted to another to edite, and prepare for the public eye), but I have relied upon, and am indebted to the many public channels of information, to those publications, such as the *Herald of Peace*, the organ of the Peace Society, and which he edited for the greater part of his public life ; the *Nonconformist*, the organ of Nonconformity ; Hansard, the reliable mirror of Parliamentary debates ; to his many public writings, and to the press of England and Wales, and not less to my own personal recollections and reminiscences, as his colleague in the service of the Peace Society, from 1866 to 1880.

From these, and many other varied sources of information, from which I have gleaned, in order to illustrate the life and labours of our lamented friend, it must not be supposed that these pages, or indeed that any record that may be written, can adequately set forth the wide range of his prodigious labours in the cause of peace and freedom.

His public utterances, replete with eloquence, pathos, and valuable facts, delivered, not alone in England and Wales, in Scotland and Ireland, but throughout the Continent of Europe, in its capitals and cities; the vast number of valuable articles in the columns of the *Herald of Peace*, the *Nonconformist*, and other journals, as well as his correspondence in the public press throughout the kingdom ; his intimate relations and communications with eminent statesmen of his own country and of foreign lands; these, and many other public and private labours, would swell into a portentous volume, alike valuable to the student and lover of historical political records, and recollections, as they are a noble testimony to his ceaseless efforts, and useful public services.

In the political career of Mr. Richard, his triumphant

election for Merthyr Tydvil in 1868, was one, if not the most important event in his life, for he gained thereby considerable accession of political strength, and as representing the aspirations of the Welsh people, and possessing the confidence of his countrymen, he was hailed as the trusted leader and champion of their civil and religious liberties; and, as has been truly said, "amid all his manifold duties, his varied aims and labours, he always kept his right hand stretched out to the ancient land of his fathers."

As the leader and Apostle of the Peace party in Parliament, his motive power was inspired by the loftiest and purest of principles, that of morality and religion; and it was under the influence of these principles, that his conduct as a public man was recognised, acting upon Christian ethics, in direc opposition to the policy of expediency, and built on this foundation, he faltered not, nor flinched, for the realisation of a better, because a freer and more pacific policy in the relations of nations.

In considering the personal characteristics of Mr. Richard, the secret of his successful career in public life, and his many achievements, much might be written, for it is an interesting and an instructive study. Close acquaintance with him for many years, and under varied circumstances, both private and public, enabled me to arrive at one decided conclusion—he never changed; he was always the same in temper, in disposition, in conviction, in power, and in energy; and if ever the motto *sans changè* can be appropriately applied to any man, most certainly he was deserving of this distinction.

He was the happy possessor of an equable disposition not easily ruffled, his honesty and tenacity of conviction not to be shaken, loyal and firm in personal friendships, and with a purpose and aim in his every thought and action, that was direct and resolute.

As an orator, whether in Parliament or on the platform, he had few superiors, and upon the questions of peace and religious freedom, without exaggeration, it may be said, he was unrivalled, capable of moving alike the vast audience, or the select circle, by his varied gifts of pathos, dramatic energy, power of declamation and massive eloquence, for whenever and wherever he spoke he carried conviction to his hearers.

He wielded the pen of a ready writer in a marvellous degree, for it was with him his *tour de force*, and the main-spring of his great achievements and of his formidable power, which he wisely and effectively exercised against the citadels of monopoly, corruption, and despotism, and he spared them not, and when he thundered against them, they tottered and fell.

Truly his death has left a void that few can fill; and to the young men, and the strong men of this generation—aye! and of coming generations too, he has left a noble legacy of devotion to duty, of loyalty to principle, and of brave and noble deeds in the sacred cause of humanity, of civilisation, and of freedom.

May it be ours to follow him in the path which he trod; for assuredly, in the language of Longfellow,—

" Lives of great men all remind us
We can make our lives sublime,
And, departing, leave behind us
Footprints on the sands of time."

# ERRATA.

PAGE 1 *for* "*1* refer," *read* "*we* refer."

  ,, 12 *for* "*1849*," *read* "*1850*."

  ,, 13 *for* "22nd August, *1849*," *read* "22nd August, *1850*."

  ,, 33 *for* "*whereby they*," *read* "*which*."

  ,, 72 *for* "*in* the high road," *read* "*on*."

  ,, 72 *for* "*Chargè d'affairs*," *read* "*Chargè d'affaires*."

  ,, 82 *for* "*he* had proved," *read* "*the Emperor had proved*."

  ,, 83 *for* "*observes*," *read* "*observed*."

  ,, 87 *for* "*was* based," *read* "*were* based."

  ,, 91 *for* "*was* estimated," *read* "*were* estimated.'

  ,, 93 *for* "*as* a candidate," *read* "*to be* a candidate."

  ,, 107 *for* "*in* the free," *read* "*for* the free."

  ,, 181 *for* "*uring*," *read* "*During*."

# CONTENTS.

## PORTRAITS.

# HENRY RICHARD,

## The Apostle of Peace.

NUMEROUS as have been the contributions from various pens, pourtraying the distinguished career, in the cause of civil and religious freedom, of the subject of this memorique, Henry Richard, the late member for Merthyr Tydvil, yet, interesting and faithful as these records have been, it is noteworthy how little has been published of his eminent services in the great life-work to which he has consecrated his noble gifts, and in which he has won an enduring, because an honorable, fame—I refer to the cause of international peace.

It is forty years since that Mr. Richard (then the minister of Marlborough Chapel, London), appeared for the first time on the platform of the Peace Society, and then and there, surrounded by George Thompson, Joseph John Gurney, Charles Hindley, M.P., J. S. Buckingham, M.P., and other eminent friends of the cause, publicly proclaimed his conversion to its principles and policy, closing a vigorous denunciation against war as in "direct, implacable, and everlasting antipathy to the whole spirit and genius of the Gospel."

Four years after this public declaration, on the retirement of the Rev. John Jefferson as the Secretary of the Peace Society, Mr. Richard was unanimously chosen, in the words of the Resolution, "as the able and efficient successor to the arduous and important post which has been vacated," and at the Anniversary Meeting, May 23, 1848, he presented the Report, the first prepared by his own hand.

At this period, forty years ago, the President of the Society was Charles Hindley, M.P. for Wigan, its Treasurer Samuel Gurney, and now, out of the thirty-four members of the Executive, not one survives.

Mr. Richard entered upon his career at a period of general disturbance in Europe and America, which soon involved him in considerable anxiety and labour.

Abroad, war had been proclaimed between Austria and Italy, and between Germany and Denmark. A desolating war also was raging between the United States and Mexico, and presumptuous as might have been considered by many, Mr. Richard urged his Committee to address by memorial the respective Presidents of the belligerent Governments, in a spirit of earnest but respectful remonstrance, and at the same time an appeal was sent to the chief European Govern- ments imploring their friendly mediation. In Switzerland, where a devastating civil war was raging amongst the Swiss cantons, an address was issued to the people urging a cessa- tion of the sanguinary conflict. But it was in France, chiefly, that the friends of peace were specially directed, arising out of the merciless "Reign of Terror," and the oppor- tunity was availed of to address in a Christian spirit the people of France, in the hope of kindling a more humane feeling; and not in vain, for it tended to calm the upheavings of the popular frenzy for revenge and massacre.

Not only abroad, but also at home, this eventful year of 1848 brought anxious labour for Mr. Richard and his Com- mittee. The absurd cry of "England in danger" was raised, which, fanned by the public Press, and fomented by alarming letters of timid persons of rank and influ- ence, tended to awaken alarm and jealousy of some imaginary foe.

Against this craven fear, a timely warning was made which helped to assuage the shrieks of the panic-mongers, and to defeat the wild project for an enormous addition to the military establishments.

---

## PEACE CONGRESS AT BRUSSELS, 1848.

It was in the midst of these social and political convulsions at home and abroad, at a time of great tumult and much violence, that Mr. Richard was called to the helm of the Ark of Peace, tossed as it was on the stormy sea of European affairs ; and calmly and resolutely did he stand to his post of duty. In this responsible position his energy and zeal soon told on the Executive, and ere the first year of his career in office was closed, he had made 1848 a memorable one, saddened though it was by hateful memories, in the history of Europe.

Conjointly with the distinguished American Apostle of Peace, Elihu Burritt (a man honored in his own and in other lands for his steady and unceasing advocacy of the cause of peace), and with that eminent philanthropist, the lamented Joseph Sturge, Mr. Richard threw himself with all the warmth of his early enthusiasm into a project for assembling in one of the capitals of Europe an International Peace Congress, which should be the means of gathering up the scattered forces of peace in Europe in a grand solidarity against the demon of War. To undertake such a task, at that time, was one of great responsibility, and required a wisdom in council, and a courage in action, which the pioneers in this enterprise nobly exemplified. It was the first occasion that there had assembled such a conclave for Peace, and insurmountable as at the onset seemed the obstacles in its way, yet they were eventually overcome, and this bold initiative to arouse the conscience of Europe, and to energise into action the slumbering longings for peace and hatred of war, was crowned with a triumph little

anticipated. On the 20th of September, 1848, in the land of
Belgium, where blind and brutal war had so often decided
the fate of Empires, in the city of Brussels, within a few
steps of that field where was fought the most sanguinary
battle of the warrior—the field of Waterloo—Mr. Richard and
his colleagues unfurled the standard for peace, and assembled
an army of men, speaking different languages, living under
different forms of government, and holding diverse political
and religious opinions, yet actuated by the *one* all-embracing
faith, the brotherhood of man and the fatherhood of God—

> "A holy gathering, peaceful all,
> No threat of war, no savage call
> Of vengeance on an erring brother ;
> But in their stead, the God-like plan
> To teach the brotherhood of man
> To love and reverence one another,
> As sharers of one common blood,
> As children of one common God,"

At this Congress it honorably fell to the lot of one of the
most distinguished members of the Belgium Government,
M. Adolphe Visschers, to preside, who was supported by
several members of the National Assembly of France, and
of the English Parliament, besides members of Academies
of Literature, Professors of Universities, *savants* of Spain,
Italy, and America, and last, though not least, ministers of
the Gospel of the Prince of Peace. The spirit displayed
throughout the sittings of its four sessions was worthy of the
cause and of the occasion.

The inaugural address of the President, the speeches of its
most eminent members, of such men as M. François Bouvet,
William Ewart, M.P., J. S. Buckingham, M.P., Henry
Vincent, M. Bertonalli (Italy), Henry Richard, and others,
full of energy and interest, were received with great enthusiasm. In addition to these, papers were read, prepared
specially for the occasion, by Edmund Fry, William Stokes,
and Elihu Burritt; but the most important work accomplished by the Congress was the adoption of an appeal

addressed to the peoples and the Governments of Europe and America, deprecating war, as condemned alike by justice and humanity, and urging the necessity of a simultaneous disarmament, and the importance of introducing into all Treaties clauses providing for the settlement of all differences by arbitration, and the adoption of an International Code as an effective means of promoting the peace of the world.

It was at this Congress we are able to read the first reported speech Mr. Richard publicly uttered on that question which, for an eventful life, has since absorbed his best energies, and to which he has consecrated his remarkable talents. As one reads it, after this interval of 40 years, one cannot fail to observe the ring of the genuine metal which has ever distinguished all his speeches, of his resistance to war, on the fundamental ground of its glaring outrage, to the spirit and genius of the Christian religion. It bristles too, as he was ever wont to interweave, with those apt illustrations, drawn from the pages of inspiration, and the endless store of his favourite and beautiful Milton. Nothing can be more vigorous than his closing words :

" We must exhibit war in its true colour, we must have the courage with a bold hand to tear the mask which it has thrown over its face, and regardless of the pomp and circumstance with which it is enshrouded, the sounding phrases of honour, patriotism and glory with which it is wont to conceal its true character, we must present it to the eye of the world, as it truly is—a gigantic murderer, drunk with ambition and lust, and hideously stained with the blood of its myriad victims."

A few months after this demonstration at Brussels, an influential Committee was nominated consisting of thirty-two gentlemen, of which but one survives, staunch and true, George Wm. Alexander, who were appointed to watch over and direct the operations of the Society, more especially in reference to the parliamentary campaign, and the proposed second Congress in Paris.

## MR. COBDEN'S MOTION, 1849.

It was evident this successful Peace Congress had stirred to its depths the dormant spirit of peace throughout Europe, and Mr. Richard resolved to keep public attention well fixed on the coming question of the day, and with the co-operation of his colleagues, he actively organised meetings, colossal in

· RICHARD COBDEN.

those days, in the great cities, beginning with the Metropolis, and thence embracing Birmingham, Manchester, Bristol, Hull, Rochdale, Bolton, Preston, Shrewsbury and Chester &c., which brought together triumphant demonstrations, rarely seen, proving the rapidity and power with which the principles of peace were taking hold of the public mind.

These series of public meetings throughout the country had a practical object in view, being in support of the resolution of Richard Cobden to bring before Parliament, early in the session of 1849, the urgent necessity of entering into communications with Foreign Governments with a view to the establishment of a system of international arbitration. Into this great work of invoking for the first time the sympathy of Parliament and the sanction of the Crown of England in this principle, Mr. Richard threw himself with great ardour, and for a period of six months, laboured unceasingly on the platform before immense assemblages in England and Scotland, no less by the active wielding of his trenchant pen.

In this vigorous agitation he was greatly assisted by capable men, whose names are household words, one of whom is still spared to labour on in this holy peace crusade to which he has dedicated his life, venerable now by service and years, the bold champion, Arthur O'Neill of Birmingham, and some too, whose loss we deplore, who have entered long since into Rest—John Bright, Joseph Sturge, Edmund Fry, Charles Gilpin, William Stokes, and many others, clouds of witnesses of whom it may be said, "the world was not worthy."

One must not forget to refer also to the valued services rendered by one who was rapidly rising into public estimation, as an able and eloquent advocate, Alfred B. Stevens, whose voice some of us still remember, inspiring the hearers with the enthusiasm of his own soul stirred as he evidently was with an ardour and zeal which carried conviction to the people. It was not permitted to this valiant soldier to be spared to labour with his co-patriots as had been fondly hoped, for at an early age he was called up higher, but he has left an enduring monument, which will stand further into the dim future than marble or bronze, a record imperishable, by those who knew and loved him well.

The day was now approaching when for the first time in the Parliament of England the important subject of International Arbitration was to be submitted to the judgment of

the representatives of the people, and in the hands of
Richard Cobden, who had become the acknowledged
Apostle of Peace, no more fitting advocate could the cause
have been confided.  The night preceding the memorable
debate, a demonstration of popular enthusiasm was witnessed
in Exeter Hall, attended by many Members of the House,
encircled with a number of the leaders of the movement,
amongst whom stood the sturdy and resolute Henry Richard,
all brimful of enthusiasm, which echoed and re-echoed over all
that vast assemblage of peace reformers.  Great was the
cheering when honest John Bright, then in the zenith of his
oratorical fame, thrilled his hearers with one of his most
forcible and impressive speeches, and there is no doubt,
conjointly with others, rendered good service to the cause
and paved the way for its thoughtful consideration the
following evening within St. Stephen's.

In the limited space of this brief memorial it will be only
possible succinctly to refer to the course of this parliamentary effort of Mr. Cobden, intimately associated as it was
with the labours of Mr. Richard.

On Tuesday, the 14th June, 1849, we have to chronicle
this eventful page in the annals of peace.  The speech of
Mr. Cobden, in introducing the motion, was admirable, skilfully adapted to his cynical auditory, courageous nevertheless,
trenchant with argument, and eminently practical.  To his
support in debate rallied some well-known men, William
Ewart, Milner Gibson, John A. Roebuck, Joseph Hume,
speaking with their characteristic boldness and sterling good
sense.  Opposing the resolution, were Lords Palmerston
and Russell, who, honourably be it said, performed their
chilling duty with courtesy, and plausibility common to
statesmanship, eulogising the motive of the enterprise, and
whilst desiring success to so humane an endeavour, yet
regretting their intention to vote against it.

But though this resolution was defeated, the moral victory
was great.  Independent of the espousal of the question of

international peace by a statesman of Mr. Cobden's distinguished ability, and eminent political services—a great accession in those early days of its unpopularity—the advocacy of the question for many months preceding its introduction in the British legislature had fixed its hold on the public mind, and though but 81 members voted in its favour, they represented a far larger constituency of electors, and non-electors, than the majority who voted against it, and as Mr. Cobden stated in a letter to his friend Joseph Sturge,

"I never knew a question make such rapid progress in the House," and as *Punch* observed in an article of keen satire, and lively but friendly humour, "the olive twig placed by Cobden in Westminster will flourish, despite the blighting wit of mess rooms, and will rise and spread into a tree that shall offer shade and security to all nations."

To Mr. Richard and his vigilant fellow-labourers, this advance may be largely due, and to them was given to realise twenty-six years later the partial fulfilment of the prophetic words of *Punch*, and let us hope, bye-and-bye, "to all nations."

---

## THE PARIS CONGRESS, 1849.

The next important movement which Mr. Richard backed by his indefatigable Committee, addressed themselves to, and with the same practical energy, was the Peace Congress which assembled in the City of Paris. Great as were the difficulties and labours involved in the arrangements of the Brussels Congress, still greater were they in connection with the Congress at Paris. They were justly described at the time as months of anxious labour, and the difficulties, which those only who watched and toiled on in spite of them, can adequately appreciate. Into this conflict Mr. Richard threw himself with all his wonted ardour and strategy, and with such a leader it is no wonder a great success crowned the enterprise. Addresses followed addresses signed by himself and Elihu Burritt, which ringing with an enthusiastic chord, stirred the friends of peace everywhere, and rallied them from afar, from hamlet and city, at home and abroad, to the standard unfurled.   Visits followed visits to Paris, where interviews were obtained with the most eminent leaders of political and religious thought in France—of such men as Garnier, Chevalier, Bouvet, De Cocquerel, Horace Say, Victor Hugo, the eminent De Tocqueville, Minister of Foreign Affairs, and Dufaure, Minister of the Interior, all of whom entered into their project with considerable "*esprit de corps*," and especially the Minister, De Tocqueville, who showed a cordiality and a friendliness, earnest and sincere, that must have astonished, as it gladdened their hearts. Well might they say, "the news of the Congress is flying through all parts of Europe and is awakening a great interest amongst all classes," and though the City of Paris was then in a "state of siege," the French Government displayed from the beginning a generous accord, admitting the peace party from England without passports, and without examination of their luggage.

The Congress assembled August 22nd 1849, under the presidency of Victor Hugo, representatives being present from all parts of Europe and the American Continent.   Its sittings continued for three days, and judging by the speeches delivered and papers read, the proceedings proved of unsurpassing interest.   Conspicuous for their eloquence and power were the harangues of Victor Hugo, the "Tribune of France," M. Visschers, of Belgium, Emilie Girardin, Richard Cobden, Henry Vincent, the Abbé Deguerry, curé of the Madeline (cruelly murdered by the Communists in 1871) Amasa Walker, member of the American House of Representatives, Edward Miall, and Athanase Cocquerel, the eminent Protestant Minister.

The Congress was most successful whether viewed in the character of those assembled, the remarkable display of eloquent orators, or the deep moral impression which it exercised throughout Europe. Great credit was due to many whose voices were not often heard, on whom devolved the arduous labours that brought so much success—such were Henry Richard, Joseph Sturge, and Elihu Burritt.

One of the most interesting features of the Congress was the Soirée given by the Minister for Foreign Affairs, De Tocqueville, to the members and delegates, and which came off with great *éclât*. It was attended by the *élite* of Paris, including many of the Foreign Ambassadors, and members of the French Government, which may be taken as a proof of the profound impression produced on the minds of the people of France and of their deep sympathy for the cause of international peace.

## "RAJAH" BROOKE AND BORNEO.

Reference should now be made to the lead Mr. Richard took in conjunction with Joseph Sturge, in face of much un-merited obloquy, against the outrageous massacre perpetrated by Sir James, *alias* "Rajah" Brooke, on the Dyaks of Borneo on the miserable plea, never substantiated, that they were a piratical tribe. When it is remembered that 1,500 of those unhappy people perished at the hands of these "*soi disant* champions of freedom, of commerce, and avengers of humanity," perished without one tittle of evidence having been submitted of their guilt of piracy, we shall not be surprised at the shout of indignation which was raised against these Borneo Butchers.

Under the auspices of the Peace Society, Joseph Sturge and Henry Richard convened a public meeting in the City of London, which was overwhelming in its condemnation against what Mr. Cobden justly called "a gratuitous, and cold-blooded butchery," and especially against the author of that cruel massacre. At this meeting Mr. Richard delivered

a powerful speech, being a calm statement of the whole facts
of the case, wherein he conclusively showed who were the
*real pirates*—not the Dyaks under the Sultan of Borneo, but
the expedition of Rajah Brooke sailing under the prestige of
the British Flag, that these outrages were the result of the
large number of restless military adventurers, wanderers on
the seas, "nothing particular to do," "looking out for a job,"
the deposing of Rajahs and Sultans, and the aping of
Warwick the King-maker in the Eastern Waters.   Amid the
approving cheers of this great meeting, he declared there
was no shadow of a pretence that these unhappy Dyaks
ever molested an English vessel, and he charged Sir James
Brooke with the committal of a criminal act, that was an
outrage of all law, human and Divine, and concluded a
powerful speech by an eloquent appeal to the Bishops and
clergy who invited this Rajah of Borneo fame to the Hanover Square rooms, that they might present him with a
snuff-box, "caress, and bless him," that if they wished "to
spread Christianity among the heathen, it must not be by
-canister and grape-shot."

The results of this meeting, and the general protests
raised throughout the country, soon told on the Government,
and though unhappily these destroyers of the aboriginal
tribes of Borneo and Celebes were not arraigned for trial,
yet the abominable "blood-money reward" which they
claimed, amounting to £20,000, was refused them, and the
Act which granted such a foul subsidy of £120 for every
head of a Dyak slain, was for ever unconditionally repealed.

---

## THE FRANKFORT CONGRESS, 1849.

The next important movement with which Mr. Richard
was prominently associated was the Peace Congress at
Frankfort, the last of the Congresses convened in the

European Capitals. The arrangements for this international meeting devolved mainly on Mr. Richard, assisted by his coadjutors, M. Visschers, Elihu Burritt, and William Stokes, and judging by the success of the project, these labours reflect great credit on their energy and skill. Consequent on the want of acquaintance by the leading men in Germany with the aims and policy of the Peace party in England, it was found necessary that a tour should be paid to Berlin, Darmstadt, Mannheim, Worms, Leipsic, Dresden, Hamburg, Hanover, Nuremburg, Munich, Stuttgard, and many other towns, where interviews took place with distinguished Politicians, Professors of Universities, and eminent writers of the day. These interviews were of the most cordial character, and helped largely to direct the attention of some of the foremost minds in Germany to the question of peace with fresh and deep interest.

The Congress met August 22nd, 1849, and it is not too much to say of it that it was a memorable meeting, worthy of its predecessors. It was presided over by the Prime Minister of Hesse Darmstadt, and amongst the eminent men who supported him were various members of the National Assembly of France, and of the English Parliament, Professors of Universities, Ministers of Churches from various countries in Europe and America, and attending the Congress were representatives of almost all the civilized nations of the world, gathered, not for mutual hate or destruction, but mingling their sympathies and counsels to advance the great work of international peace. Of the proceedings of the Congress, space will not permit to refer. For several weeks these proceedings occupied a foremost place in the records of the European Press, and it was evident they excited great interest, especially on the thoughtful Germanic mind, as it was natural it should do in all its grandeur, as one of the most pressing questions demanding their attention.

We must now turn from these encouraging records of the triumphs of Peace to the inglorious Kaffir War, which excited, at the close of the year 1850, considerable interest, and which involved Mr. Richard and the peace party in England, in an active opposition to the policy which sanctioned one of the most iniquitous wars Great Britain ever waged. This war of 1850 proved the truth of the language of Bacon,

"But what does war, but endless wars produce,"

as it was the result of the embittered feeling which the previous wars of 1811, 1819, 1830, and 1846, had left in their blood-stained track. From the first day of British connexion with the Cape of Good Hope in 1806, British possessions there had steadily increased, not by right but by might, not by justice but by a cruel policy of extermination. Under the various administrations of Lord Charles Somerset, Lord Glenelg, and Sir Harry Smith, the grip of England had steadily tightened, until in 1846 it was described as exceeding the territory of any one of the largest States in Europe. It were difficult to explain or defend the causes which led to this gradual policy of unjust annexation, and its concomitant evils, the extermination of the various aboriginal tribes. Sometimes it was explained on the ground of the encroachments of Europeans, the restless adventurous spirit of Englishmen; sometimes to disputes as to the boundaries of territory; sometimes by the straying of the cattle of settlers, and in this war of 1850, by the stealing of an axe, or the straying of an ass, the property of an English colonist; but above all, and herein lies the main cause of these humiliating wars at the Cape, by the presence of British troops, which encouraged the encroachment of Europeans on the Kaffirs' territory. The Kaffirs naturally resented; they stole the cattle of the colonists, and committed depredations by way of reprisals. Then · followed retaliation, and war ensued, and thus, with the termination of each war, England's dominions advanced, step by step, sowing the seeds of further wars and further encroachments.

It was against this unjust policy of aggrandisement that Mr. Richard bestirred the country, and truly there was good ground of opposition, when a war of extermination was raging on the miserable pretext of a stolen axe, and the straying of some donkey; a war which involved Great Britain in an expenditure of three millions sterling, and a terrible Bill of Blood. Into this most opportune protest Mr. Richard devoted unceasing efforts. Articles of a most trenchant character, teeming with startling facts, and resonant with an eloquent indignation, flowed from his facile pen; meetings were convened and addressed by him in Birmingham, Bristol, Sheffield, &c., and in various parts of the Metropolis, by which united agency the eyes of the people of England became opened as to the true origin of these deplorable conflicts, which checked this restless spirit for territorial aggrandisement that was disgracing the fair fame of England.

## THE GREAT EXHIBITION, 1851.

We now come to the year 1851, a year for ever memorable, as the opening of the Palace of Industry. It was natural that with the mingled throng of the Rulers of the Earth, the galaxy of Emperors, Kings and Queens, Princes and Princesses, scions of Royal blood, amid the gathering too of Warriors and Statesmen, that the Peace Party should vie likewise, in greeting with a hearty " All Hail!" this Palace of Concord, so full of good omen to their cause. By their presence at its inauguration, by their pæans of rejoicing, and by memorials and congratulations to the Royal Commissioners, we find Mr. Richard ever alert, in turning to the most favourable advantage so grand a festival of Industry, so gorgeous a Banquet of Peace. One of the most gratifying evidences of the good impress on the public mind was the emphatic language at the inaugural ceremony of that Prince among Princes, Albert the Good, that

"It has for its end the strengthening of the bonds of peace and friendship among all Nations of the earth ;"

and of the significant reply from her own lips of Her Majesty the Queen, to the prayer of that address :

"That it might encourage the Ark of Peace, strengthen the bonds of union amongst all nations, and promote a friendly and honourable rivalry for the good and happiness of mankind."

Such impressive declarations evoked similar utterances from Statesmen of both parties in the State, from eminent Ministers of Church and Dissent throughout the land, and even military men caught the contagion for Peace, and to crown all, a sign appeared in the Heavens, the appearance of a new planet, which was looked upon as the harbinger of a better time coming, and Sir John Herschel gave vent to the public enthusiasm, and called the new-born star, Irene, the Grecian for Peace. One good move taken by Mr. Richard and his colleagues deserves notice. They prepared a memorial to the Royal Commissioners urging that no prizes should be given to weapons of destruction, and when the awards of merit were distributed, "not one prize was given for instruments of war," the distinguished jurors considering that as the object of the Exhibition was to save life rather than destroy it, that therefore this strictly humane principle should be maintained throughout.

----

## THE MILITIA BILL, 1852.

In the beginning of 1852, the country was roused by the Militia Bill, introduced into Parliament by Lord John Russell. Against this measure Mr. Richard by voice and pen vigorously protested, and for several months, supported by Cobden and Gibson in Parliament, he waged a vigorous, though hopeless, resistance to this obnoxious measure. Considering the utterly groundless reasons brought forward by the War party in its support, the action of Cobden and Richard, in and out of Parliament, appears reasonable and just. The panic was a senseless one, originating as usual with the military and naval officers on half-pay in their restless propensity to write anonymous letters in the public journals, speaking of the fate of England being sealed. They declared a deep-laid conspiracy existed among continental despots, headed by the Emperor of Russia, to crush liberty in Europe, and to aid its accomplishment, the overthrow of England was indispensable. Again, that a French invasion was confidently predicted, that France was burning to revenge Waterloo, because the Prince de Joinville had written a terrible pamphlet shewing how easily England might be surprised, and ridiculous as it seems, Austria it was said was angry with our treatment of Hungary, the thrashing of infamous Haynau, and the ovations to Kossuth, and that she was meditating reprisals, or in other words, war against England.

Against these preposterous dangers and monstrous alarms, the country was driven by certain naval and military alarmists, to improve the defences of the country, and accordingly the Government pandering to this baseless apprehension, brought forward military measures and voted, wasted! millions of money.

Mr. Richard and his friends directed public attention, mainly against the Militia Bill, and by a spirited agitation all over the country, they evoked a general outcry in opposition to the measure. Meetings were held in the chief centres in England and Scotland, most of which Mr. Richard addressed, and though this agitation was not crowned with success, still, it was so far satisfactory, that when the question was tested in Parliament 165 members voted its

C

rejection, a significant homage to the strong feeling in the
country.

-----

## THE MANCHESTER CONFERENCE, 1853.

In the beginning of 1853, we find Mr. Richard busily
engaged in organising a National Conference in Manchester,
to consider the general question of war, its burdens, and its
dangers.    The circular convening this Conference was
signed by upwards of 200 influential men in various parts of
the realm, including 19 Members of Parliament, amongst
whom we find the names of Cobden, Bright, and Gibson,
the celebrated trio who led the van and conquered against
the Corn Laws.    Considering the object of the Conference
was general rather than specific, and that it was held in the
winter under the canopy of a murky atmosphere, it is
remarkable that, as regards numbers and interest, it surpassed
the assemblies of the kind ever held, whether at home or
abroad.    Under the presidency of the veteran George
Wilson, whose eminent services as Chairman of the Corn
Law League will long be gratefully remembered, this
memorable meeting was continued into four sessions, the
last session culminating in a magnificent demonstration in
the Free Trade Hall.

The proceedings of the Conference were distinguished by
remarkable speeches from George Wilson, Richard Cobden,
John Bright, Joseph Sturge, Samuel Bowly, and others,
directed chiefly against the system of large armaments, and
resenting the ignoble panic which had seized the nation.
The demonstration in the Free Trade Hall has rarely, if
ever, been equalled for numbers and enthusiasm, and no
wonder considering the stirring harangues of Cobden, Bright,
and Gibson, which thrilled not only that great audience, but

the country generally, and unjustly brought down upon these devoted men of peace such a prodigious explosion of ridicule, invective, and abuse, from *Punch* to *Chronicle*, that was disgraceful to the writers whose pens had evidently been dipped in gall.

## THE EASTERN QUESTION, 1853.

We now approach an eventful period in the records of Mr. Richard's career. Hardly had the Conference at Manchester closed its labours, than the attention of the nation was turned with deep solicitude to the complications of the East, and for several succeeding years, the labours of Mr. Richard and his colleagues were heavily taxed in their endeavours to avert the disastrous and deplorable Crimean War.

As early as July 1853 Mr. Richard sounded the tocsin of alarm by a powerful contribution from his pen on the Eastern question, wherein the nature of the difficulties between Russia and Turkey were clearly set forth, and assuredly never did an international difficulty of so trivial a character, assume such gigantic proportions, or culminate in a greater catastrophe. It would appear to have arisen on this wise—The French Government (apparently intoxicated by the wicked "*coup d'* *état*" of Dec. 1851, which enthroned a Bonaparte, and engulphed France into an abhorent militarism) appear to have originated the mischief in the East by a series of intrigues at Constantinople, ostensibly for the purpose of securing certain privileges for her fellow Christian subjects, the Roman Catholic devotees at Jerusalem. Russia, who was anxious for a quarrel with Turkey, likewise intrigued on behalf of the members of the Greek Church scattered over the Turkish dominions, and out of these miserable squabbles, which may

be called a wrangle for the keys of the Holy Places, sprang a
mine, that in the following year burst with terrific fury, and
involved Europe in a blaze.

The question naturally arises, wherefore did England
intervene ?  What rights, or privileges, or interests had she
to safeguard?  The answer is obvious.  None whatever,
except this, and so far as can be discovered it was the only
pretext, namely, that vaunted "spirited policy," of a bygone
time, and that proud prerogative of intervention, to maintain
the "balance of power" in Europe.  Into the intricate
mazes of those prolonged and mysterious negotiations—a
marvellous record of bungling diplomacy, beginning with
this contemptible quarrel for the keys of the Holy Places at
Jerusalem, and ending with the lamentable failure of the
celebrated Vienna Note, a period of twelve months—it will
be impossible here to enter.  Against this policy of intervention by England in the affairs of Turkey, and of blind un-
natural hatred of Russia, which precipitated the Crimean
War, Mr. Richard nobly stirred himself, and of these efforts
by voice and pen, by press and platform, a glorious record
might be made.

The times were eminently critical, and great as were the
forces against which the Peace party had to contend, they
fought nobly and unflinchingly to the last ; an heroic band,
Cobden and Bright, Sturge and Richard, and a host of
others, whose deeds will ever live in grateful recollection,

"On the bead-roll of time
Worthy to be filed."

From the pen of Mr. Richard, at the earlier period of the
threatened danger in the East, followed in quick succession
various articles in the Press, laying bare with pitiless severity
the intrigues of the War party, and exposing the flimsy
character of the "*casus belli*," and by such an array of facts
and arguments the Party of Peace were soon stirred into
vigorous action to stave off the impending trouble.

As an effectual way for holding aloft the banner of peace in

the midst of the tumult, a great demonstration, to protest against
the popular clamour, was held at Edinburgh in October, 1853,
and mainly owing to the active exertions of Mr. Richard, this
Conference proved an immense success. Similar to the
great meetings at Manchester, it was eminently representative,
with this addition that the chief towns of Scotland sent their
leading men to stand side by side with the English friends
of peace in that crisis, and the presence of the eminent
leaders of the Peace party, Cobden and Bright, who, with
admirable moral courage, dared to confront the tempest of
obloquy, and by their masterly eloquence gave considerable
*éclat* and interest to the proceedings. The sittings of the
Conference, presided over by the Lord Provost of Edinburgh,
Duncan MacLaren, late M.P. for that city, continued two
days, and closed with an enthusiastic demonstration in the
largest hall in Edinburgh. At this great meeting Richard
Cobden spoke at considerable length a speech of commanding power, "a clear stream of facts, arguments, and
illustrations, arranged in the most perfect order, enforced
with the most severe logic, and in a style so terse, compact,
and forcible, that there was scarcely a waste word from
beginning to end." He was followed by a gallant Admiral,
Sir Charles Napier, who came down from London expressly
to oppose the resolutions, but whose courage failed him in
the trysting hour. Then followed Mr. Bright in a speech
of wonderful power, which thrilled and swayed that vast
audience " like the ocean, when moved by the wind," and
inspiring all, as they gazed on his erect and resolute form
like a pillar of state, and listened to the burning words
stream from his lips, words of emphatic protest against the
popular clamour, which was gradually drifting England into
the dire calamity of war.

Immediately after this great meeting, whilst the public
feeling was fairly roused by the vigorous speeches of the
Conference, Mr. Richard, joined by Mr. Bowly and Mr.
Stokes, entered on a campaign of public agitation in

Scotland, and addressed enthusiastic meetings, chief amongst which were Cupar, Dunfermline, Dundee, Perth, Aberdeen, Arbroath, Montrose, and Stirling. But the public mind was gradually becoming inflamed to the highest degree in favour of war, and public meetings in this state of boiling heat became dangerous, exasperating where they should have calmed the popular fury.

During this period of national intoxication, when the voice of reason, the shriek of humanity, and the thunders of Heaven were drowned in the wild and passionate tumult for war, Mr. Richard, placed in a most trying position, displayed in an eminent degree a calmness and a courage most commendable. Whilst the nation was seething with a frenzied foam for war against Russia, he did not shrink from lifting his voice in language of stern admonition and rebuke, and when public utterances were crushed by the maddened shouts of infuriated mobs, maddened by drink and impelled by loot, then he wielded his eloquent pen, which

> " Supersedes the sword,
> That right not might shall be the word."

Sometimes these effusions from his pen were a tractate, sometimes in the more formidable because arduous character of a pamphlet, but alike inculcating the true Christian principle of peace, and the untold because unspeakable calamities which war inevitably inflicts upon those dearest of British and world-wide interests—the interests of religion, morality, civilisation, and commerce.

Addresses likewise were prepared and issued under his signature to various corporate bodies, and in the hope of withstanding the rising tide of a wrathful and warlike spirit, which was threatening to submerge the conscience of the nation, he indited an address to the Christian Ministers of the land, not only entreating them to restrain the revengeful and hateful passions, but exhorting them to besiege the Throne of the Most High to avert from Europe the terrible scourge of war.

This opportune appeal, couched in fitting language and full of touching pathos, received from not a few a cordial response, was read by them to their assembled congregations, and inspired not a few from their exalted positions to preach the truth, " On earth peace, and goodwill to men," and to invoke the sacred name, that " the plague might be stayed."

One of the most valuable contributions of Mr. Richard's pen during this trying period of the war, and which deserves especial mention, was a " History of the Origin of the War," drawn from parliamentary documents, issued in a pamphlet form, consisting mainly of a simple record of historical facts, eminently adapted for the crisis.

It was a masterly production, based as it was on official documents, and received a most extensive circulation, and greatly assisted to modify the opinions of waverers as to the merits of the war, and to dispel the vague impressions and prejudices which, unhappily, the people of this country had formed so erroneous a judgment. Though the war fever was at its height, and the danger of addressing meetings was considerable, yet on several occasions, at the close of the year 1855, and at the beginning of 1856, Mr. Richard felt it to be his duty to brave the popular frenzy, and in London, and in Manchester, Norwich, Bristol, Cardiff, Newport, Luton, Dunstable, and Leighton Buzzard, and other places, he addressed large and often stormy meetings. In this campaign he was aided by Mr. Samuel Bowly, who displayed a devoted zeal and valiant spirit worthy of the cause, and at Nottingham, Coventry, Worcester, and Leicester and other towns lectured to large audiences in favour of peace, and by the power of his persuasive eloquence, and the justice of the arguments, carried conviction to his hearers.

At Cardiff, where a panic had well-nigh seized the town in anticipation of the meeting, Mr. Richard met with considerable opposition, and his reception may be characterised as threatening. He was placarded in the town as an emissary of the Czar, and the magistrates were compelled to take precautionary measures to keep the peace. Undaunted by this display of rowdyism, true to his mission, "his spirit failed him not," he faced the turbulence of the mob, and for two hours, in spite of much violent interruption, nobly advocated the great principles, not as an "Emissary of the Czar," but as an emissary of the Prince of Peace, and at the close to avoid further violence and tumult, the Mayor wisely dissolved the meeting.

Such exhibitions of frenzied zeal, amidst his own Welsh countrymen, in favour of the prosecution of the war, happily were not repeated, and he was permitted in several of the towns of the Principality to continue his campaign. Thirty-six years have passed away, and not alone in Cardiff, but throughout the kingdom, a great and remarkable change in opinion has dawned. The teaching lessons of history, the bitter fruits of experience, have brought home to the conscience of the nation the justice and the wisdom of the noble stand which Mr. Richard and the friends of peace then made against the folly and wickedness of the Crimean War. Cardiff and its honourable citizens pre-eminently have long since buried the hatchet of war, they have long since and amply condoned for that violence and wrong to one, who has been for many years hailed as their foremost chieftain in the cause of Peace and Freedom. A noble reparation has been made, and we rejoice to know that Cardiff is sound to the core for the great principles of peace which they once despised, and loyal to a man, to the memory and worth of a fellow-countryman whom they once reviled and persecuted.

In 1856 a gleam of sunshine burst through the clouded sky of European affairs, and shed a bright ray of hope for peace over the blood-stained battle-fields of the Crimean peninsula, where a million of men were echeloned in hostile array engaged in the horrid work of wholesale human carnage.

In France, especially in the capital, Paris, where little

enthusiasm prevailed in favour of war, and where deep
suffering was felt, and loud murmurs were raised, this movement for peace was universally received with a sentiment of
joy and satisfaction.  The French press, in giving vent to
the public enthusiasm, severely censured the tone of distrust
and defiance assumed by the leading articles of the London
press, who were to their discredit doing all they could to
prolong the war by heaping insults on Russia, by snarling at
the pacific tone of the press of France, and everywhere
sowing suspicions and objections against everything and
everybody favourable to peace.

This preposterous swagger and brag on the part of England
was happily crushed by the moderation of the Allies, and at
St. Petersburg the acceptance of a basis for pacific negotiations
dissipated the fears and raised high hopes for the conclusion
of this dishonourable war.

The heavens cleared, the waters of fierce conflict began to
abate, the dry land was discovered whereon the Ark of Peace
might safely anchor after the storm, and soon on Ararat's
plateau was seen the fulfilment of the dearest hope of the
friends of peace, for

"A voice angelic !
Telling that no more the cannon
    Shall be heard along the shore,
Nor the charging squadrons trample
    Fellow-creatures in their gore.

"A voice angelic !
Telling that the fratricidal
    Strife and bloodshed now shall cease,
And again the busy millions,
    Cultivate the arts of peace."

## THE CONGRESS AT PARIS, 1856.

In the prospect of the assembling of the Congress at Paris
of the Plenipotentiaries of the Great Powers, Mr. Richard and

his allies stirred themselves, and measures were promptly
taken to secure the recognition by the Congress in the Treaty
of the principle of arbitration in place of the brutal arbitrament of the sword.  With this object in view a deputation was
arranged, consisting of Richard Cobden, M.P., Milner Gibson,
M.P., Lord Robert Grosvenor, M.P., George Hadfield, M.P.,
and others, to present to the Prime Minister, Viscount
Palmerston, a memorial.  The Prime Minister received it
with marked courtesy, and listened to the able memorial with
much interest, for how could it be otherwise, containing as it
did the practical and reasonable proposition that "a provision
might be introduced into the Treaty of Peace, binding the
respective Governments to refer misunderstandings hereafter
to the decision of an impartial arbitrator."

Viscount Palmerston, in reply to this Memorial, and
to the observations Mr. Cobden, Mr. Gibson, and Lord
Grosvenor, gave a general approval of the principle, and
said "that it was the duty and interest of Governments
to adopt it, and he was quite sure that whoever might be
charged with the government of this country, not to allow
matters to involve them in a state of war," and further
expressed a cordial sentiment in favour of the usefulness of
associations for peace, in influencing the general opinion of
mankind to prefer "the solid advantages of peace to the
more dazzling results of war."

Encouraged by this successful interview with the Premier,
and the favourable opinions expressed by him on the main question, Mr. Richard and his coadjutors, impelled by a high sense
of obligation to their own consciences, as well as in the justice
of the sacred cause they stood forward as champions, they
decided to advance one step further, a step it must be admitted
the most responsible and important, full of the utmost
gravity, and requiring the exercise of the keenest judgment
and moderation, that can possibly be conceived.

This mission was none other than to go to Paris, and in
his own person, and by his own voice, to submit to the

Sovereigns represented at the Congress and to their respective Plenipotentiaries, a Memorial, praying the Congress to
recognise by Protocol the grand principle of international
arbitration, as a means of settling international differences.
The conception of such a mission, bold in design, the execution of the intricate details, the preparing of the memorial,
performed with such delicate wisdom, a task of no ordinary

JOSEPH STURGE.

character, it is needless to say was the work of a master-mind,
and to the subject of this memorique, under the blessing of
God, must the renown be given.  He was nobly sustained in
this most important mission by the counsel and labour of two
men with a devotion and zeal not less remarkable to the cause
of peace, both of whom have long since passed to their great
reward, Joseph Sturge, and Charles Hindley, the latter M.P.

for Wigan, and president of the Peace Society.  All honour to
this brave triumvirate, the heroic and historic three, who may
well be compared to the "dauntless three" immortalized by
Macaulay when he wrote,

> "And straight against that great array,
> Forth went the dauntless three."

These men are the world's best and truest heroes, a
nation's glory, and worthy to be imitated.  They desired
not renown, they aimed at no monumental tablet ; not like
the martial hero, who wins his laurels amid the din and
carnage of the battlefield, emulating his comrades in deeds
of slaughter and of bloodshed, heedless of the cries of the
wounded, and the wholesale butchery of ten thousand
fellow-creatures,

> "Who rush into an eternal state,
> Out of the very flames of rage and hate."

Their's was a nobler and a grander because a more
humane and Christian deed ; their's was a conflict for
humanity without bloodshed, a struggle for freedom and
for peace, by the gentle but all powerful agency of reason
and of justice founded on the great decree of the Most
High, "who hath made of one blood all peoples to dwell in
peace on the face of His earth."

A few details of this important mission may not be without
interest, closely identified as it was with the unwearied
industry of Mr. Richard himself.

It was in the month of April, 1856, Mr. Richard, Mr.
Sturge, and Mr. Hindley, journeyed to Paris, in order to
lay before the assembled Congress there, the subject of
International Arbitration.  They were the bearers of a
memorial to the Emperors of France, Russia, and Austria,
the Kings of Prussia and Sardinia, and the Sultan of
Turkey.  This memorial, signed by Joseph Sturge as Chairman of the Peace Conference Committee, and by Henry
Richard as Secretary of the Peace Society, set forth the
widespread moral and material desolation inflicted by

war, it enforced the hazards inflicted on Europe by the absence of any system of " amicable reference," and urged that when the representatives of the Great Powers were assembled to arrange the future relations of Europe, the opportunity should be availed of to decide on a system of International Arbitration, and entreated individually each Plenipotentiary to promote the introduction into the Treaty of a provision for referring any disputes between Nations to an impartial and peaceful umpirage. A copy· of this memorial was placed in the hands of each Plenipotentiary, and, in addition, an interview was obtained with each severally in support of its prayer.

Happily, the president of the Congress, Lord Clarendon, was an enlightened statesman, ever favourably disposed to listen to counsels for peace, and to advance the common cause, so that when the deputation submitted the subject to his notice, he assured them that he would make an effort to bring the matter under the consideration of his colleagues. Lord Clarendon, on the 14th of April, faithfully fulfilled his trust, and having secured permission to bring the proposition before the Congress, he introduced the subject in a spirit that was most honourable to his character. An entire sitting was devoted to its discussion, and in the report of the proceedings of this discussion, Count Walewski, Ambassador for France, cordially concurred in the proposition as " being fully in accord with the tendencies of the Epoch." Count Buol, Ambassador for Austria, Baron Manteuffel, Ambassador for Prussia, Count Orloff, Ambassador for Russia, Count Cavour, Ambassador for Italy, orally supported the proposal, and accordingly a protocol was framed, the 23rd of the Treaty of Paris which declared as follows :

"Whereupon the Plenipotentiaries do not hesitate to express, in the name of their Governments, the wish, that States between which any serious misunderstanding may arise, should, before appealing to arms, have recourse, as far as circumstances might allow, to the good offices of a friendly Power," and further,

"the Plenipotentiaries hoped that the Governments not represented at the Congress will unite in the sentiment which·has
inspired the wish recorded in the present protocol."

Although this declaration was not all that was desired,
being optional and recommendatory, rather than positive and
obligatory, still, bearing in mind that this was the first time
that this happy innovation had been seriously considered by
statesmen for incorporation into a Treaty between the Great
Powers of Europe, bearing in mind also that at that time, so
recently as thirty-two years since, the principle of Arbitration
was looked upon as Utopian and visionary, and that its
recognition by the Congress was accomplished in face of
many difficulties, such a success must undoubtedly be considered as an immense triumph, "the moral effect of which,"
as was observed by Joseph Sturge, "it was impossible to
estimate;" an opinion which has been amply borne out
during the period that has intervened.      ·

Emphatic and influential were the testimonies of such
men as the late Earl of Derby, who declared in his place in
the House of Lords, to be "to the endless honor of that
Congress," and, of William Ewart Gladstone, who, in the
course of a speech in the House of Commons described
it as "a very great triumph."    And an honorable gentleman, who moved the address in reply to the speech from the
throne, rendered still more eloquent testimony when he said
that it "throws around peace an additional bulwark, and
sets a landmark in the progress of civilization and humanity."

Thus ended this inglorious Crimean War, a war, which
not only involved the enormous expenditure of 340 millions
sterling, but above all, and to which no amount of treasure
can compare, involved the sacrifice of one million of precious
lives, the manhood, the bread-winners of Russia, France,
England, Turkey, and Sardinia, a war, which instead of
settling, unsettled the Eastern Question, which gave that
most effete and corrupt nation Turkey, a new lease of cruel
and despotic power over the subject races in her Empire, a

war, which more than anything else consolidated in a neighbouring nation France, the dynasty of the Bonapartes, that in 1870 well-nigh brought her to the verge of ruin, a war, which prepared the way in 1876 for the terrible massacres in Bulgaria, and the ruthless destruction of human life in the insurrections of Montenegro and Servia, and finally precipitated the Russo-Turkish War of 1876 and 1877.

No thanks to the Government which declared that devastating Crimean War, nor to the Parliament of England which sanctioned it. But to the men who opposed it, preeminent amongst whom stand the names of Cobden, Bright, and Gibson in Parliament, and of Richard, Sturge, and Bowly out of Parliament, is due the imperishable renown for having resisted it almost alone, in the face of unmeasured obloquy. In the eloquent language of the brave champion for peace, the unmitred because incorruptible statesman, John Bright, *theirs* is the great consolation that "not one word of mine hath ever, shall ever, sanction the squandering of my country's treasure, or the spilling of one single drop of my country's blood."

---

## WAR IN CHINA, 1857.

Scarcely had the pæans of exultation ceased, scarcely had the ink dried on the parchment roll of the Treaty of Paris, which concluded the war with Russia, when the nation was stirred, and stirred painfully, by the shout of a war in China, and the terrible bombardment of Canton, with its defenceless and innocent population of a million-and-a-half souls, by a squadron of the British Fleet under the command of Admiral Seymour. And wherefore? For a cause the most trivial and unjustifiable that history has ever recorded.

It appears on the evidence of the Official documents and

by the statements of the Ministers of the Crown, to have
arisen in consequence of the seizure by the Chinese Authorities at Canton in October 1856, of the piratical Lorcha,
called the "Arrow," which was manned by a gang of
notorious pirates under the command of an Englishman,
but an alien to his country and her fair fame.

The career of this smuggler, told in the boastful recitals
of the crew, and corroborated by several merchantmen, had
been for some time engaged in scuttling and massacring whenever and wherever the opportunity presented itself. To the
discredit of the Flag of England, she had hoisted the British
Ensign as a cloak for her dark deeds, and to shield her
from capture in her depredatory exploits, an illegal act,
justified only on the ground of her having an Englishman,
a vile adventurer on board who was directing her operations
of smuggling and reprisals. Immediately on her seizure,
the English Consul at Canton, Mr. Parkes, addressed a
peremptory demand to the Governor-General of the Canton
Province, Commissioner Yeh, for her release, requesting
also an apology, and compliance therewith within 48 hours,
at the peril of the bombardment of the City.

Never was such an outrageous demand made by a repre
sentative of England, and never was the intervention of the
power of England more grossly abused, for on the evidence
of Sir John Bowring, the British Plenipotentiary at Hong-
Kong, the "Arrow" had no right whatever to hoist the
British Flag, her license had expired a month previously,
and he declared she was, on that account, to say nothing
else, in no way entitled to the protection of the English Flag.

With such irrefragable testimony, and in face of the
revolting deeds of pillage, loot, and wholesale human
carnage which followed, no wonder Mr. Richard stirred
himself, and by the scathing power of his pen, and the
energy of his influence, moved Parliament and the country
towards an indignant condemnation, as severe and merited,
as ever befell the actors in that diabolical transaction, the

representatives as well as the Ministers of the Crown who defended, and even gloried therein.

Mr. Richard incontestably proved that the " Arrow " was not an English vessel, as she was built by Chinese, owned by Chinese, manned by Chinese, with the exception of this *soi disant* Englishman on board; and remarkable to say, when the vessel was boarded no flag was flying, but that immediately on her seizure this counterfeit British flag was hoisted, in order to shield her in her illegal character as a smuggler from her just fate; and the conclusion which he arrived at was this, that the seizure was a *pretext*, not the justifiable reason, for forcing on a quarrel with China, substituting another "*casus belli*," in the language of Admiral Seymour himself, which was none other than to compel the Chinese Government to declare the port of Canton open, not for legitimate commerce, Oh! no, but for the compulsory traffic, in the very teeth of the wishes of the Chinese Government, of that most detestable opium traffic, a traffic verily "in pestilence, poverty, vice, madness, and death."

Well may Englishmen blush at the recital of such a deed, forced on not by diplomacy and negotiation, bad enough as that would be, but forsooth, forced at the mouth of the cannon, belching forth desolation and destruction, until the whole city was enveloped in flames, "in the horror of which men and women and children, innocent infancy and helpless, were ruthlessly immolated."

The nation was moved, the press had the courage to denounce this outrage on humanity, including such organs as *The Saturday Review The Spectator, The Examiner, Daily News, Morning Advertiser, Leeds Mercury*, and a score of others, all of whom lifted their voices in severe condemnation of this bombardment, whereby they poured red-hot shot and shell into the city of Canton, crushing and pounding in one indiscriminate massacre its population, without justification, based on pretensions the most false,

D

and therefore as the most wanton and treacherous deed with which the British name was ever identified.

Parliament too was moved. In the House of Lords the question was introduced in a most masterly speech by the late Earl of Derby, powerfully supported by Lord Lyndhurst and Earl Grey, and in the House of Commons on the motion of Mr. Cobden, a debate extending over four nights followed, which will long be memorable, from the fact that nearly every man of weight and influence off the Treasury Bench joined in denunciation, a debate worthy of the occasion, full of intellectual power, lofty, earnest, and severe.

Two grand speeches deserve notice, those of Mr. Cobden and Mr. Gladstone. The former for two hours and-a-half seized the attention of the House, holding it in willing and delighted captivity by an eloquence of charming simplicity, logical facts and truths, which carried conviction and admiration to the assembled senators of England.

The speech of Mr. Gladstone was, as might be expected, the most brilliant of all, distinguished by the truest eloquence, masterly, full of high principle and earnest conviction. A few quotations may be permitted.

"There is not war with China, no Sir, but there is hostility and bloodshed, a trampling down of the weak by the strong, a terrible and abominable retaliation. (Cheers.) War taken at the best is a frightful scourge to the human race, and because it is so, the wisdom of ages has surrounded it with strict laws and usages. You have dispensed with all these precautions. (Cheers.) You have turned a consul into a diplomatist, and that metamorphosis is forsooth to be at liberty to direct the whole might of England against the head of a defenceless people. You go to China and make war upon those who stand before you as women and children. You can earn no glory in such warfare. We hear of calamity heaped upon calamity, of cruelty heaped upon cruelty."

He closed by a powerful appeal as follows :—

"With every one of us it rests to shew that this House, which is the first, the most ancient, and the noblest temple of freedom in the world, is also the temple of that everlasting justice without

which freedom itself would be only a name, or only a curse to
mankind. And, Sir, I cherish the trust and belief, that when
you rise in your place to-night to declare the numbers of the
division from the chair which you adorn, the words which you
speak will go forth as a message of mercy and of peace, as a
message of prudence and wisdom, to the farthest corners of the
world." (Loud cheering.)

Such speeches as these, marshalled by an array of incon-
trovertible facts, appealing powerfully to the sentiments of
humanity, of justice, which dwells so securely in the breasts
of Englishmen, appealed not in vain to the House of Commons, and when on the 14th of March, the division took
place, the words of hope expressed by Mr Gladstone received
their fulfilment, for a message went forth that a majority of
the English Parliament refused to sanction the diabolical
deeds committed against Canton, with which the names of
Sir Michael Seymour, Sir John Bowring, Mr. Consul Parkes,
and Lord Palmerston himself were associated, and by that
message of condemnation, the responsible advisers of the
Crown of England, defeated and disgraced, appealed from
that decision to the electors throughout the country.

This dissolution of Parliament, and appeal to the Nation
to ratify or nullify the decision of Parliament, brought Mr.
Richard to the front, in the hope that by the issue of statements of facts on the whole case, drawn from official sources,
and by appeals to the conscience of the electors against what
he believed and shewed to be an outrage upon justice and
humanity, of deeds committed *in their name*, the decision of
Parliament might be the decision of the Nation, and result
in the defeat of the confidence trick, which Lord Palmerston
made the hustings cry.

Unhappily in spite of justice disgraced, the appeals of
humanity outraged, the fair fame of England sullied, the
electors ˙of the Empire allowed themselves to be carried
away, first by a blind and furious hatred of the "barbarians," ·
whom they considered ought to be exterminated like wild
beasts ; and secondly, by a senseless clamour about the

honour of the British flag, which they considered of paramount importance to the eternal principles of truth and righteousness. The result was that not only the Government of Lord Palmerston secured a majority, not only the people of England pronounced against a policy of peace and in favour of a policy of war, but, humiliating fact, a majority which excluded from Parliament three at least of the foremost men of England, foremost for their political integrity, distinguished ability, and disinterested patriotism, such were Richard Cobden, John Bright, and Milner Gibson. No higher testimony was offered to these eminent men in their temporary exclusion from the senate by a temporary revulsion of feeling of the Nation, than the lofty language penned at the time by Mr. Richard :

" They have that light within which no outward reverses can darken. There is no cloud upon their consciences. There is no taint of blood on their hands. On the contrary, recalling the fidelity with which they have sought to promote the interest of humanity and peace, how steadfastly they sacrificed power and popularity rather than swerve from their loyalty to truth and conscience, how in the hour of their defeat, a willing and cordial homage has been paid by all classes to the purity of their motives, the integrity of their public character, it may truly be said whether there are any men living who occupy at this moment a position more honourable, or enviable than that of Richard Cobden and John Bright."

## PERSIAN WAR, 1857.

Not only was Mr. Richard's anxiety and labours during the year 1857 directed to this miserable embroglio between England and China, but also near the close of the year, ere the troubles of that disgraceful war had come to a termination, his attention was turned to the outbreak of hostilities in Central Asia, wherein the British forces in India were moved without the knowledge and certainly without the sanction of Parliament on a filibustering expedition into the

Persian dominions, ostensibly for the occupation of the city of Herat. A brief reference to the causes, the objects, and results of that Asiatic war is necessary here, not only on account of the action taken by Mr. Richard in the matter, but also because herein was generally accepted at the time to be one of the ruling if not dominant causes which precipitated, as it preceded, the terrible mutiny in India, and the appalling massacre at Cawnpore, which so moved the English mind, and threatened to shake to its foundations the sway of the British sceptre in the Empire of India.

In the debate in the House of Commons on this Persian war, which took place in the month of July 1857, we find some important particulars on the subject. It would appear that whilst the object of the war was to compel Persia to evacuate the city of Herat, and to render compensation for injuries inflicted there, yet owing to the haughtiness of the foreign policy of Lord Palmerston a demand was made that the Prime Minister of Persia, whom the English Government held responsible for that occupation should be summarily dismissed, and a Minister appointed more favourable to friendly relations with England. Herein was the sole cause of that war which involved a great sacrifice of men, and money,—and strange to say which was finally concluded by a Treaty of Peace in the same year, in reference to which, to quote the declaration of Lord John Russell and of Mr. Gladstone, who used these remarkable words:

" It stands upon record, and is beyond all doubt, that we made peace upon terms decidedly less favourable to England, and less unfavourable to Persia, than those which Persia herself had offered before the war broke out."

In November and December 1858, Mr. Richard, accompanied by Joseph Sturge of Birmingham, and Edward Smith of Sheffield, visited Liverpool, Manchester, and Leeds, and addressed conferences of the Friends of Peace, for the purpose of stimulating renewed activity and support, and at each of those important centres Mr. Richard subsequently delivered public lectures, choosing for his subject, " Does War tend to promote Christianity," and he also took part in several meetings on the " Anti-Opium Question."

---

## WAR IN ITALY, 1859.

The War in Italy in 1859, between France and Sardinia on the one hand, and Austria on the other, was vigorously assailed by Mr. Richard, for he considered it had no reference to the well-being of nations, but was the offspring of diplomatic and dynastic intrigues, a sequence of the Crimean War of 1854, stimulated by the ambition of the Emperor of the French to play an imposing part in Europe, as well as by the ambition of Victor Emmanuel, King of Sardinia, in virtue of his alliance with France, England, and Turkey in the Crimean War, by which he hoped to obtain territorial aggrandisement, and thus enable Sardinia to enter into the family of European powers.

In this impending struggle on the Italian peninsula for the freedom of Italy from the Alps to the Adriatic from Austrian and Papal domination, Mr. Richard and the Peace Society lost no opportunity and spared no effort to create a powerful public opinion in favour of the absolute non-intervention of England; and within a few weeks after the outbreak of hostilities, an influential meeting in favour of non-intervention was held in Exeter Hall, under the presidency of Mr. Samuel Morley, at which Mr. Richard, Mr. Benjamin Scott, Rev. Newman Hall, Mr. H. E. Gurney, Mr. George Thompson, and others took part; and a Memorial was adopted to Lord Palmerston, which deplored the sanguinary War being waged by three professedly civilized and Christian nations, deplorable not only on account of the slaughter and misery involved, and the international hatreds engendered, but on the ground of future disquietude and danger to the peace of Europe, and they therefore appealed to the Government to adhere strictly to the principle and practice of non-intervention, and that thus England might be enabled to fill the honorable office of friendly Mediator between the contending States.

In the following month Lord Palmerston received the Memorial at the hands of an influential deputation, introduced by Mr. Edward Baines, M.P., and after Mr. Richard had read it, the Prime Minister replied, concurring in the views expressed, and promising support of the policy recommended, but believed it would be better for Italy to be relieved from the power of Austria, and he hoped for a satisfactory solution by the emancipation of Italy.

The policy of Lord Palmerston and Lord John Russell strongly favoured the alliance of France and Sardinia, against the despotism of Austria, and the possession by Austria of any portion of the Italian peninsula ; and their accession to power in 1859, on the defeat of Lord Derby after an appeal to the country, turned mainly if not entirely on Foreign Affairs, especially the respective opinions and policy of Conservative and Liberal statesmen on Italian affairs ; Lord Derby having declared in favour of Austrian domination, and Lord Palmerston and Lord Russell in favour of the independence of Italy and of an Italian Kingdom under the rule of the House of Savoy.

The policy of Lord Palmerston, judged by his despatches to the Ministers at Foreign Courts, his correspondence with his colleagues in the Cabinet, and his public utterances, were unequivocally to give the moral support of England to the Franco-Sardinian alliance; and his declaration to the deputation, organised by Mr. Richard, at the Foreign Office in favour of England's neutrality was conditional, as his words imply the defeat of Austria, and the emancipation of Italy.

Fortunately for Italy and the general peace of Europe, the arms of France and Sardinia were victorious ; and the

Emperor Napoleon foreseeing the probable intervention of Prussia, and anxious for peace after the sanguinary conflicts of Solferino and Magenta, instructed Count Persigny, the French Ambassador at London, to invite the good offices of the British Cabinet as Mediator; but Lord Palmerston objecting to the terms of peace proposed by Persigny, declined the overtures of France, and the French Emperor thereupon dispatched General Fleury to the Austrian head-quarters, and proposed an armistice, which being accepted, a Conference of the two Emperors took place at Villafranca, and on the 11th July a Provisional Treaty of Peace was signed, on the basis of an Italian Confederation under the Presidency of the Pope, the cession of Lombardy to Sardinia, and the restoration of the Grand Dukes of Tuscany and Modena. These proposals led to the resignation of Count Cavour and the opposition of the Prime Minister of England.

For several months subsequently the intervention and the influence of England directed by Lord Palmerston was visibly and powerfully felt, notwithstanding his pacific assurance to the contrary, addressed to Mr. Richard and his friends; and although the position taken up, and the policy pursued by the English Premier may have been disinterested, anxious only for the realisation of the noble aspirations of the Italians for a united and independent Italy, and her freedom from a foreign yoke and from Austrian rule, yet at the same time the resolute determination of Lord Palmerston and Lord John Russell, whose views were identical, throughout this prolonged diplomatic quarrel, not confined simply to the Cabinets at Paris, Vienna, and Turin, but with the other great European Powers, it may without exaggeration be said well-nigh involved Great Britain into an open rupture, an outbreak of a European War.

In a remarkable despatch penned by Lord Palmerston, dated January 7th, 1860, the position of England at this juncture was plainly stated :—

"The English Government," he said, "have determined, in

regard to Italian affairs, that England should not abdicate its position as one of the Great Powers of Europe.

"It considers that what is at issue is not the interests of the Emperor Napoleon, but the interests of the people of Italy, and through them, the welfare and peace of Europe.

"The policy of England is in accordance with those principles which English Statesmen in our times have professed and acted upon, and which are the foundation of public opinion in England.

"We take our stand upon the principle that no force should be employed for the purpose of imposing upon the people of Italy any form of government or constitution, that the people of Italy should be left free to determine their own political existence.

"To accomplish this England ought to come to an understanding with France and Sardinia, a joint determination to prevent any forcible interference by any Foreign Power in the affairs of Italy.

"But such an engagement might lead us into war. War with whom? War with Austria. Well, suppose it did, would that War be one of great effort and expense? Clearly not. France, Sardinia and Italy would furnish troops enough to repel any attempt which Austria could make to coerce Sardinia or Italy.

"Our share in such a War would be chiefly if not wholly Naval; and our Squadron in the Adriatic and a couple of Regiments to garrison some point on the Adriatic would probably be the utmost of our contribution.

"My own deliberate opinion is that the course now recommended would be highly approved by the country, that it would be approved by Parliament, but if by any combination of parties an adverse decision were come to, it would in my opinion be the duty of the Government to appeal from Parliament to the country."

Such was the remarkable declaration in January, 1860, on the settled policy of Lord Palmerston on the affairs of Italy, differing very considerably from the pacific declarations made to Mr. Richard and the deputation in June, 1859, in favour of neutrality and friendly mediation, and how the noble lord or his colleague, Lord John Russell, reconciled this divergence of opinion and policy it is difficult to say. Happily however for the honour of English Statesmanship and the interests of England, this threatened triple alliance of the Western Powers against Austria and its consequence an European War, was averted, for the ultimatum of England was practically accepted, by which France and Austria agreed not to interfere for the future in the affairs of Italy, the evacuation by France of her troops in Rome, the several States in Central Italy to declare their choice of allegiance by a plebiscite, and although subsequently France annexed Nice and Savoy, as her share in the plunder of a reconstructed Italy, their annexation was assented to rather than risk the danger of War.

In March 1859 Mr. Richard, accompanied by Joseph Sturge and Edward Smith, visited several of the large towns in the North of England, with a view to re-organize the Auxiliaries to revive the interest in the cause of peace.

The special interest attaching to these labours of Mr. Richard, accompanied by the President of the Peace Society, were rendered memorable from the fact that it was the last "labour of love" that that eminent philanthropist Joseph Sturge rendered to the Cause of Peace to which he was so devotedly attached, and no less to which he had rendered such signal services.

"None who heard him," writes Mr. Richard, "can ever forget the earnestness, the humility, the pleading and pathetic tenderness which marked his address. They were listened to by many there with throbbing hearts, and tearful eyes ; but Oh ! if we had known that he was standing so near the threshold of heaven, when he spoke to us how we should have caught and treasured every word that fell from his lips."

"Soon after his return home on the 14th May," on that early May morning soon after the break of day, he heard his Master's voice saying, "Come up hither," "and he was gone."

# THE WAR PANIC, 1859 TO 1862.

Late in the year 1859, Lord Palmerston became alarmed, mainly arising out of a dispute between Spain and Morocco, for the possession of disputed territory on the African Coast, and frightened Lord John Russell and his colleagues into the belief that France was aiming to obtain, through Spain, certain fortified points near Gibraltar, which in the event of War, might shut England out of the Mediterranean.

In a letter to Mr. Gladstone, then Chancellor of the Exchequer, dated 15th December 1859, Lord Palmerston gave vent to all his alarmist fears and unworthy suspicions of France, and he strongly advocated the fortifying of the naval arsenals, and the dockyards on the ground ;—

" That if by a sudden attack by an army, landed in strength, our dockyards were to be destroyed, our maritime power would for more than half a century be paralysed, and our colonies and our commerce would be at the mercy of the enemy, who would be sure to show us no mercy.

" That such a landing is in the present state of things possible must be manifest.  No naval force of ours can effectually prevent it."

There is no doubt that at this juncture Lord Palmerston had in addition, become painfully distrustful of the Emperor Napoleon, in spite of his personal friendship for him, and his former confidence in him as an ally, a suspicion accelerated by the occupation of Syria by French troops, and the annexation of Nice and Savoy; in fact he spoke of "the Emperor's mind as full of schemes as a warren is full of rabbits."

In a letter to Lord John Russell of November 4th, 1859, he says :—

" Till lately I had strong confidence in the fair intentions of Napoleon towards England, but of late I have begun to feel great distrust, and to suspect that his formerly declared intention of avenging Waterloo has not died away.

" Next, he has been assiduously labouring to increase his naval means evidently for offensive as well as for defensive purposes, and latterly great pains have been taken to rouse throughout

France, and especially amongst the army and navy, hatred of England."

In a letter also to the Duke of Somerset he says —

"I have watched the French Emperor narrowly and have studied his character and conduct. You may rely upon it that at the bottom there rankles a deep and inextinguishable desire to humble and punish England, and to avenge, if he can, the many humiliations—political, naval and military—which since the beginning of the century England has by herself and her allies inflicted upon France."

And later on, Lord Palmerston wrote to Mr. Gladstone condemning the action of Cobden and Bright for their speeches against the increased military expenditure, and adding :—

"We have on the other side of the Channel a people who, say what they may, hate us from the bottom of their hearts as a nation, and would make any sacrifice to inflict a thorough humiliation upon England.

"They are eminently vain, and their passion is glory in war; they cannot forget or forgive Aboukir, Trafalgar, the Peninsula, Waterloo, and St. Helena."

Under the fear of this baseless "invasion panic" Lord Palmerston urged forward gigantic preparations of defence, the construction of fortifications, and the development of the Volunteer Rifle Movement.

A Confidential Committee had ·been appointed in 1858 by Lord Derby's Government to enquire into the comparative state of the Navies of England and France. The report of this Committee embracing six years, 1852 to 1858, was laid before Parliament, January, 1859.

This alarmed the Peers of England, Lord Lyndhurst declaring that ;—

"From information which I have received, and the accuracy of which I do not doubt, that the French are at the present moment building steamers for the purpose of transporting troops, each of which is constructed to carry 2,500 men with all the necessary stores. . . . I will not consent to live in dependence on the friendship or forbearance of any country ; are we to sit supine on our own shores, and not prepare the means necessary in case of war to resist that power ?"

Lord Ellenborough caught the contagion and exclaimed;—

" My Lords, it is not safe for the country to remain unarmed in the midst of armed nations."

Lord Stratford de Redcliffe, the author of the Crimean War, declared;—

" It was a just cause of shame, and an intolerable humiliation that a great empire like ours should appear, though it were only for an hour, to exist by suffrance, and at the good pleasure of a forbearing neighbour."

In the House of Commons Mr. Horsman delivered a downright panic speech in which he said;—

" The Emperor of the French acted for the interests of France; it was ours to guard the safety of England. . . . Not a moment must be lost in making the country safe against any accident, and until it was so we must act as if the crisis were upon us. No human tongue could tell how soon or how suddenly it might arise."

It was under such a fusillade of abusive speeches such as these, hurled at the Ruler of a Great and Friendly Power, so recently our ally, that Mr. Cobden visited Paris for the express purpose of negotiating a Treaty of Commerce, which was intended to bind the two nations in amity and concord, and he observed that this popular delusion might have been an element of danger to the peace of the two countries, had it not been for the character of the Emperor, who throughout those provocations displayed a perfect equanimity and self-control.

On the 23rd July, 1860, Lord Palmerston brought forward the Government measure for the construction of works for the defence of the Royal dockyards and arsenals and of the ports of Dover and Portland, and for the creation of a central arsenal, at the cost of £11,000,000, when he delivered one of the most serious and alarming speeches ever delivered by a Minister of the Crown in a time of peace, and the following alarmist utterance will suffice :—

" It is impossible for any man to cast his eyes over the face of Europe, and to see and hear what is passing, without being convinced that the future is not free from danger. It is difficult to say where the storm may burst ; but the horizon is charged with clouds which betoken the possibility of a tempest, and in the main I am speaking of our immediate neighbours across the Channel, and there is no use in disguising it."

It was at this critical and important moment, writes Mr. Cobden ;—

"When a commercial Treaty with France upon the liberal arrangement of which depended the whole success of the measure, that this speech burst upon the negotiators in Paris. Had its object been to placé the British Commissioners at the greatest possible disadvantage, it could not have more effectually accomplished the purpose. *   *   *   *   *

" It cut the ground from under their feet of seeking to strengthen the friendly relations of the two countries as represented by their Governments.   *   *   *   *

" Had the Emperor seized the occasion for instantly suspending the negotiations, he would have undoubtedly performed a most popular part, but on this, as on other occasions, his habitual calmness and self-mastery prevailed, and to these qualities must be mainly attributed the successful issue of the Treaty."

Well might Mr. Disraeli to his great credit exclaim ;—

"What is the use of diplomacy ?   What is the use of Governments ?   What is the use of cordial understandings if such things can take place ?

" Truly there is a vacant niche in the Temple of Fame for the Ruler or Minister who shall be the first to grapple with this monster evil of the day."

Early in the incipient stages of this Palmerstonian alarm of invasion from France, Mr. Richard, in December 1859, came to the front, and assisted by his valued colleague, Mr. Edmund Fry, endeavoured to counteract the suicidal folly which Ministers and Parliament were plunging, scared as he said by an article in the *Times,* with not a fragment of justification save

" The baseless fabric of a vision."

On the one hand, in France this monomania rested on the shallow foundation of a restless faction, who cherished the hope of scrambling into Power by a political convulsion that might shake the authority of the Emperor, and on the other hand, encouraged and supported in England by a formidable combination of Whigs and Tories, who hoped thereby to divert the thoughts and aspirations of the people from Parliamentary Reform and other remedial legislation by a craven fear of France and sinister designs of her Ruler, and the absurd cry of "England in danger."

During 1860 and 1861 Mr. Richard by the press and

EDMUND FRY.

platform laboured hard to stem the rising tide of terror of France, and alarm at the defenceless condition of England. Article after article from his active pen followed one another in rapid succession on the Armaments of Europe, especially their costliness, in which he shewed that from the year 1815 to 1860 Great Britain had spent the enormous sum of £821,000,000 in preparations for War, and the equally enormous sum of £915,634,000 for the interest of her National Debt, contracted for War and by War, making the immense total of £1,737,186,000 poured into the unfathomable abyss of War; and yet in spite of this gigantic outlay for securing the strength of the Empire, England was still in danger, and that therefore greater sacrifices and a greater military outlay must be made, not born of any actual necessity, but born of passion and greed, from personal considerations of the Military Classes. Well might Mr. Richard strive at this juncture to expose the ruinous folly of such a gormandising system, and to rouse the nation to demand that the Government should enter into negotiations with the other Governments of Europe, and especially of France, with a view to the mutual and simultaneous reduction of those armaments which oppress the people, and fill Europe with so much alarm and disquietude.

He was stimulated in this action, in the belief, well founded, that there was a coalition in France and in England of the Military with the Protectionist party, to circumvent the noble and disinterested efforts of Mr. Cobden, to bind England and France in the bonds of amity and goodwill by a Treaty of Peace, through Commerce, and if possible to defeat and crush the great scheme, lest peradventure, to their eternal shame be it said, this noble Treaty of Free Trade and Bond of Union, should bar the way of those two great and mighty Nations from plunging into the unspeakable horrors of a bloody War.

Mr. Richard, on the contrary, highly eulogised that Treaty, and the great Statesman who had so skilfully and successfully negotiated it, as having done more, yes, a thousand times more, to prevent War between these two countries, than all the iron-cased vessels, all the rifled cannon, all the bristling fortifications, and all the heroic volunteers in knickerbockers and shakos that the panic-mongers can produce ; and further, adopting the eloquent language of Lord John Russell, that as ;—

" This Treaty of Commerce would tend to lay broad and deep foundations in common interest, and in friendly intercourse, for the confirmation of the amicable relations that so happily exist between the two countries, and thus make a provision for the future which will progressively become more and more solid and efficacious."

Therefore such being the case to make an attempt for France and England to come to some accord, in the language of Mr. Disraeli ;—

" To terminate this disastrous system of wild expenditure by mutually agreeing, with no hypocrisy, but in a manner and under circumstances which admit of no doubt, by the reduction of armaments, that peace is really our policy."

The activity of Mr. Richard, by the press and platform, on this question was remarkable, keeping two objects steadily in view, the one to inform and arouse the popular mind in England on the absurdity and folly of the military panic, and the other to bring to bear the reciprocal feeling of friendship and good neighbourhood with France, and shatter thereby the foundation for the unworthy alarmist fears of the War party in England.

During the years of 1861 and 1862 he laboured hard on the platform, and delivered Lectures and addressed Public Meetings in various parts of the country; and amongst other places, at Leeds, Bradford (2), Huddersfield, Birmingham, Bristol, Cambridge, Southwark, York, Highflatts, Selby, Halifax, Tottenham, Barnsley, Dewsbury, Darlington, New-castle-on-Tyne (2), Sheffield, Hull, Brighton, at all of which memorials or resolutions to the Government and the representatives of those towns were adopted, deprecating the mistrust of France, and in favour of disarmament.

In the month of April, 1861, Mr. Richard, accompanied by Mr. Joseph Cooper (an ardent and devoted friend of freedom for the slave, and peace amongst nations), formed a deputation on behalf of the Peace Society to France, carrying a conciliatory Address to the People of France, which referred with satisfaction to the recent Treaty of Commerce negotiated by Mr. Cobden, as evidence of the mutual

E

desire of the two peoples for friendly relations, and for
Union ; regretted the sinister influences at work by certain
sections to impair this friendship, and urged the importance
of the people of the two nations to come to the front, and
express their determination to maintain the cordial alliance
of England and France, and to lead the way—

"Not in deeds of violence, not in armaments for War, but a
rivalry in those beneficent triumphs of peace which are attended
with no remorse to the victor, and no humiliation to the vanquished."

The deputation, as missionaries of Peace, were received
in Paris by those to whom they were accredited with
marked courtesy and cordiality, and by the favour of the
editors of the various daily and weekly Journals, the Address
was published in full in most, if not all the leading papers,
from the semi-official organ of *Le Journal des Débats*, to the
popular paper, *L'Opinion Nationale;* and from these it was
reproduced in many of the provincial and foreign Journals
throughout Europe, a result which the *Nonconformist* thus
refers to :—

"At a juncture when the horizon of Europe is black with a
threatening storm, Mr. Richard, on behalf of the Peace Society,
has been able to address wise counsels to the foremost Continental Nation, and we may reasonably hope helped to deepen
that aversion to War among the French people which is one of
the best safeguards of international amity."

Exactly a year after this pacific mission to France, (and it
is a forcible proof of its beneficial results, in conjunction
with other influences, that during the interval France made
no hostile movement, whether of menace or action,) the
International Exhibition in London was inaugurated when a
great procession of the Nations to England was witnessed, a
veritable invasion from France in a special degree, not as
the prophets of evil omen such as Palmerston, Horsman
& Co. had predicted, of embattled hosts intent on avenging
Waterloo, and of effacing the humiliating memories of the
defeat and captivity of the First Napoleon—no ! but of the
*élite* of France, the vanguard of civilization and peace of

that great Nation, marching in overwhelming numbers to
the Metropolis of the world, to exchange personal greetings
with English men and English women, and to prove by
their presence in the capital of England that they have no
sympathy with the insane rivalry of Statesmen, the jealousy
of Governments, and the ambitions of Rulers, and that in
industry, and commerce, and civilization alone,

" Peace hath her victories,
Thrice more renowned than War."

It was fitting therefore, that at this international festival
of industry, the opportunity was not forgotten by Mr.
Richard and his friends to greet the foreign visitors with a
cordial reception, not only with missives of peace, translated
into various languages, not only by inviting many of the
distinguished visitors to an open assembly for an interchange
of friendly sentiment and feeling, but also, and above all, to
present them with an Address as a friendly token to treasure
as an eternal bond of union, on their return to their own
land.

This address was signed by Joseph Pease the President,
and Henry Richard the Secretary of the Peace Society, and
in effect, it declared, that this *re-union* of the Nations of the
world, was designed to draw the peoples nearer together ;—

" In mutual intercourse and dependence, and thereby to fulfil
one of the great purposes of Christianity in promoting Peace
on Earth, and Goodwill among Men " ;—

that steamships and railways, electric telegraphs and a free
Commerce, favors the unity and brotherhood of nations ;
that an attitude of mutual jealousy and suspicion by the
civilized Nations of Europe is an anachronism and a crime ;
and it appealed therefore to all, to form in their respective
countries, a power of public opinion that will compel the
Governments of Europe, in the words of the late Sir Robert
Peel ;—

" To reduce those military armaments which belong to a
state of War rather than of Peace."

Following close upon this international Exhibition of all
Nations, came from an unexpected quarter a crushing defeat
of the war party, in overwhelming proof of the just
and strong position taken up from the first by Mr. Richard,
by a remarkably pacific speech delivered by the Ruler of
France at the opening of the French Chambers at the close
of the year 1863, and which was soon afterwards followed
by a definite proposal from him for the holding of an International Congress at Paris, in order to place if possible on a
safer and firmer basis the peace of Europe.

By this stroke of diplomacy the Emperor of the French
gave the lie direct to his enemies and detractors in England,
who for a period of three years had exhausted their
vocabulary of abuse, hurled not alone at himself as the head
of the most powerful nation in Europe, but also levelled
without a shade of a shadow of foundation against the
people of France.

It is well-known that as far back as 1860, when Lord
Palmerston and his Government were doing their utmost to
excite in the minds of the English people prejudices,
suspicions, and even enmity against France, on the absurd
ground of a supposed intention of Napoleon III. to avenge
Waterloo by an invasion of England, that the Emperor
had addressed to Count Persigny, the French Ambassador
in London, a dispatch, a straightforward and courteous
declaration, utterly denying the charges and schemes
attributed to him, and nothing could have been more frank.

" Tell Lord Palmerston from me in the most explicit manner,
that since the Treaty of Villafranca I have had but one thought,
one object—to inaugurate a new era of Peace, and to live on
the best terms with all my neighbours, and especially with
England.'

And yet notwithstanding this important disclaimer from
the French Emperor, and in spite of the Commercial Treaty
between the two Nations, the War party in England, led by
Lord Palmerston, as his letters and speeches testify, ceased
not year after year to mistrust, misrepresent, and malign the

people, the Parliament, and the Ruler of a Mighty Nation, our ancient ally.

All these fears and prognostications were unfounded, and as a crowning proof of the sincerity of the French Emperor, to inaugurate as he declared, an era of Peace during his reign, he comes forward in 1863 in the *rôle* of the pacificator of Europe. Mr. Richard hailed with satisfaction this speech of the Emperor when he declared ;—

" Have not the prejudices and rumours which divide us lasted long enough? Shall the jealous rivalries of the Great Powers unceasingly impede the progress of civilization? Are we still to maintain mutual distrust by exaggerated armaments? Must our most precious resources be indefinitely exhausted in a vain display of our forces? Must we eternally maintain a condition of things which is neither Peace with its security, nor War with its happy chances? Let us have the courage to substitute for a sickly and precarious condition of things, a situation solid and regular, even should it cost us some sacrifices. Let us assemble without pre-conceived system, without exclusive ambition, animated alone by the thought of establishing an order of things founded for the future on the well-understood interests of both sovereigns and peoples."

M. Drouyn de L'Huys, the French Minister for Foreign Affairs, following close upon this pacific utterance of the Emperor, opened up communications with the British Government, reminding them of the recommendations of the Paris Congress of 1856, in favour of a reference of any misunderstanding between the States to the friendly offices of a Neutral Power, before appealing to arms.

This important dispatch was followed by a practical proposal of the Emperor, addressed to the Sovereigns of Europe, to convene an International Congress at Paris for the discussion and settlement of the questions in dispute, and thus secure the pacification of Europe ; but Lord Palmerston refused to accede to the proposal, and his reasons for doing so are contained in two important letters which he addressed, November 15th, 1863, to the King of the Belgians, and to Lord Russell in a subsequent letter dated December 2nd, 1863.

In the former he wrote as follows :—

"The functions of a Congress if now to be assembled might be two-fold, and would bear either on the past or the future, or both.   As to the past the functions of the Congress would either be unnecessary, or barred by insurmountable difficulties. As to the future, would the Congress have to range over the wide and almost endless extent of proposed and possible changes, or would it have to confine itself to questions practically pending ?

"In the face of all these difficulties my humble opinion is that no Congress will meet; for its failure will give Europe some danger and some embarrassment."

To Lord Russell, December 3rd, 1863, he wrote :

"It is quite certain that the deliberations of a Congress would consist of demands, and pretensions, put forward by some and resolutely resisted by others, and that there being no supreme authority in such an assembly to enforce the opinions or decisions of the majority, the Congress would separate leaving many of the members on worse terms with each other than when they met."

This opinion of the Prime Minister of England was not shared by the other European Powers, for we find that Russia, Prussia, Italy, Denmark, Belgium, Spain, Sweden and Norway, Portugal, Greece, and several of the States of Germany, gave their unqualified support to the proposal, and even the Pope of Rome ; but the decision of England was unfavourable, and the project fell through.

Mr. Richard warmly supported the idea, which he considered a noble one, for this realisation might have inaugurated a change in the Policy of Europe of great value to the Nations; and he gave effect to this opinion by the address which was sent on behalf of the Peace Society to the Emperor, wherein he said in conclusion,—

"Should your Majesty succeed in leading the Powers of Europe into the path of arbitration and disarmament, it will confer upon your Majesty's reign, a glory far brighter and more enduring than any that can be reaped from the most brilliant military achievements, because it will be a glory derived from the gratitude of nations, and the well-being of universal humanity."

To this address the Emperor sent a most gracious reply,

expressive of his warm appreciation of the sentiments it contained, and of its recognition of his constant solicitude for the maintenance of the general peace.

---

## THE AMERICAN WAR OF SECESSION, 1861.

No record of Henry Richard's labours in the Cause of Peace would be complete without a reference to the persistent, and from his standpoint of consistent opposition to the great struggle between the Northern and Southern States of America, based as it was on his undeviating hostility to all War, and all exercise of force in national or international affairs.

In the first place a brief reference to the causes which precipitated that great War is necessary.

The culminating point of the American crisis was the Presidential Election, at the close of the year 1860, of Abraham Lincoln, and this choice by a majority of the American people drew a direct line of demarcation between the Northern and Southern States, as it was stated that not a single Southerner voted for, and not a single Northerner voted against him. The Abolitionists of the North not satisfied with the results of their victory, indulged in exasperating language towards the Pro-slavery party of the South, and the latter, smarting also under the injustice of a prohibitive tariff, looked upon the Union as a tremendous evil, and resolved to exercise what they considered their lawful right to secede, and to declare their independence.

The feeling in the South was decidedly opposed to the commercial policy of the North, which was prohibitive, for it pressed heavily on the commercial classes, but the social and political question of slavery was the chief cause of contention ; for the Southern States clung tenaciously to it, and were alarmed at the feeling of hostility displayed by the press and political parties in the North.

This conflict of opinion was brought to a test in Congress by the vexed question, whether slaveholding territories should be admitted into the Union, and on its being decided in the negative the Southern representatives withdrew, and the Secession followed, South Carolina, Virginia, and Georgia taking the lead, and their first act was to seize the Federal arsenals and fortresses in the disaffected States.

On the 9th January, 1861, the first shot was fired from the batteries of Fort Sumpter against the Federal Fleet, which was in effect the declaration of disruption and War, and on the 18th February, Mr. Jefferson Davis was inaugurated President of the Confederate States, on which accession he declared :—

"We have entered on a career of independence, which must be inflexibly pursued through many years of controversy with our late associates of the Northern States."

On the 4th March Mr. Abraham Lincoln delivered his inaugural address as President of the *dis*-United States, in which he declared:—

"A disruption of the Federal Union, heretofore only menaced, is now formidably attempted.   I hold that in the eye of universal law, and of the constitution, the Union of these States is perpetual."

At the onset of this terrific conflict Mr. Richard promptly sounded the note of alarm in the columns of the *Herald of Peace*, and he justified his intrusion in the controversy on the grounds :—

"That we on this side of the Atlantic are better able to form a clear and correct Christian judgment of American affairs than the American people themselves, whirled about as they were in the mad mäelstrom of the fierce political excitement which seems to have sucked almost everybody into its vortex."

During the four years that this fierce tornado raged in all its fury from " the frozen North in unbroken line to the glowing South, and from the wild billows of the Atlantic westward to the calmer waters of the Pacific main," Mr. Richard strenuously opposed and vigorously condemned the policy of the North and of the Federal Government at Washington to maintain the Union by force; and whilst dissociating himself and his friends from any sympathy for slavery, but on the contrary avowing "a strenuous, consistent, and persevering" hostility to that abomination, yet he declared that infinite as is the iniquity of slavery, to attempt to abolish it by War is only an attempt to cast out devils by Beelzebub, the Prince of the Devils. He considered that the anti-slavery party in America committed two capital errors—of policy and of principle.

"First, the act on the immoral and unchristian axiom that in order to punish or to destroy crime we are at liberty to commit another; * * * * but they forget that the two spring from one source, muster under one banner, and are intimate allies. * * * And they commit this other error, they accept as of Divine origin and sanction events merely because they occur. They see the universal outbreak of the war spirit in the North against the South, and they straightway exclaim, 'This is of God.' What indications are there about this uprising of the North that should entitle them to trace it to a Divine source? Has it sprung from sympathy with the oppressed, from righteous indignation against wrong? They know, none better, that it is, to a large extent, the mere offspring of national pride, and bellicose passion, and if they trust to this as a means of abolishing slavery, as sure as they are living men they will find that they are trusting in the staff of a broken reed."

Mr. Richard sincerely believed that the object of the war was not the abolition of slavery, though remotely it might be the cause;—

"But that the great bulk of men who are now swelling the war-cry, and rushing into the ranks to fight, are men who despise the 'nigger' and hate the abolitionists as cordially as ever. * * * * *

In truth it is difficult for us who look at the matter calmly from a distance, to resist the impression that the fierce war excitement, now raging in the North, is far more a matter of pride and passion than of any principle whatever."

As early as May 1861 Mr. Richard penned an Address on behalf of the Peace Society to the United States of America, of earnest sympathy and respectful expostulation on the perilous crisis, which in general terms, boldly declared that

the worst of all solutions that can be attempted is a fratricidal war; "and it appealed to the friends of peace" to avoid
the fatal mistake of imagining that you can decide questions
of disputed right by conflicts of brute force; and especially it
appealed to the Christian Churches of all denominations, and
emphatically to the Ministers of the Prince of Peace, to stand
between the living and the dead, that the plague be stayed.

This Address and the articles from Mr. Richard's pen in
the *Herald of Peace* condemnatory of the War and the action
which the Anti-Slavery Party who had hitherto professed the
principles of peace were taking, roused their vehement indignation, especially from the pens of W. Lloyd Garrison, Henry
Ward Beecher, Harriett Beecher Stowe, and others.

"Nothing" said Mr. Richard "that has occurred since will
induce us to recall or qualify the words that we then employed.
What we say is that the moving impulse which has heaved the
great mass of the community into such violent agitation is not
the question of slavery at all but the preservation of the Union,
the constitution of 1787, the insult offered to the American
flag."

In support of this position Mr. Richard quotes from the
last message of President Lincoln, who declared that the
North is fighting to bring back the South into Union with the
North.

"The simple fact is," writes Mr. Richard, "with regard to our
ardent anti-slavery friends in America they can only see one
evil in the universe and that is slavery." * * Heaven forbid
that in saying this, we should seem to try to extenuate the
enormities of slavery, for we believe it to be an abominable and
accursed thing which degrades man and dishonours God. But
then we say precisely the same thing with yet deeper emphasis
of War. * * * And is it to be supposed that we can look
with pleasure when we see men whom we honour so blinded by
their hatred of one sort of wickedness as to rush with open arms
into the embrace of another equally atrocious?"

At the commencement of the war Mr. Richard strenuously supported the action of the British Government in
the question of the recognition of the South as belligerents,
action which was severely condemned by the North, and
cordially approved by the South; and the argument and

facts arrayed by Mr. Richard in support of the declaration of Lord Russell "that the Southern Confederacy must be treated as belligerents" was, he considered, historically and juridically correct, and if any Government was responsible for the unfortunate dilemma in which the great Maritime Powers were placed, undoubtedly the Federal Government at Washington were alone and severely to be blamed.

Prior to the Congress which met at Paris at the close of the Russian War, all the Maritime Powers of the world recognised and exercised the right of privateering, and the issuing of Letters of Marque to any Neutral Nation to equip and arm privateers, to capture and confiscate the mercantile marine of the belligerent Nation.

But at the Congress at Paris in 1856, it was declared by all the Powers assembled, that "Privateering is, and remains, abolished;" and the protocol further bound the Governments "to bring the declaration to the knowledge of the States which have not taken part in the Congress of Paris, and to invite them to accede to it;" but unfortunately the invitation to the United States was rejected, on the ground that it was not compatible with its interests; but it made a counter proposal that private property at sea should be totally exempt, unless contraband, from seizure during war, not only by privateers, but by the navy of belligerents; and the proposal being rejected by England, although accepted by the other European Powers, the original proposal in accordance with the Declaration of Paris was only binding between those Powers who had acceded to it, and thus the practice of privateering by the United States remained a part of the recognised laws of War.

When, therefore, President Lincoln issued his proclamation declaring the South in a state of revolt, Mr. Jefferson Davis replied by issuing "letters of marque" for privateers to prey on the merchant-marine of the North, and the South were thereupon declared to be pirates by the North, a declaration that the British Government could not accept;

and Lord John Russell soon after announced in Parliament that the Government had come to the unanimous opinion that the Southern Confederacy of America must be treated as belligerents ; and this declaration was followed by the proclamation of Neutrality by England between the belligerents, to the effect, that she was at peace with all Nations, but war unhappily existing in the United States, she commands all the subjects of the Queen to observe the duties of neutrality towards the combatant Powers, and to respect the exercise of their belligerent rights.

Mr. Richard approved of the action of the British Government in the recognition of the South as belligerents, and he stated his views very forcibly in an article, July, 1861, wherein he shewed it was not only in accordance with the opinions of Wheaton and Phillimore, but also with the historical precedents, during the War of Greece against Turkey, of the South American Colonies against Spain, as well as of the North American Colonies against Great Britain.

The unfortunate position taken up by Mr. Richard was the logical and inevitable result of the sympathy and support which from the beginning he extended to the Secession, and *ipso facto* to the rebellion of the Southern States ; but in doing so he involuntarily, possibly unconsciously, committed himself, not simply to the possession by the South of the rights and privileges of belligerents, but to their recognition as a Nation, and to their right of secession by War, thus re-echoing in effect the memorable declarations of two of the most eminent members of Lord Palmerston's Government, the first by Lord John Russell, in 1862, at Newcastle-on-Tyne, affirming that

" This was a struggle on the one side for supremacy, and on the other for independence ; "

which was followed soon after by the assertion of Mr. Gladstone at Liverpool that :

" Mr. Jefferson Davis had already succeeded in making the Southern States of America a Nation ; "

and these declarations indicated the dangerous tendency of the policy of Lord Palmerston and his Cabinet, to render the powerful moral and material aid of Great Britain in favour of the Southern Cause.

This action of Mr. Richard (examining into and criticising it after an interval of 26 years), is perplexing in the extreme, and is not more astonishing than his support of the Southern cause (for the former was the consequence of the latter), for unfortunately he was unable to recognise anything good in the policy of the North, whilst for the South and its actions he was undoubtedly an ardent supporter.

This recognition by the British Government of the South as belligerents came upon the country, and especially upon the Government of the North, like a clap of thunder in a clear sky, and was followed by the rejoicings of the aristo-cratic and ruling classes ; for it was believed by them to herald the downfall of free institutions and of the Republican Government across the Atlantic.

It was as sudden as it was precipitate, for it followed within a fortnight of the fall of Fort Sumpter, which took place on the 14th April, 1861 ; and on the 21st May following, the British Cabinet decided on immediate recognition, with all the rights of belligerents applicable on the ocean, as well as on land, which practically lifted the South to an equality with the North, constituted them *de facto* and *de jure* a Nation, with all the privileges of municipal and international law, to make peace or war, to negotiate treaties, to raise loans, and opened to them the ports, ship-yards, and foundries of England, and gave them a flag co-equal with the Stars and Stripes.

It was an inconsistent act for England, and especially at the bidding of a Minister of Lord Palmerston's antecedents, who had himself repeatedly pledged her to the abolition of slavery, to recognise the Government of the Southern

Confederacy, whose main purpose was, in the words of its vice-president, Mr. Stephens, "to found an Empire with Slavery as its chief corner-stone." In face of such a false position, well might Charles Sumner, from his place in the Senate at Washington, condemn in scathing indignation the policy of the Ministers of the British Crown ; and the following are the closing words of his celebrated speech :—

"At a great epoch of history in the United States, not less momentous than that of the French Revolution, or that of the Reformation, when civilization was fighting a last battle with Slavery, England gave her name, her influence, her material resources, to the wicked cause, and flung a sword into the scale with Slavery."

The recognition of belligerency was no less deplorable in its results, for it not only transferred American trade to foreign and especially to English bottoms, led to the out-fitting of rebel cruisers in English ports, to the destruction of upwards of twenty million dollars of the Northern Merchant Marine, rendered the blockade of the Southern ports a costly and hazardous undertaking, raised to a high rate of premium the assurance of the Northern Marine, but it led to the building, equipping and escape of the Alabama and Shenandoah, and other cruisers, to serious complications between England and America, that for a long time threat-ened to involve these two great Anglo-Saxon races in War.

On the contrary, had recognition not been made, no vessel could have been built in England for the South, for by the laws of Nations the building or equipping of a vessel against the United States would have constituted an act of piracy. England would not have been converted into the Arsenal and base of War operations for the South; no munitions of War could have been furnished, not one single blockade runner, laden with supplies, could have left the British shores except under a penalty, and the War with all its fearful cost of blood and treasure would not have been so prolonged.

Whatever may be our views as to the wisdom or the

justice of the position taken by Mr. Richard at this great crisis in the history of the Great American Republic, there cannot be two opinions on the course which he adopted, and the action which he took in favour of the non-intervention of England in that deplorable internecine War, not simply by force of arms, but also by any declaration of moral or any display of material aid.

" Our concern," says Mr. Richard, " on this side of the Atlantic is to do what lies in our power to prevent the evil, already sufficiently appalling, from being aggravated by England being implicated in the strife. We believe the strongest wish of the British Government and the British people is to stand altogether aloof from the unhappy struggle, to maintain a strict neutrality."

For England to maintain that policy of strict and impartial neutrality and to conform faithfully to the municipal and international, law of nations, was undoubtedly the difficulty of the position; because in the desire of the British Government to maintain a friendly and not a hostile attitude to the *de facto* Government of the South and the Federal Government of the North, lay the danger of her being dragged into the conflict; and, as it subsequently proved, the danger when the war was concluded, of having as a neutral State, not satisfied the requirements of international obligations and international law.

## THE TRENT DISPUTE.

At this juncture a crisis arose that roused Mr. Richard into action, for it put closely to the test the pacific utterances of Ministers, and for a brief interval strained to a hair's breath, the peaceful relations between England and the Northern States of America, consequent upon the seizure on the high seas of Messrs. Sliddell and Mason and their associates from the British mail-packet the " Trent," by order of Captain Wilkes of the San Jacinto of the United States Navy.

The facts are briefly these : The Government of the South, despatched two ex-Senators of the United States, Sliddell and Mason, the former the author of the Fugitive Slave Land, and the latter of the filibustering system organised by the Confederacy, as ambassadors respectively to France and England ; and these two gentlemen embarked from Charleston on a blockade runner, and under cover of the darkness reached Cuba, whence they took passage on board the "Trent," bound for England, viâ St. Thomas, and *en route* the steamer was over-hauled by the San Jacinto, the ambassadors were arrested, and conveyed back to America and incarcerated in Fort Warren.

Immediately on the facts becoming known, an angry outburst of public opinion was heard, demanding their release at the peril of War. The Minister for Foreign Affairs, Lord Russell, echoing the National sentiment, in a despatch to the British Minister at Washington, Lord Lyons, declared ;—

"That they were taken from on board a British vessel, the ship of a Neutral Power, whilst such vessel was pursuing a lawful and innocent voyage, an act of violence, which was an affront to the British flag and a violation of international law."

This communication was backed up by the despatch of the Guards and other troops to Canada, before a reply to the demand for a surrender of the Envoys to Europe had, or could have been received.

To allay this feverish excitement against the North, and the frantic cry for War, Mr. Richard spared no effort to avert the peril by issuing an Address to the various religious bodies in England, which was a powerful appeal, noble in language and pathetic in tone to the ministers of the Prince of Peace "to stand up amid the storm, and, in the name of their Divine Master, rebuke the raging tempest of human passion."

A Memorial to Lord Palmerston was also indited by Mr. Richard, and signed by him and Joseph Pease, and Samuel Gurney, which proposed that the disputed question, being one of international law, should, in the event of the failure of diplomatic negotiation, be referred to the decision of some friendly and impartial Arbitrator.

Fortunately, at this moment of anxiety, when the great issues of peace and war hung in the balance, the French Government came to the rescue, and assisted to pull the two countries out of the dilemma into which the rashness of the United States' Commodore, and the bellicose attitude of Lord Palmerston, had involved them ; for the late Emperor Napoleon, to his great credit, instructed the Minister for Foreign Affairs, M. Thouvenel, to support the judicial position of Great Britain, and in effect to insist that the emissaries of the South, not being military persons actually in the service of the South, were not subject to seizure on board a Neutral ship.

The peaceful settlement of this untoward incident was also largely promoted by a great speech delivered by Charles Sumner on January 9, 1862, in the United States Senate, in which he powerfully supported the language of the despatch of the French Government, and after appealing to the President to let the men go, said ;—

" There are victories of force. Here is a victory of truth. If Great Britain has gained the custody of the two rebels, the United States have secured the triumph of their principles. But this triumph is not enough. The sea-god will in future use his trident less ; but the same principles which led to the present renunciation of early pretensions naturally conduct to yet further emancipation of the sea. The work of maritime civilisation is not finished. And here the two nations, equally endowed by commerce, and matching each other, while they surpass all other nations in peaceful ships, may gloriously unite in setting up new pillars, which shall mark new triumphs, rendering the ocean a highway of peace instead of a field of blood."

The settlement of the "Trent" dispute was a great satisfaction to Mr. Richard, and one that he might with just pride rejoice over, not alone that the personal and public efforts he had put forth were crowned with such conspicuous success, but because, being a disputed question of international law, it was settled as he claimed for all such questions, by those precedents and principles that should ever be the guide and arbiter for nations.

---

## THE AMERICAN WAR OF SECESSION.

### (Continued.)

Whilst however the danger of War between England and America was happily averted, the tremendous conflict between North and South raged with increased fury, and for three years all efforts stimulated by Mr. Richard and the friends of peace, at one time in Memorials to the Government in favour of Arbitration or Mediation, at another time, powerful appeals to the people of the United States to arrest the destructive struggle, were unavailing to stay the whirlwind of passion, or bid the avenging sword return into its scabbard.

Mr. Richard, undaunted and undismayed, laboured hard with his pen in many directions on this one engrossing and deplorable conflict, and during the years 1862, 1863, and 1864, in fact from the beginning to the close of the War, he wavered not in his heroic attitude even though brave men and true fell away from his side, nor faltered in his unsparing rebukes, even though the religious press of England were arrayed against him.

In May 1862 we find him writing a vigorous article and asking, What are the objects for which this War is waged by the Federalists ?—First, the Restoration of the Union, in which they are sincere.  Secondly, the Abolition of Slavery, in which he doubted the sincerity of a large part of the North.

But were either of these ends likely to be obtained by War, or to be so attained as not to mock them in the shadow?

As regarded Union, he believed they were expecting a result that was contradicted by the history of the world, and as regarded the Abolition of Slavery, he believed that to proclaim emancipation in a storm of blood and flames could come to no good.

In November 1862 he writes:

"We," speaking for himself and the Peace Society, "are pledged to the doctrine that all war is unchristian and unlawful, and cannot, whilst condemning it in the abstract, defend it in the concrete; moreover, we do not believe that this war is waged for freedom; and if we did, we do not believe they can attain their object by fighting, or give it our sanction without an utter abandonment of our principles."

He believed it was waged not for freedom but for "Union and Empire," and in support of this he cites the language of President Lincoln:

"My paramount object in this struggle is to save the Union, and it is not either to save or destroy slavery. If I could save the Union without freeing one slave, I would do it; and if I could do it by freeing all the slaves, I would do it. What I do about slavery and the coloured race, I do because it helps to save the Union; and what I forbear, I forbear because I do not believe it would help the Union."

This declaration and the subsequent emancipation proclamation of President Lincoln he severely condemned, and supported it by the language of Mr. Gladstone, when he said:

"We have no faith in the propagation of free institutions at the point of the sword. It is not by such means that the ends of freedom are to be gained. Freedom must be freely accepted, and freely embraced. You cannot invade a nation in order to convert its institutions from bad into good; and our friends in the North have, as we think, made a great mistake in supposing that they can lend all the horrors of this war to philanthropic ends."

"No," said Mr. Richard, "I cannot lend my sanction to do all this evil that good may come, even if there was the slightest probability of its ever coming by such infernal means. I am not prepared to buy the freedom of the Slaves at so tremendous a cost."

At this period of the struggle, England was divided into two opposite camps, Cobden, Bright, and Forster in antagonism to Palmerston, Russell and (strange as it may appear) Richard; and with this alliance the royal and aristocratic classes of England, backed up by the *Times* and other powerful organs of public opinion.

The anti-slavery party, and the sympathisers with the North, united their forces and constituted a powerful factor, powerful in numbers, and in oratorical ability; for they not only perceived that a break-up of the American Union and the dissolution of the Republic of the West would be a heavy blow to the cause of political freedom, and of free institutions all over the world, but that the success of the South would cancel the emancipation proclamation of President Lincoln, would destroy all hope for the abolition of the accursed system of human bondage, and would bind ·irrevocably, and with tenfold more cruelty and oppression, the galling shackles upon the four millions of the coloured race; for had not the fiat gone forth from the lips of the Vice-President of the Southern Confederacy, Mr. Stephens, by which he endeavoured to rally the classes against the masses, that slavery was the chief corner-stone of the Confederacy!

No wonder then that with such tremendous issues at stake, and that with such clear and definite aims in view, that the announcement of the President's Policy of Emancipation roused throughout Great Britain the ancient fires of freedom for the Slave; and day by day the anti-slavery feeling gained in strength as evidenced by the rush for meetings everywhere, no matter how obscure or how distinguished the orators, for it shewed how deep and wide was the sympathy for the North and for human freedom in the South, in the breasts of the English people.

Towards the end of the year 1863, one of the most distinguished men in the United States—distinguished alike for his courageous and eloquent advocacy of the anti-slavery cause,—Henry Ward Beecher, arrived in England, and from many platforms delivered orations of great power and ability in support of the North and the policy of the North, and, as it was to be expected, rallied wherever he went and wherever his speeches were read, the friends of freedom and humanity to the popular cause.

Mr. Richard attended one of these meetings at Exeter Hall, and to counteract the commanding influence of this fearless advocate, or rather to defend his position of apparent hostility to the North, he wrote an article on the subject of that address, which appeared to him utterly lacking in any Christian sentiment or principle, but on the contrary to undermine and discredit the teachings of the Great Founder of the Christian Faith.

Mr. Richard was sadly moved by the declaration of Mr. Beecher, that "the firm invincible determination of the North, deep as the sea, firm as the mountains, but calm as the heavens above us, is to fight out this war through, at all hazards, and at every cost," for it opened up to Mr. Richard's mind a "terrible vision of blood and vengeance"; and in virtuous indignation, he rebuked in powerful language, Mr. Beecher and Mr. Newman Hall who supported him, and the following is one of the most striking passages in that article ;—

" Those amongst ourselves who give in to this spirit are far less excusable than the men who are in the midst of the war, and have drunk of the maddening cup of its enchantments.     *     *

" On what page of God's Gospel do we find any warrant for sustaining men in their avowed determination to exterminate five millions of people, unless they submit to their will or be themselves exterminated in the attempt ? If the Northern people had received a commission direct from Heaven, attested by ' signs and wonders and mighty deeds ' commanding them to do this thing, they might even have hesitated and shrank back from its execution.  But for those who are the professed disciples of Him who came not to destroy men's lives but to save them, to imagine they are doing God's service by undertaking this ferocious project, *out of their own mere will*, to uphold a particular form of political government, or—still more monstrous plea!—to promote the cause of Christian philanthropy on the earth, is one of the most extraordinary instances of the delusion by which the god of this world blinds the eyes of men, that is recorded in the history of the race."

Throughout the year 1864, the course of the American War was happily not interrupted by any serious complication with England, and Mr. Richard, unwilling to stir up amongst his countrymen the slumbering embers of hostility,—hostility more sentimental than real,—against the one side or the other, maintained a dignified reserve; for he felt, as he expressed it, "a vain hope to make the still small voice of reason and religion heard amid the hurricane war of passion that deafened all other ears on the other side of the Atlantic;' nevertheless he frequently exercised his great power as a writer, wherewith to keep before the public eye the manifold evils inseparable from the continuance of the murderous strife and the imminent dangers, lest the people and Government of the United States, hitherto so free from the military traditions and its inevitable intoxication for military glory, should seek with its vast armies and navies to arrogate to itself the position of a great military power, and become a menace to the peace of the world.

At the beginning of the year 1865, there were evidences of the approaching termination of this terrible fratricidal struggle, and Mr. Richard was able, in the Annual Report of the Peace Society, to say with what—

"Inexpressible satisfaction we see the dreadful and disastrous civil war which has so long desolated America coming to a close. No imagination can conceive, no language can adequately express, the amount of evil which it has inflicted on that country, and the world.   Probably not fewer than 1,000,000 of young men have perished prematurely, and in every conceivable form of horror and agony, by sword, and famine, and pestilence, and misery.   As to its cost in money, we shall certainly be within the mark if we say that on both sides not less than £1,000,000,000 have been withdrawn from the service of civilisation to be squandered in mutual butcherings and blood.  *  *  *  Heaven in its mercy grant that the evil effects may not extend beyond the line of actual conflict.  *  *  *  One bright spot, however, remains amid the wide waste of material and moral desolation, one result of the war to offer some consolation for its manifold and incalculable evils. No result, indeed, can justify or atone for the use of unlawful means. Still it may be permitted even to those who most strongly disapproved of the war, to rejoice over the fact, or what they hope will become a fact, that as one consequence flowing from it, the great abomination of slavery bids fair to perish out of the land for ever. * * * But it would have been far better to have seen the garland of victory for this great deliverance placed on the brow of the Prince of Peace, instead of being transferred to the head of

' Moloch—horrid king ! besmeared with blood,'

to enhance his glory and perpetuate his brute dominion over the minds and hearts of men."

## WAR IN JAPAN.

In 1863 Mr. Richard aroused the energies of the friends of peace into action in consequence of the alarming intelligence from Japan, which in the month of July foreshadowed a renewal of one of those unjustifiable wars in the East, such as the recent China Wars to which reference has been made.

Well might Mr. Richard say, "*It is not possible for Englishmen to go anywhere without marking their steps with fire and blood*," and this remark, if true, has a certain application in the causes of the war with Japan in 1863.

Our intercourse with Japan shows that, first of all, we thrust ourselves upon them in the teeth of all their strong prejudices, and then compelled them at the mouth of the cannon to enter into a Treaty of Commerce with us, but, further, we affront their feelings, and violate their customs ; and having by these means provoked them, we exact from them demands, and in default we scatter havoc and ruin amongst them.

The war against Japan in 1863 may be traced to these causes, and the incident which provoked this war was as contemptible as it was disgraceful. It appears three English gentlemen and a lady, whose names deserve notoriety, Mr.

Richardson, Mr. Clarke, Mr. Marshall, and Mrs. Borrodaile, were riding in the high road leading from Yokohama to Yeddo.

At a distance of several miles from Yokohama they met a procession of Princes, and it is customary for all people who meet such processions to retire at their approach or to kneel while it passes, neither of which they would do though they had been warned repeatedly of it; and the result was they were attacked and one of the party killed.

Immediately on Lord Russell receiving information of the incident, he wrote to Lieut.-Colonel Neale, the representative of England, to make a demand for reparation.

(1) An ample apology for the offence.

(2) The payment of £100,000 as a penalty on Japan.

(3) The trial and capital execution of the guilty parties, in the presence of the Naval Officers of the British Squadron, and in the event of refusal the Admiral of the Fleet on the station to declare War, and to take what measures he thought necessary for the vindication of the honour of England.

This ultimatum was sent in April by Colonel Neale, the British *Chargé d'affairs* to the Tycoon or Prime Minister of the Emperor, and twenty days only were allowed for compliance therewith; and during this interval great alarm naturally prevailed at Nagasaki, and other towns, where foreign merchants and their families were residing.

The difficulty of the situation was intensified by two insurmountable obstacles—first, the immense distance to the scene of disturbance, and the absence of direct and rapid communication with the authorities there; and secondly, the absolute authority exercised by the representatives of the Government of the Queen, the Consuls and Generals and Admirals in Eastern waters and stations, whenever and wherever they considered the personal and private interests of Englishmen and the public or imperial interests of England demanded reparation.

Mr. Richard, heavily handicapped by these obstacles, was not dismayed, and lost no time in vigorously protesting against this threatened barbarous war; in the first place by a slashing article from his pen immediately the news reached England, which he followed up by a Memorial which was signed by Mr. Joseph Pease and himself on behalf of the Peace Society, for presentation to Earl Russell, Secretary of State for Foreign Affairs, which reminded the Government that the Treaty of Commerce with Japan, upon which armed intervention was based, was obtained under coercion, and in opposition to the prejudices and traditions of the people; and further, that the Treaty stipulations had been violated by lawless Englishmen, whose action the authorities could not restrain, and that this coercive policy against Japan, and unscrupulous conduct of foreigners, could not fail to lead to grave complication, and to a succession of ignoble and costly wars, and the memorialists advised a withdrawal of Englishmen and the armed forces of the Crown from Japan.

The Government of Japan conceded two of these demands, the apology and the payment of £100,000; but this not being sufficient, and without attempting any further negotiation, Vice-Admiral Kuper was ordered to enforce the demand. The British squadron, consisting of the Euryalus, Pearl, Perseus, Argus, Coquette, Racehorse, and Havoc, appeared on the 11th August before Kagosima, and demanded full compliance with the ultimatum, and on the 12th and 13th carried on a series of mock and abortive negotiations; and on the 14th the British Admiral commenced operations by bombarding Kagosima, with its population of 180,000 souls utterly innocent of complicity in the alleged insult, and soon the whole town was in flames, and laid in ruins.

The bombardment continued two days. At the end of the first day's operations the ships in the harbour and one half of the town were in flames, and the following day the bombardment was continued, and the palace of the Prince shelled, and, says the Admiral, "the entire town of Kagosima is now a mass of ruins." Well might Mr. Cobden, in writing on this barbaric act of the British Admiral, denounce this cruel proceeding.

" Picture," said Mr. Cobden, "this great commercial centre reduced in forty-eight hours to a heap of ashes, try to realise the fate of its population, and then ask what great crime they had committed to bring on themselves this havoc and destruction."

To our shame and confusion the answer must be that this is the way in which Englishmen, under the command of Admirals Kuper and Neale, administer justice for the murder of an individual 10,000 miles away, of which crime the inhabitants of Kagosima were guiltless of all knowledge and complicity, and afterwards the chief actors in this outrage on humanity cooly laid claim to the approbation of the British nation.

When the details of these diabolical proceedings of the British Squadron on the coast of Japan reached London, Mr. Richard indited a memorial to Her Majesty the Queen, which was signed by Samuel Gurney, and Joseph Pease, and himself, acting on behalf of the Peace Society, expressive of their deep sorrow and shame, in which he declared that this " tremendous act of vengeance inflicted by British arms cannot be justified on any ground," and in effect declared that acts like these create an insurmountable barrier to the progress of civilization and Christianity in the East, and that on these and other grounds the Memorial entreated Her Majesty " to withold her Royal sanction from this great outrage " perpetrated in her name on the unoffending people of Kagosima.

" It is an ill wind, verily, that blows no good ; " and this deplorable bombardment, and armed intervention by the British Admiral, forced on the attention of Her Majesty's Government the peril to England of entrusting to irresponsible men, far removed from control, the declaration of war, and led to a great and urgent reform. Hitherto, in our foreign relations with such nations as China and Japan, every British official claimed and exercised the right to call into action the military or naval forces of England without the authority of the responsible Government at home ; and therefore, in order to prevent a recurrence of those deplorable events which had so long disgraced our relations with Eastern nations, Lord Clarendon issued an important dispatch, dated January 28, 1869, addressed to the consular and military representatives of England abroad, and which declared :—

" Her Majesty's Government cannot leave with Her Majesty's Consuls or naval officers to determine for themselves what redress or reparation for wrong done to British subjects is due, or by what means it should be enforced. They cannot allow them to determine whether coercion is to be applied by blockade, by reprisals, by landing armed parties, or by acts of even a mere hostile character. All such proceedings bear more or less the character of acts of war, and Her Majesty's Government cannot delegate to Her Majesty's servants in foreign countries the power of involving their own country in war."

## THE DANISH WAR.

At the beginning of the year 1864 the Schlezwig-Holstein question agitated Europe, and at one time threatened to involve England in war against Prussia and Austria, on behalf of Denmark, who claimed a sovereignty over the Duchies. Owing to the prominent and successful part that Mr. Richard took in favour of non-intervention in this quarrel, a brief historic reference is necessary.

In 1848 an insurrection broke out in Denmark for the avowed object of establishing the union of Schlezwig-Holstein under a constitutional system distinct from the Danish Crown, and Germany being appealed to, assisted the insurrection, and by the Treaty of Peace of 1850, which followed, it was expressly stipulated by Denmark and approved by Prussia, that the Duchies should not be incorporated with the Danish Kingdom; and when King Christian ascended the Throne in November 1863, this stipulation, and the recognition of the Duke of Augustenberg as Duke of Schlezwig-Holstein, was claimed by Prussia and Austria and the Duchies, in accordance with the Treaty of London of 1852.

On the other hand, King Christian claimed to be Sovereign of all the territories under the sway of his predecessor, and Suzerain of the Duchies, and the German Diet thereupon decreed an administration of the Duchies of Commissioners acting ostensibly for the Duke of Augustenberg; and the latter in support of this right occupied Kiel with a military force, as the rightful Sovereign, and herein was the course of the quarrel, and of the war which followed.

The first step taken by Mr. Richard, and his promptitude is worthy of mention, was in January, 1864, when he forwarded a Memorial to Lord Russell, Minister for Foreign Affairs, in favour not only of abstaining from an armed intervention between Denmark and the Austro-Prussian allies, but also from any menacing demonstrations of force, or any diplomatic engagements without the sanction of Parliament.

In the meantime War was declared, the allied forces of Austria and Prussia advanced, and the Danish troops fell back upon Düppel; and at this juncture, to avoid further bloodshed, Great Britain offered her mediation, which being accepted, an armistice was concluded, and a Conference of the Great Powers assembled in London; but after sitting for two months, owing to the exacting demands on the one side, and the obstinacy on the other, it broke up without coming to a satisfactory result, and hostilities were resumed.

The question that agitated England was whether she should go to the help of Denmark in the struggle, Lords Palmerston and Russell leaning to intervention under certain conditions, but the Peace party, led by Mr. Cobden in

Parliament, and by Mr. Richard outside, were too strong for
the Noble Lords; and added to this, France, upon whose
alliance England had relied, at the last moment hesitated,
and finally withdrew, which left England in the lurch, and
Lord Palmerston was obliged to announce to the House of
Commons, on 25th June, that there would be no War, to
the immense satisfaction of the Peace party, who were in
a majority, but to the bitter chagrin and humiliation of the
minority who favoured intervention and War.

This result was a triumph of non-intervention and neutrality, and from this date it became a turning point, the
watchword and accepted doctrine of the foreign policy of
England; and it was with justifiable pride and satisfaction
that Mr. Richard rejoiced over it, and pressed it home by a
series of brilliant articles from his pen to the mind and
conscience of the Nation.

To no man was this great triumph,—this great revolution
in the foreign policy of England—more justly due than to
Mr. Cobden, a just tribute to those masterly articles which
for many years emanated from his pen, and to the influence
of that "unadorned eloquence" in favour of a wiser and a juster
foreign policy; and it is a noteworthy fact that his famous
speech in the House of Commons, July 1864, on the Dano-
German question, was one of the last, as it was one of the
best efforts, and will long be remembered by those who heard
it, the first and last occasion that the writer of this memorique
listened to the voice of that great and good man, pleading in
gentle and silvery accents for peace; and an extract from
that speech is well worthy of being quoted :

"The present system of diplomacy has broken down (cheers).
Our Foreign Office has lost its credit with foreign countries.
(Opposition cheers). You cannot approach at this time a foreign
country on any question of foreign politics on which you will
not be looked upon with want of confidence and indeed with
mistrust (Opposition cheers). And why? Because foreign
countries feel that whilst they are dealing with the Foreign Office,
the Foreign Office has not the power—the power is here (cheers).
I maintain it behoves us to adopt, ourselves, a different foreign

policy, and to let it be known that it is our intention to make the Government feel that it is necessary to act up to our views (hear, hear). The present system cannot go on ; it requires a change in the interests of our neighbours ; it requires a change on higher grounds—in the interests of peace, civilisation, and humanity (loud cheers)."

## INSURRECTION IN POLAND.

No sooner was the danger of intervention by England in the Dano-German difficulty averted than another question of international difficulty and danger to European peace presented itself, arising out of the historic complications of Poland ; and Mr. Richard determined that the policy of non-intervention adopted in the Danish war, and accepted as an axiom of foreign policy by both parties of the State, should be tenaciously maintained in the affairs of that unhappy kingdom.

It may be useful to a right appreciation of the Polish question to pass rapidly in review the history of the dismemberment, in fact, of the effacement of Poland as a Sovereign State from the number of the families of European nations.

When the first partition of Poland was accomplished in 1772 by the base treachery of Russia and Prussia, Edmund Burke, foremost among the statesmen of England, emphatically condemned it as "an infamous deed," and exerted his great oratorical powers to secure the alliance of France and England to avert the catastrophe that was threatening to subvert the liberties and independence of one, if not of the most ancient nationalities of Europe ; but the Ministers of George III., anxious to prevent English intervention in Continental affairs, (would that they had continued steadfast to that doctrine), resolutely resisted the appeal of Burke; in fact, they deemed the security of Polish independence

unworthy even of notice in the King's Speech at the opening
of the Parliament, 1772.

The dismemberment of Poland in 1772 by Russia,
Prussia, and Austria, may be traced to the armed interference of Russia in 1763 in the choice of a successor to
the Throne, on the death of Augustus III. in favour of
Poniatowski, a favourite of the Empress Catherine II.
By the Treaty of Warsaw between Russia and Poland (24th
February, 1768), the liberty, constitution, and integrity of
Poland was guaranteed; and the miserable plea put forward
by the Empress Catherine of Russia, in 1772, for interference and occupation of Poland by Russian troops, and
which led to its subsequent partition, were the avowed
interests of the Greek religionists, precisely the same plea
put forward by the Emperor Nicholas in 1853 as a justification for Russian interference in Turkey, and for the subsequent attempt, by war, to secure her overthrow.

In Poland, prior to 1772, the great majority of the Poles
were Roman Catholics, and it cannot be denied that they
grievously oppressed their fellow-countrymen, who, under
the name of Dissidents, had, by the constitution, been
guaranteed all the rights and privileges of free citizens; and,
unfortunately for Poland's independence, in their distress
they appealed to Russia and Prussia for their friendly
mediation, and England, believing in the sincerity of these
Powers, that they had really the interests of the Dissidents
at heart, joined in the Memorial to the Government at Warsaw;
but the fact was, as events subsequently proved, neither
Russia nor Prussia cared one jot or tittle for the religious
welfare of Greeks, Calvinists, or Lutherans, for their intervention was but a pretext for the extension of empire.

The Russian troops surrounded Warsaw, resolutions were
dictated by the Russian Ambassadors, her armies intersected
the country, and measures were taken to achieve the final
blow of the national existence of Poland.

In this dismemberment the Imperial Courts of St. Petersburg, Berlin, and Vienna, were the three participators, without one word of reprobation from England or France for so flagrant an act of spoliation.

By the convention signed at St. Petersburg, August 5th, 1772, the boundaries of the territories allotted to the three Powers respectively were definitely settled and guaranteed to each other. Russia obtained for her share, Livonia, Witepsk, and Polotsk, the Palatinates of Mocislaw and Minsk. Prussia secured the states of Great Poland, and the whole of Polish Prussia. Austria was assigned the 13 towns which Sigismund, King of Hungary, had mortgaged to Poland in 1412, half of the Palatinates of Cracow, Sendomire, Belz, Pocatia, and Padolia.

The second partition of Poland, in 1793, was as disgraceful as the first partition in 1772, for it was accomplished with the expressed purpose of preventing reform in her administration.

King Stanislaus Augustus, the nominee of the Government of St. Petersburg under the reconstitution of Poland in 1772, had endeavoured to give to Poland a liberal constitution ; the most violent abuses were remedied, order was established, the privileges of the nobles were abolished, legislative chambers instituted, and a bright future for Poland seemed destined to dawn ; but the jealousy and resentment of Russia were roused, and at the very time the allies affected horror at the atrocious deeds of the French Republicans, Russia, Prussia, and Austria determined on crippling still further the independence of Poland.

Unlike the first partition in 1772, it was not accomplished without a severe struggle and great bloodshed. Under the patriotic leadership of brave Koscuiszko, Poland declared war against the invaders of their rights and liberties, and at Reslavice and Warsaw defeated the Russian troops, but soon afterwards he succumbed to the superior forces of Suwarrow in which 6,000 of the Polish army perished, and

" Freedom shrieked, when Koscuiszko fell ; "

and when Suwarrow made his triumphal entry into Warsaw, after terrible slaughter, the insurrection was quelled, and subsequently (Oct. 24, 1795) a new Treaty of Partition was signed which dethroned King Stanislaus, and Poland was dismembered still further by the three Imperial powers.

Russia obtained the whole of Lithuania, Samogitia, Courland, and Semigallia, in all an addition of 2,000 square miles, comprising 1,000,000 inhabitants.

To Austria was assigned the Palatinates of Sendomire and Lublin, with part of Brzesci, Podolachia, and Masovia, comprising square miles and population nearly equal to Russian annexation.

To Prussia was assigned the other parts of the Palatinates of Masovia and Podolachia, the port of Troki and Cracow, representing 1,000 square miles, with a population of 1,000,000.

One of the causes of the insurrection in Poland in 1864 was the Emancipation Act of the Emperor Alexander, which gave a deadly blow to the supremacy of the nobles in the western provinces of Poland ; and had they renounced their pretensions to these provinces of Russia, wrested from Poland by the partitions of 1772 and 1793, they might have obtained the complete autonomy of the Poland of 1815, but they unwisely determined to make a last effort for the re-conquest of the Russian provinces, and thus to re-establish the oligarchy which was the soul of ancient Poland prior to 1772.

, Determined upon an appeal to arms they relied for support on the discontent of the Russian nobility, the weakness of the sovereignty of the Emperor in the conquered provinces and the existence of elements of a revolutionary character ; and they relied also on the sympathy and support of the Western Powers in their struggle for the achievement of Polish independence.

The insurgents in Poland in the rebellion of 1864 were not the people, nor had they any sympathy with the popular

G

mind; they were an exclusive and aristocratic class, full of religious bigotry, whose objects were to restore the supremacy of the Roman Catholic Church, to suppress the interests of the Greek Church, and therefore the establishment of a great Catholic Power in Northern Europe, at the sacrifice of the suppression of the liberal institutions and reforms introduced by the Emperor Alexander of Russia.

The policy of Russia in Poland previous to the outbreak of the rebellion was generally acknowledged to be one of wisdom and conciliation,—by the introduction of municipal institutions and local self-government, by placing members of the patriotic party into positions of confidence and power, and especially by the enfranchisement of the serfs, he had proved his sincerity for promoting the happiness and security of his Polish subjects; and these enlightened reforms, there is no doubt, however much we may deplore the partitions of 1772 and 1793, had helped to lay foundations of constitutional freedom in that unhappy country.

Mr. Richard naturally deprecated this appeal of the Polish nobility to force of arms, for achieving their independence; and believing as he did in the liberal and conciliatory policy of the Emperor Alexander towards the Poles, he cordially supported Russian policy and claimed for Russia the sympathy of England on the ground that she was struggling, as England had struggled in her earlier history, for civilization against feudalism; and he utterly discredited the charges of oppression Poland brought against Russia, and that the Poles far from being goaded by oppression, it was precisely the reverse, for he considered that the mild rule of the Emperor Alexander, and the emancipation by Russia of 25 millions of serfs, had furnished both the cause and the opportunity for the organising of a formidable conspiracy against Russian rule.

Mr. Richard also considered that the engagements entered into by England in 1815 by the Treaty of Vienna were not binding, as Russia, Prussia, Austria, France and the other

Powers had openly violated many of its provisions, and to interfere on the higher ground of justice and humanity was pregnant with mischief and misery, for it would, he said, constitute England the Don Quixote of universal humanity, and he hailed with satisfaction the declaration of Lord Russell, Minister for Foreign Affairs, in which he said :—

" For my part I see no advantage that could arise from armed intervention on behalf of Poland. I can see nothing but confusion and calamity likely to arise from an interruption of the peace of Europe. I cannot see what clear or definite object which a British Government could propose to itself, would justify them in entering into such hostilities, and I enter my protest against engaging in any such contest."

Lord Palmerston expressed similar views, and the Government being firm against intervention the policy advocated by Mr. Richard was adopted.

---

## THE WAR IN NEW ZEALAND.

In 1860 and 1864 England was engaged in an extermi_ nating War against the Maories in New Zealand, and Mr. Richard, on its first outbreak, wrote a series of articles on the subject, and he justly observes that " It would be diffi-cult to put one's finger on a single year within the century when Englishmen were not engaged in War ; " and this terrible charge alas ! is too true, for from the day of our colonisation in New Zealand, British policy in New Zealand has been to exterminate the noblest aboriginal race which British adventure and British prowess has subjugated ; and this fate of the Maories is all the more shocking when we remember how much Missionaries have done to effect their civilization.

Mr. Richard justly asked, What is the cause of the New Zealand War ? The answer is obvious, for like all Colonial

Wars of England, it arose out of a purchase of land estimated at 600 acres, from one chief called Teira, which was
claimed by another chief called Kingi, a tract of land purchased by the Governor of New Zealand, Sir George
Browne, and the invalidity of the purchase was generally
recognised, and therefore the injustice of the War. A
sanguinary struggle in the province of Taranaki was the
result, and at its close, Governor Sir George Grey, who had
succeeded Governor Browne, ordered that the land should
be restored to its lawful owners, but before this act of resti-
tution was done, irreparable mischief had been effected.

The New Zealanders had made up their minds that
whatever might be our professions, our intention was
" *slowly but surely* " to despoil them of their rights to the
soil. The war in 1864 was therefore the sequence of the
war in 1860, as the Maories considered they were not really
defeated, that they were in possession of Tátaraimaki, which
they regarded as a conquest.

The result was that when military force was sent to resume
possession of Taranaki, the military escort were attacked and
killed, and this being the first shot fired, war was inevitable.

The war cry raised in Taranaki was the signal for the tribe
of Waikatoo, who sympathised with their fellow-countrymen,
to rise in rebellion.

For a time Auckland was in danger, but by the energy of
General Cameron it was saved, and the war confined to a
narrow limit.

The New Zealanders were treated as " *rebels*," taunted as
" *niggers*," and branded as " *traitors*," and threatened with
spoliation, they naturally rose in arms; and who will blame
them, for England might have ensured their loyalty by a
policy of justice and conciliation.

The policy of England was to exterminate the Maories,
and thus secure peace, but it was, as Mr. Richard said, "the
peace of the tomb, a peace that could only cover England
with dishonor," and he warmly supported the address of the

Aborigines Protection Society to the Duke of Newcastle, the Secretary of State for the Colonies, against the absolute confiscation of the land of the Maories, estimated to be eight and a half millions of acres, by a monetary compensation of three millions sterling, advanced by the Colonial Government and guaranteed by the Crown, on the ground that it would drive the Maories into a state of hopeless despair.

---

## JOSEPH STURGE.

In June 1864 Mr. Richard completed the Memoirs of Joseph Sturge, a work of surpassing excellence of one of the noblest and spotless characters of the Nineteenth Century, an ardent advocate of peace, a friend of freedom, and an unflinching opponent of injustice, oppression or wrong wherever, and by whomsoever committed, whose life was one constant stream of benevolence and philanthropy ever on the alert, to promote and secure the greatest happiness for the greatest numbers unlimited by frontier, race, or colour.

He died in May 1859, in the 67th year of his age, and for four years, Mr. Richard devoted his unrivalled powers of lucid and graphic description in writing the life of his lamented friend, and fellow-labourer in the cause of peace and goodwill amongst the peoples and nations of the world, and nobly did he execute the great trust committed to his charge. For as Mr. Burritt beautifully wrote in reviewing the Memoirs, " His life was a priceless treasure to the land, and the age it brightened and blessed." *

---

* I commend the memoirs of Joseph Sturge, as worthy of being read by every friend of peace, for his example is worthy of imitation.

## RICHARD COBDEN.

In 1865, Mr. Richard and the friends of Peace suffered an irreparable loss by the death of that truly great and good man Mr. Cobden, whose services to the cause of Peace, over a period of thirty years, must ever be held in grateful remembrance, which was well expressed by Fréderick Passy, the eminent French economist, at the graveside of that illustrious man.

"Cobden has done more for allaying international hatreds, for the extinction of those jealous rivalries which have so often armed people against each other, and for promoting the fundamental interests of humanity, than any of the statesmen who have hitherto taken part in the government of nations."

Mr. Richard keenly felt this great bereavement, personally, as a faithful friend and able coadjutor; and especially on public grounds, as a statesman of the first rank, unadorned and undecorated, and as an orator and writer, whose "unadorned eloquence" carried conviction to the people.

Mr. Richard paid a splendid eulogium to his departed friend, one amongst the many eulogiums by pen and speech that he inscribed to his memory, of which the following is an extract:—

"How can we estimate the value of his sound judgment, his sagacious council, his resolute spirit, his great reputation? Where again shall we find the fearless independence of mind, which did not shrink from adopting and avowing opinions however widely at variance with the traditions of the class among whom he moved; the lofty courage which stood up, with scarcely even a consciousness of the sacrifice it was making, against "the world's dread laugh," when in pursuit of objects and measures which he thought right; the patient gentleness with which he bore the prejudices and littleness of inferior men, provided only he was convinced of their insincerity; the sovereign sweetness of nature which saved him from either sourness or despondency in the day of defeat; the dauntless tenacity of purpose with which he clung to his convictions in the face of all discouragement, and returned again and again to the work in which he had been previously baulked? When we think of all that he was to those who knew him intimately— the brave man, the true gentleman, the genuine practical

Christian, the generous friend, the true patriot—we must fairly avow that our heart is nearly broken, at the immensity of the loss we have sustained." *

## CONFERENCES AT MANCHESTER, 1864-5.

In 1864 and 1865, two important and influential Conferences, (the latter being a continuance of the former), were held at Manchester, which Mr. Richard attended and took a prominent part, for a conviction prevailed that there was much in the aspect of events in Europe, and in the tone and tendency of public opinion in England, to encourage the friends of peace to renewed activity in the promulgation of their principles.

Representatives were present from Manchester, Liverpool, Oldham, York, Bradford, Ashton-under-Lyne, Rochdale, Bolton, and other places, and the proceedings were of especial interest, varied by able speeches and addresses; a paper by Mr. Joseph Rowntree, of York, on the influence of the press for peace advocacy; by Mr. William Stokes, the Secretary of the Conference, on the duty of the friends of peace at the approaching General Election; by Isaac B. Cooke, Liverpool, on the importance of enlisting the support of the peoples in Europe, upon each of which topics valuable addresses were delivered.

Towards the close of the conference Mr. Richard spoke at some length on the principles upon which the Peace Society was based, and on the application of those principles to the relations and intercourse of States, and on this subject he said :—

"The doctrine they sought to teach was, that war was inconsistent with the spirit of Christianity, and the true interest of mankind.   *   *   *   With respect to the policy

* "The Life of Richard Cobden," by John Morley, should be read by all who desire international concord.

which they had sought to inculcate, one of its great principles was, that it was the duty of nations, when disputes arose, instead of having recourse to the sword, to try and settle their differences by a resort to arbitration, on the great basis of reference to reason and justice rather than brute force. Another principle was, the practicability of nations being enabled to reduce the enormous military armaments with which they now burdened themselves ; a third was the duty of non-intervention in the

WILLIAM STOKES.

affairs of other nations ; and a fourth principle was the cultiva-tion of friendly relations by commercial and social intercourse, and by a right use of the press between States, and especially between England and France."

.The following month Mr. Richard also took a prominent part in a Conference at Brighton, which was convened for the purpose of "promoting by all legitimate and practicable means the settlement of international disputes by friendly arbitration, instead of by the sword," and was presided over by Mr. Marriage Wallis, and attended by several ministers of religion and local friends of the Cause, and in the evening Mr. Richard addressed a large public meeting in support of the resolutions adopted at the Conference, which was presided over by the Mayor.

Following up the two Conferences at Manchester, Mr. Richard, in 1865, also took part in influential Conferences at Bristol and Newcastle-on-Tyne, the former one presided over by the veteran in the Cause, Mr. George Thomas, and the object of which was, mainly, to rally to the banner of peace the "few faithful men" who, during the crisis of the Russian and American Wars, had "steadfastly refused to bow their knee to the military Baal," and amongst those "few faithful men" who were present and took part in this Conference may be mentioned the names of Robert Charleton, J. H. Cotterell, the Revd. David Thomas, Thomas Pease, William Tanner, all of whom have now passed away, entered into rest.

At the Conference at Newcastle-on-Tyne, presided over by Mr. J. C. Lamb, representatives were present from Sunderland, Shields, Darlington, and other places, and amongst the speakers, in addition to Mr. Richard, was Joseph Pease, who had succeeded the late Joseph Sturge as President of the Peace Society, whose persuasive eloquence and powerful influence was a great accession of strength to the Cause that Mr. Richard was straining every nerve to advance.

In the evening of the day of this Conference Mr. Richard addressed a public meeting presided over by Mr. Mawson, and concluded an eloquent speech in these words, spoken with much feeling :—

" Last Friday I stood over the grave of Richard Cobden, and to confess to you my weakness, when I looked into the vault, and saw his coffin lie there, and called to remembrance how long that man had been like a tower of strength to me, upon

which I could always lean—his wisdom in council, and his undaunted courage in action—the first impulse of my weakness
was, as if I must retire from all share in public matters, and give
them up in despair and despondency. A few months before, I
had walked by his side along the same road where the funeral
procession went on Friday, and I could remember the precise
remarks he made to me by the particular points of the road, and
my feeling was, as I said, that having lost such a pillar of strength
in the cause of peace, that I could no longer persevere ; but my
second reflection was, that such is not the lesson which the
life and example of Richard Cobden should teach, to any of his
surviving friends ; that man who, twenty-five years ago, lifted up
his voice in the midst of this nation in favour of free trade and
international peace, and who continued till the last day of his
life faithful and unflinching to the principles of his youth. Was
it right, then, that I should retire from the work which Provi-
dence has given me to do ? No ; but as the Carthagenian
General, taking his little boy to the altar to swear eternal enmity
to Rome, so I felt disposed, standing over the grave of my
honoured and beloved friend, whose friendship had been for
fifteen years the privilege and pride of my existence, to swear
et ernal fidelity to the cause of Peace—a cause for which he had
do ne more than any man of his time, and I would, if it had been
in my power, have taken hundreds of the rising youth of England,
and there, over the grave of the man of Peace, have sworn them
all to an unflinching fidelity to the same cause." (Cheers).

The following evening, accompanied by Mr. Pease, Mr.
Richard attended and addressed an enthusiastic public
meeting at Sunderland. Meetings were also addressed on
the Peace question by Mr. Richard during 1865, at Graves-
end, Tottenham, Deptford, Greenwich, and three in the
Metropolis.

---

## THE GENERAL ELECTION OF 1865

Proved of two-fold interest to Mr. Richard—firstly, in his
efforts to influence the Electors to a right choice of candidates
favourable to " Peace, Retrenchment, and Reform ; " and
secondly, it was the first occasion that an opportunity was
presented to him to be a Parliamentary candidate.

Parliament was prorogued July 1865, having reached its

full term of existence, and Lord Palmerston appealed to the
constituencies for a renewal of trust and of power, the
seventeenth and last Parliament that the octogenarian Premier
was elected to serve, for in October, 1865, his long political
career closed.

At this election of 1865 there were few, if any, burning
questions of political interest claiming the attention of the
country, it was therefore especially a favourable opportunity
to turn the attention of the electorate to questions of fiscal
and foreign policy, and Mr. Richard availed himself of this
political lull to the fullest advantage, and it may be said,
with considerable success.

Mr. Richard issued on the eve of the elections an appeal
to the electors of the Three Kingdoms, and he gave promin-
ence to the question of international arbitration for the
settlement of questions of dispute between Great Britain
and the United States, arising out of the Civil War in
America.

The United States Minister for Foreign affairs, Mr. Seward,
had in a dispatch dated October 1863, suggested an arbitral
reference of the Alabama dispute, which had been contemptu-
ously refused by Lord Russell, and this made the question
one of some practical importance for pressing on the attention
of the electors and candidates.

The appeal of Mr. Richard also referred to the enormous
military expenditure, and to the excessive number of military
men, which was estimated at 327 Members that constituted
the War element in the last Parliament.

On the former subject Mr. Richard stated at some length
in the *Morning Star* more fully his views, and gave some
striking figures in support of retrenchment, and he warned
the electors not to be led away by stereotyped phrases,—" I
am for all possible economy in the Public expenditure, consistent with the safety of the country,"—which he considered
meant a blind and reckless squandering of the Public money
for defence, and that it was not for the security of the

nation, to build wooden ships, nor to manufacture Arm-
strong guns, nor to have an unlimited extension of armaments, for it was proceeding on a mistaken foundation, and
that the best way for national security, quoting Peel, Disraeli
and Cobden, was to bring about a proportional and simultaneous disarmament.

When the General Election of 1865 was over, placing the
Liberal party once more in power, Mr. Richard justly
credited the Peace party with this political triumph, and for
this reason : the Members of the Government, and Leaders
of the party, and pre-eminently Mr. Gladstone, based a
renewal of support on the ground that they had preserved
peace, and that through all the periods of the American, the
Danish and the Polish Wars, a policy of non-intervention
had been adopted, and not only thereby averted the armed
intervention of England, but that also they had negotiated
the Commercial Treaty with France as a powerful factor for
peace between the two nations; and lastly, the Ministerialists
declared they had under the wise financial administration of
Mr. Gladstone reduced three millions of taxation, which
they declared would have been nine millions but for the
expenditure of six millions sterling to restore, as Mr. Gladstone termed it, " our position in China."

These pacific results had been, it is true, achieved during
the seven years' administration of Lord Palmerston, but they
were due, and due alone, to the firm and determined stand
of the Peace party in and out of Parliament ; they were
triumphs won by Cobden, Bright, and Richard, against
almost overwhelming opposition, and in this triumph of all
public men, they were most entitled to the renown, not
simply in the return of the Liberal Administration to power,
but what was of far greater moment, converted to a pacific
policy abroad, and pledged to the adoption of non-intervention in foreign quarrels from which they had so narrowly
escaped becoming involved in the American and European
troubles from 1859 to 1865.

The General Election of 1865 was especially memorable for Mr. Richard in a personal direction, from the fact that he was invited for the first time in his public career as a candidate for a seat in Parliament.

The strong recommendation for this position came from the press of the Principality of Wales, the land of his birth, and in the columns of the *Cymru* appeared an earnest appeal to elect Mr. Richard for Cardiganshire, from which the following is an extract :—

" Honour yourselves, your country, and your religion, by determining to elect Henry Richard, the Apostle of Peace, the friend of Richard Cobden, to represent you in the next Parliament."

Mr. Richard accepted this call under a high sense of duty, and proceeded to Aberystwith to take the field against the sitting Member, Colonel Powell, and his appearance so frightened the Whig party that they immediately withdrew the Colonel and substituted for him a strong supporter of Lord Palmerston in the person of Sir Thomas Lloyd, and it was rendered more complicated by the candidature of Mr. David Davies ; and Mr. Richard, rather than cause a division that would have endangered the Liberal seat, retired, much to the disappointment of his friends, but his chivalry for the party was amply rewarded three years later, as is subsequently shown.

---

## THE INSURRECTION IN JAMAICA, 1865.

In January, 1866, intelligence reached this country of a deplorable outbreak in Jamaica, the causes of which forcibly illustrates the saying of Solomon, "*Behold, what a great fire a little spark kindleth,*" and this outbreak, and the tornado of passionate revenge which followed, involved Mr. Richard and his friends of the Anti-Slavery Society, in much labour and anxiety, and a reference to these events is necessary.

It appears to have originated, partly from the arrest of a
man brawling in the Court of Petty Sessions at Morant Bay,
who was afterwards rescued by the populace, and partly by a
trespass case on a plantation that had no owner, and the
attempted arrests, and subsequent rescue of the prisoners
were the accelerating causes of the outbreak.   The Sessions
House was defended by eighteen volunteers, and the rioters,
who numbered 600, quickly overpowered them, massacred
the Magistrates and Officials, and on the following day
the mob occupied and plundered several towns in the
Island, and much property was destroyed, and many lives
were sacrificed.

On the same evening, Governor Eyre held a Council of
War, and proclaimed Martial Law, and for several days the
Militia and Volunteers hunted down the " rebels," and those
who were not killed in the open were captured, tried by Court-
Martial, found guilty, and shot or hung; and in this
indiscriminate manner the rebellion was crushed.

Governor Eyre then proceeded to the arrest of the Hon.
G. W. Gordon, a popular leader and member of the Assembly,
who gave himself up voluntarily, when he was placed on the
*Wolferine*, and despatched with troops to Morant Bay for
trial.

The charge made against Gordon was, that he advised and
incited the insurrection at Morant Bay on the 11th October,
1865, and that consequently he was responsible for the
wholesale massacre which took place, and especially of Baron
Von Ketelhodt, the Magistrates, and other officials assembled
at the Court House at Kingston, and upon this charge he
was arraigned before a Court-Martial, which consisted of
three young Officers, and in a few hours, without Counsel or
legal assistance, or time given for a proper defence, the Court
adjudged him guilty of high treason, and sentenced him to
be hung the following day, without any chance of an appeal
either to the Government at home, or to the clemency of
the Crown.

As soon as possible, on the facts becoming known, Mr. Richard prepared a Memorial, which was signed by Mr. Joseph Pease and Mr. Samuel Gurney, and forwarded to Earl Russell, Her Majesty's Secretary of State for Foreign Affairs, imploring the Government to put a stop to the "Reign of Terror" in Jamaica, and to institute a searching Enquiry into the whole of the deplorable business, that those who had been guilty of the reckless effusion of blood should be brought to justice. Mr. Richard also published a pamphlet giving all the leading facts of the case, and copies of it were sent to Members of Parliament, to Editors, Ministers, and other gentlemen of influence throughout the country, and by such efforts as those, backed by the eloquent pleadings of the Press, the conscience of the nation was touched, and public opinion was roused to redeem the national honor and character from complicity in so great a crime.

The month following the report of the extraordinary trial of Mr. Gordon for High Treason and of his execution reaching this country, Mr. Richard denounced it in the strongest terms, for he said :—

" It was impossible to read this shameful record without feeling the pulse throb with indignation, and the brow flush with shame, at such a grotesque farce enacted in the name of justice, at such a wicked wrong inflicted on an innocent man, at such deep dishonor done to the British name."

It was firmly believed by Mr. Richard, and the Committee of the Anti-Slavery Society, that poor Gordon had been foully put to death, nay, that in consequence of his foremost and unflinching advocacy of the Rights of the colored people, a deep-rooted animosity prevailed against him, and a determination on the part of his political opponents, by fair or foul means to remove him, and therefore, strong efforts were put forth to compel Her Majesty's Government to institute an Enquiry into the whole circumstances connected with the terrible events in Jamaica, the wholesale executions, estimated at upwards of two thousand persons ; the alleged conspiracy, prior to the riot, at Morant Bay; and especially into the alleged justification for the arrest, trial, sentence and death of the Hon. G. W. Gordon.

As a preliminary step, for the purpose of securing this Enquiry, a powerful Deputation, of which number Mr. Richard was one, waited on the Colonial Minister, Mr. Cardwell, which was introduced by Mr. Samuel Gurney, M.P., and the right hon. gentleman, in his reply to the Memorial and speeches addressed to him, declared that Her Majesty's Government had determined upon a *"full, an impartial, and an independent Enquiry"* into the deplorable events in Jamaica, and into the causes which had occasioned them, and this Deputation to Ministers was followed by an imposing demonstration in Exeter Hall, at which Mr. Richard delivered an effective speech, concluding as follows :—

" The men who are the true friends of the honor of England are not the men who are trying to make England responsible for what has been done in Jamaica. We trust that public opinion will clear England from that responsibility. We want to wipe away from the fair brow of our motherland the stain of blood which has been fixed upon it by Governor Eyre and his compeers. We shall best honor England by bringing those men to justice who have violated all equity, who have disgraced humanity, and tarnished the lustre of the British name."

This demonstration, and other efforts, stimulated the immediate action of the Government, and accordingly the Royal Commission, consisting of Sir Henry Storks, Charles S. Roundell, Russell Gurney, J. B. Maule, and Lieutenant Strahan, set sail for Jamaica ; and they were accompanied by a delegation of the Jamaica Committee, namely, John Corrie, J. Horne-Payne, and William Morgan, all members of the legal profession; also by a Commission of Enquiry from the Society of Friends, Thomas Harvey and William Brewin, all of whom, it was acknowledged, were admirably fitted for the special duties entrusted to them.

The Royal Commission arrived in Jamaica January, 1866, when Sir Henry Storks was sworn in as Governor of Jamaica, in place of Governor Eyre, and from the 23rd January to the 30th April the Enquiry proceeded, and the conclusions arrived at for submission to Parliament agreed in the main with the published facts which originally led to their appointment, as to the details of the insurrection, its causes, and results, but they considered the punishments inflicted on the coloured people were excessive ; that the summary executions were cruel, and the floggings barbarous, and Her Majesty's Government were compelled to express their entire concurrence with this Report, and moreover, that the responsibility of ex-Governor Eyre, especially in regard to the illegal trial by Court-Martial, and the precipitate and cold-blooded execution of poor Gordon was proved, and the decision of the Government was unanimous in declaring :—

"That they do not consider they should discharge their duty by advising the Crown to replace Mr. Eyre in his former government of Jamaica."

Accordingly Sir John P. Grant, K.C.B., who had served in India as Lieutenant-Governor of Bengal, was appointed to succeed him.

The Jamaica Committee went further than the Report of the Royal Commission, guided by the independent information of Messrs. Corrie, Horne-Payne, and Morgan. They were of opinion that ex-Governor Eyre was amenable to the law for the illegal acts committed by him during the continuance of Martial Law in Jamaica, and they decided to institute proceedings against him and his accomplices, and to arraign them before a judicial tribunal. Steps were immediately taken in the first instance against Brigadier General Nelson, and Lieutenant Brand, who, after a preliminary investigation, were committed to take their trial; but at this trial, though the Grand Jury were charged in a great speech of five hours from Chief Justice Cockburn in support of their committal, they nevertheless declared the Bill against the accused, " *not found.*"

The Jamaica Committee thereupon determined upon the prosecution of ex-Governor Eyre alone, and in consequence

H

of this action Mr. Charles Buxton, the chairman of the Committee, retired from the position, on the ground that shameful and even criminal as had been the acts committed by Governor Eyre, they were not such as involved him in the guilt of wilful murder.

Mr. Richard on the contrary cordially supported the prosecution in a vigorous article from his pen, in which, after setting forth the atrocities perpetrated in Jamaica, and the illegality of the 'trial and execution of Gordon and others, he declared :—

" If the accused (ex-Governor Eyre) can only once be brought into Court, and arraigned before a Criminal Tribunal, even though he should afterwards be acquitted, something will have been gained for the cause of justice and humanity."

---

## WAR IN ABYSSINIA, 1867.

When Parliament was prorogued on the 21st August, 1867, reference was made in the Queen's Speech to the unhappy complications in Abyssinia, with a view to obtain the release of British subjects, and that a peremptory demand for their release had been made to King Theodore, failing which hostile measures would be taken. King Theodore refused to surrender the captives held by him at Magdala, and the Government resolved on War, and on the 19th November, 1867, Parliament was summoned to provide the "ways and means," the Speech from the Throne declaring as follows :—

" The Sovereign of Abyssinia, in violation of all international law, continues to hold in captivity several of my subjects, some of whom have been specially accredited to him by myself ; and his persistent disregard of friendly representations has left me no alternative but that of making a peremptory demand for the liberation of my subjects, and supporting it by adequate force."

Mr. Richard, immediately on this Declaration of War,

issued an important statement, in pamphlet form, which was widely circulated on the eve of the assembling of Parliament, in which he said that the state of affairs in Abyssinia was a striking instance of the tendency of Englishmen to meddle with what does not concern them, and he set forth very clearly the facts, how that in 1840 Mr. Walter Plowden persuaded Lord Palmerston to appoint him British Consul for Abyssinia, and the year following, acting in the name of England, he negotiated a Treaty with Ras-Ali, the Ruler of Gondar, at the time he was waging a war with his rebellious subjects; that in 1854, Ras-Ali was overthrown by his son-in-law, Theodore, who of course repudiated the Treaty the former had made with England, and soon afterwards poor Plowden fell into the hands of the enemies of King Theodore, and was killed.

It would have been well at this juncture if the English Government had not appointed a successor, for the uselessness of having Consular relations with this barbaric Monarch had been amply proved, but notwithstanding the protest of the Ruler of Abyssinia, Captain Cameron was appointed, who, as it afterwards turned out, was most unfit for the position; and, as proof of it, when King Theodore refused to receive him as Consul, and desired him to leave the Capital, and when Lord Russell in 1863 instructed him to carry out the King's wishes and to return to Massowah, and there remain until further orders, Cameron refused to do so, but interfered in the public affairs of Abyssinia, for he sided with the enemies of the King, denounced him as a murderer, which invoked the jealousy of the King, and the inevitable result was that he was imprisoned.

To secure his release Mr. Rassam was sent as intercessor, but the King detained every one who went to him, and the reason assigned was, that the Abyssinian Monarch having written a courteous letter to the British Government, no notice was taken of it, and in fact it was placed in the pigeon-holes of the Foreign Office, and never answered.

In both Houses of Parliament, on its assembling in November, the debate on the Address, and the subsequent debate on the resolution moved by the Chancellor of the Exchequer for the expenses of the Expedition to Abyssinia, shewed an entire absence of party feeling, and in fact general unanimity prevailed, not even the members of the Peace party raised any protest, but gave their silent vote for the war, and the " ways and means " for its prosecution.

No doubt the Expedition was conducted with great energy and skill, and it is only just to Lord Napier to admit it was conducted in a humane spirit, no cruelty or plunder having been practised upon the people, and it was satisfactory that our Consul and the Missionaries were released from their captivity; but, as Mr. Richard declared, it must be admitted that they had no business in that barbarous land at all, and but for their folly in going, or the folly of those who sent them, the £8,000,000 sterling which that war cost, and which is now buried in the mountains of Abyssinia, would have been saved.

---

## MR. RICHARD'S CONTINENTAL EFFORTS.

In June, 1868, Mr. Richard, accompanied by Mr. Charles Pease, formed a deputation to Paris to attend the meeting of the International League of Peace, presided over by a long-tried friend of the Cause, Jean Dollfus, Mayor of Mulhouse, which was addressed, amongst others, by Augustus Visschers, Frederic Passy, M. Isidor, Grand Rabbi of the Jews, Martin Paschaud, Minister of the Protestant Church, and Henry Richard; and the latter, before he left Paris, convened a private Conference of the friends of the Cause, for the purpose of initiating a movement in France of friendly relations with Germany, and with a view to allay the mutual jealousy and suspicion existing between the two nations.

Again, Mr. Richard, during the parliamentary recess of 1869, went on a pacific mission to the Continent, and visited Paris, Brussels, The Hague, Berlin, Vienna and Florence, for the purpose of bringing about some concerted action in the direction of disarmament. Mr. Cobden, in the years 1849, '50 and '51, raised this question in the British Parliament, but without any practical issue; and Mr. Richard was of opinion that it was vain to wait for Governments to take an initiative in the direction of disarmament, and that therefore we must look to the people, through their representatives in the various Legislatures of Europe, to bring pressure to bear on their respective Governments; and the results of his labours in this important mission were highly encouraging, and fully justified the heroic efforts made.

In Holland he received a cordial welcome from the leading members of the Legislature, and he was there encouraged by their action, and especially for their efforts in favour of an International Convention for the better treatment of wounded soldiers in War, and especially for a clause which expressed the hope ;—

" That this Convention may be soon followed by others, by which the contracting parties shall engage to abolish War, as incompatible with the principles of Christianity, the interests of their subjects, with the civilisation of the age, and the peaceful wishes of the Nations."

In Belgium, the question of disarmament was ably handled by M. Couvreur, a distinguished friend of peace, who introduced the subject in the Belgian Parliament in a speech of great force and eloquence. In Germany, the results of his mission were of real practical importance, and gave earnest of much good ; for at Berlin, Dr. Virchow, one of the most distinguished members of the Reichstag, submitted a resolution in favour of international disarmament, which was supported by 99 members ; in Dresden, two members of the Saxon House of Representatives submitted a similar resolution, which was carried by a large majority. In Austria Mr. Richard was heartily welcomed at Vienna, where he

was assured that ninety-nine hundredths of the Austrian
people abhor War, and curse a policy which compelled them
to meet their fellow-men on the field of battle, and the idea
of disarmament took firm hold, and a resolution was brought
forward in the Reichsrath by Herr Mayerhoffer, urging the
Government to take steps with the European Powers to
effect a general disarmament, which was supported by 53
members.

After visiting Wurtemburg, Munich, and Florence, at all
of which important centres he was accorded by public men
and the Press generally hearty good wishes for his success,
Mr. Richard visited Paris, where the International League
of Peace organised a successful banquet to receive him,
attended by several deputies, amongst whom were, Jules
Favre, Jules Simon, Albert Tachard; also by M. Laboulaye,
Arles Dufour, and Frederic Passy. In the course of the
proceedings Mr. Richard reviewed his campaign to the
various European Capitals, and observed :—

"Everywhere I have met with a cordial reception and
encouraging assurances, and I hope that you gentlemen, the
Deputies around me, will cheerfully introduce in your own
Chamber a similar Motion."

Jules Favre responded to this challenge, and pledged his
own, and his colleagues, earnest co-operation, a pledge that
the subsequent Franco-German War prevented his carrying
out.

---

## THE SOCIAL SCIENCE CONGRESS.

At a Social Science Congress held in London 1868, Mr.
Edwin Chadwick in the chair, Mr. Richard read a paper on
" Standing Armies and their influence on the Industrial,
Commercial and Moral Interests of Nations." He referred
to the number of men under arms, estimated at 3,926,957,
able-bodied men, and including the auxiliary forces, upwards

of eight millions of men; to the cost of the military establishments of Europe, including the loss of labour and interest
on capital, equal to £282,000,000, which he shewed involved
the European States in normal embarrassment. Having
referred to the physical and moral evils inseparable from such
a system, he advocated an understanding with the Great
Powers to secure a gradual and simultaneous disarmament,
and supported the proposal from the opinions of Cobden,
Sir Robert Peel, and especially from the Emperor of the
French, who at the opening of the Chambers in 1863 said :—

" Have not the prejudices and rancours which divide us lasted
long enough ? Shall the jealous rivalries of the Great Powers
unceasingly impede the progress of civilization ? Are we still to
maintain mutual distrust by exaggerated armaments ? Must our
most precious resources be infinitely exhausted in a vain display
of our forces ? Must we eternally maintain a condition of things
which is neither peace with its security, nor war with its happy
chances ? "

And he gave an illustration of its practicability from the
Treaty of Ghent in 1814, between Great Britain and the
United States, which limited by Protocol the respective
military forces on the North American Lakes, and which he
shewed proved an effective arrangement.

The discussion which followed was of great interest, and at
the close the following resolution was adopted :—

"That the Standing Committee of the department be requested
to consider and prepare such propositions of measures as may
appear to be practicable for the reduction of the burdens of
Standing Armies, and of pressing them upon the consideration
of the Legislature and the Government."

During the same year, Mr. Richard addressed the Annual
Meeting of the London Missionary Society in London on the
pacific duties of Christian Missionaries, in which he made
an impassioned and eloquent appeal to the Ministers present
to be faithful in their propagandism, in their example, and
action to the pacific teachings of their Great Master, and he
closed as follows :—

" I am jealous for the honour of Christ in this matter. I am

jealous that when He shall conquer India and China to His
power, as I believe He will ultimately, no one shall have a right
to share His glory, no one shall have a right to say that it was
owing to the broadsides of British men-of-war, that it was owing
to the diplomacy of British Plenipotentiaries or Ambassadors, or
Consuls, that the work was accomplished. No! let Him have
the glory. Trust not in these things, dear friends. Trust in the
living God. Trust in the presence of the Master. Trust in the
influence of God's Spirit, that is the best trust, and by that only
shall you conquer.—(Loud applause)."

As closely allied with this subject, reference may be suitably made to two remarkable publications from Mr. Richard's
pen, remarkable for their boldness and vigour of language,
as they undoubtedly were for their courage and originality
of attack, as few men within or without the circle of the
Peace Party would dared to have made such a powerful
onslaught on so influential and Christian a body, or would
have sympathised with the polemic weapons wielded against
them, by Mr. Richard.

These two publications were, firstly, "A Letter addressed
to the Directors and Supporters of Bible and Missionary
Societies," and secondly, "The Effects of the Civil War in
England on the National Liberties, Morality, and Religion."

The former taking for its motto the Apostolic injunction
"not to do evil that good may come," was an eloquent
Christian appeal to the pioneers of Christianity in foreign
lands to be faithful in their missionary enterprise to the
teaching and example of their Divine Master, and this
appeal he justified on the ground that he felt that there was
creeping into the advocacy of their great cause a spirit that
was flagrantly at variance with the spirit of the Gospel, which
was evidenced by a disposition to place their missionary
Christianity under the protection of British Armaments, and
in the silence maintained in regard to military aggressions
on the rights and possessions of heathen nations, which he
illustrated by a reference to the Opium War with China,
the Invasion of Afghanistan; the Wars with Burmah and
Persia; and the Annexation of Scinde, Oude, and other

States of Hindostan to the British Crown. Believing, he said, that Christianity and War are in their sources, their principles, their spirit and tendency, as opposite as light to darkness, any attempt to mix Blood and Bible, Gospel and Gunpowder, was inexpressibly revolting to him, and he feared that this heterodox teaching so prevalent, advocated in England by eminent ministers of the Gospel, was re-acting most disastrously upon Christian ministers abroad.

Mr. Richard appealed further to missionary history, whether the triumphs of British Arms were the best means for the propagation of the Gospel, and instanced the career and labours of the missionary—Williams in the South Seas; Moffat in Africa ; and other missionaries in New Zealand, the Fiji Islands, and the West Indies.

In the second pamphlet (published in 1862) he denied that the Wars of the Commonwealth, from 1640 to 1660, against the intolerance, arbitrary taxation, and unconstitutional rule of Charles I., furnished any proof of the necessity or advantage of an Appeal to the Sword, for he considered it tended to damage, not promote, the interests of liberty, religion, and morality.

He stated that at its close every semblance of liberty was sacrificed, for Cromwell suppressed liberty of speech, parliamentary government, and enthroned a military despotism over the land, and that when Cromwell disappeared matters were infinitely worse, and in support of this view he quoted Macaulay, Evelyn, and Mackintosh.

Further, not only was liberty lost by the Wars of the Commonwealth, but England lost her love of liberty, which he attributed to the deplorable effects that Civil War produces, diffusing corruption in society, and brutalises the people.

He showed that prior to the Civil War a deep moral and religious earnestness pervaded the country, whilst subsequent to the restoration of the Stuarts, piety declined, and corruption eat like a canker into the heart of society, and he considered that it was the result of the disastrous tendency which a state of War produced in the mind of the people.

Religious liberty was sacrificed by the Act of Uniformity, the Conventicle Act, and the Five-Mile Act, and the result was 60,000 were imprisoned for conscience' sake, and from five to 6,000 perished, and thus he considered the sword was an inefficient instrument to redress wrong, to vindicate right, to establish liberty, on a secure and lasting basis.

## GENERAL ELECTION, 1868.

Towards the close of the year 1868, Parliament was dissolved, and Mr. Richard, in response to the earnestly-expressed wish of his Welsh fellow-countrymen, consented to stand as a candidate for Merthyr Tydvil, and his appearance in the constituency evoked great enthusiasm, and on several occasions during the contest monster processions with banners and music met him, and the largest buildings that could be obtained were crowded to their utmost capacity to hear him in Welsh and in English appeal to the electors for their support. His return by the votes of 12,000 electors, and a majority of 6,000 over the Right Hon. Henry Bruce, was hailed with joy by the Welsh people and by many outside Wales, and on his return to London, the Committee of the Peace Society adopted the following resolution, an expression of feeling shared by many thousands of his friends :—

"The Committee desire to convey to Henry Richard their sincere and cordial congratulations on his election as member of Parliament for Merthyr Tydvil, and express their ardent hope that he will be able from time to time to enunciate in the House of Commons those great, and patriotic, and Christian principles on which the Peace Society is founded. From their intimate acquaintance during many years with Mr. Richard's able and indefatigable exertions, both in this country and on the Continent, for the promotion of Peace, the Committee view with especial satisfaction the prospect of his participation in those parliamentary debates which may refer to the Armaments of Europe, International Arbitration, and the peace of the world."

## THE FIRST SPEECH IN PARLIAMENT,

delivered by Mr. Richard, was on the 22nd March, 1869, on the adjourned debate of the Second Reading of the Bill of Her Majesty's Government, brought into the House by Mr. Gladstone to put an end to the establishment of the Church in Ireland, and to make provision in respect of the Temporalities thereof, and of the Royal College of Maynooth.

The debate was opened on this night by Sir Roundell Palmer (now Lord Selborne), one of the few of the usual loyal supporters of the Liberal party, and the most distinguished of that small minority, who conscientiously opposed this great measure of justice to Ireland, and, having been followed by the Solicitor-General, Sir J. D. Coleridge, Mr. Charley, Serjeant Dowse, and Mr. Vance, Mr. Richard rose and delivered a very successful maiden speech, which *The Nonconformist* described as " happily conceived, well delivered, and which caught the ear of the House."

It was a speech from a Welsh point of view in favour of the Bill, for it supplied valuable information, as shewing the success which had attended the exertions of voluntary Nonconformist Churches in Wales, and commended their example to the study and imitation of the Church in Ireland.

The following evening, or rather early on the morning of March 24th, after four nights' exhaustive debate, the Bill was read a second time in a very full House, consisting of 618 members, and shewed a majority in its favour of 118.

In the same session, on July 6th, Mr. Richard championed the cause of the newly enfranchised electors of Wales in the free exercise of their political rights, especially in the county constituencies, and submitted the following motion on the subject :—

" That in the opinion of this House, the proceedings of certain landlords in Wales, towards their tenants, on account of the free exercise of the Franchise at Elections, are oppressive and unconstitutional, and an infringement of the rights conferred by Parliament on the people of this country."

The Right Hon. H. A. Bruce, at the close of the debate, on behalf of the Government, appealed to Mr. Richard to be satisfied with "the just distinction he had secured by his powerful and remarkable speech," and the impression it had produced on the House, and withdraw his motion, and, yielding to this appeal, it was by leave withdrawn.

In the Session of 1870, Mr. Richard took considerable interest in

## THE ELEMENTARY EDUCATION ACT,

submitted to Parliament by Mr. Forster, on the 17th February, for securing throughout England and Wales the provision of accommodation and appliances for the elementary education of the people, partly through the medium of voluntary schools already existing, or to be thereafter established, and partly by the establishment of rate-supported schools under public School Boards. The debate on this great Measure was deferred to the second reading, when considerable opposition arose, on the provisions establishing School Boards to permit the teaching of particular religious views in the schools under their control. This religious difficulty was strongly enforced by the supporters of the Birmingham League, who advocated unsectarian education, and their spokesman, Mr. George Dixon, the founder of the League, upon the second reading of the Bill, April 6th, moved an amendment to the effect :—

"'That no measure for the elementary education of the people could afford a permanent and satisfactory settlement which left the important question of religious instruction to be determined by the local authorities,"

and, on the third night of the debate, Mr. Richard addressed the House in its support, mainly from a Welsh Nonconformist point of view, and, at the conclusion of the debate, the Prime Minister, (Mr. Gladstone) consented to consider the strong expression of opinions of the supporters of the amendment, even to the extent that the religious clauses of the Measure should be considerably re-modelled, and Mr. Dixon, relying on this assurance, did not press his amendment to a division; but it was relying on a broken reed, as events proved, for we find that at a subsequent stage in Committee on the Bill, Mr. Richard renewed his opposition by moving on 24th June the following important amendment :—

"That grants to denominational schools should not be increased, and that in any system of elementary education, the attendance should be everywhere compulsory, and the religious instruction should be supplied by voluntary effort, and not out of public funds."

He objected to the scheme of the Government on the ground, that it aimed to make the education of the people of England for ever denominational, and to saddle the support of it upon the taxpayers, which, in the words of Mr. Cobden, was "a proposal by which everybody shall be called upon to pay for the religious teaching of everybody else." The principles of Nonconformity, he said, were opposed to the taxation of the people being applied to purposes of religious instruction and worship, and he fortified this position by declarations of Mr. Bright and Mr. Baines. To the compromise which had been suggested, to the effect that in schools hereafter established by local rates, no catechism or religious formulary should be taught, he considered there would be no security against the schools becoming sectarian and that to leave the teaching to the discretion of the Schoolmaster or to the School Boards, would be to create a new sacerdotal class to influence the country for the future, which would introduce an element of religious discord and animosity.

## THE FRANCO-GERMAN WAR.

The years 1870-71 were saddened indeed by one of the most terrible Wars of modern times, and the history of those miserable complications which plunged eventually France and Prussia into that fratricidal struggle, proves, that it was a War declared and waged on the most flimsy, and the most unjustifiable pretext, and in consequence of the prominent action which Mr. Richard took to avert this catastrophe, a statement of the facts is necessary.

Spain was anxious for a King, as the healing balm for some of her constitutional maladies, and Prim, the Cromwell of the Revolution, who had been throwing out his line, with such a tempting bait, into nearly every Royal Court in Europe, and as uniformly unsuccessful, at last secured a candidate, as. he believed in every way qualified for the position, one of those numerous Princes in Germany, a younger scion of the Royal House of Hohenzollern, Prince Leopold Sigmaringen, who, possessing but a Colonelcy in the Hussars, was naturally anxious "for promotion to the first vacant Throne in Europe."

Immediately on the. Government at the Tuilieries being informed of what they considered to be a terrible crime against the honour and the prestige of France, the exercise by Spain of her undoubted right in the choice of a King, not a moment was lost in instructing Benedetti, the French Ambassador, to the Court at Berlin, to interrogate Bismarck, and to demand an explanation. But Bismarck was absent from the Capital, on the ground, it is believed of ill-health ; his deputy declared he knew nothing of the transaction, and was, moreover, without instructions from the Chancellor ; and the King was at his favourite retreat at Ems. To Ems Benedetti is ordered forthwith to repair ; but by some inexplicable blundering in the carrying out of that important mission, he only hastens the impending rupture between the two Powers. Meeting the King as he was taking his accustomed promenade, Benedetti plunges abruptly into the delicate controversy, breaking that official reserve which the negociations at this momentous crisis required should not be rashly entered upon, and the result was, he was politely informed that Prince Leopold, at the solicitation of parental authority, and in deference to France, had renounced his candidature, and to make it clear, the official renunciation in the *Cologne Gazette* was given him to read.

The French Ambassador, not satisfied with this with-drawal, acting upon the suicidal instructions he had received from Paris, in the most undiplomatic manner, demanded that the King of Prussia should give a guarantee, a distinct assurance, that neither then nor thereafter should that candidature be revived. Neither the proposal nor the manner of presenting it was conformable to Royal usage, nor agreeable to the Royal mind ; and Benedetti was not only refused a hearing, but emphatically assured by the "Aide-de-camp" to the King that he declined giving such a promise. This remarkable interview closes, and the political horizon, which Earl Granville had declared a few days before, to be so tranquil, now appeared dark, and threatened an inter-national storm.

At this serious juncture of events, Bismarck appears on the scene, and to aggravate matters very considerably he causes to be published in the *Norddeutschen Zeitung* (the official organ of the Government) some doubtful statements, implying that the King had publicly snubbed the Imperial Ambassador of France ; and that thereupon the latter had returned the compliment, an idle squib, which was flashed by telegraph from Berlin to every Capital and Court in Europe.

To give a European publicity to such a statement, was felt to be an intentional affront and humiliation to France ; and in the inflamed and disturbed feeling of the French and German mind, was an act of great imprudence, on the part of a Statesman, who professed and sometimes practised a conventional diplomacy.

Unhappily, too, other causes were not wanting to compli-cate matters very considerably, and to jeopardise the main-tenance of Peace, for the Duc de Grammont, French

Minister for Foreign affairs, forgetful of the dignified attitude
befitting the responsible office he held, indulged in bellicose
language from the Tribune of the Corps Legislatif; the
Press too, oblivious of their delicate vocation as Instructors
of the people, lashed the public mind into an ungovernable
fury against Prussia, calling upon the soldiers of Jena to be
ready to cross the Rhine; and finally, Ollivier, the Premier
of France, recreant to his avowed love for peace, and to the
special conditions under which he accepted the Premiership
of France, amidst the frantic enthusiasm of the assembled
Senators, "with a light heart," pronounced the declaration of
war, that awful declaration, the fiat of a clique, by which
thousands and tens of thousands of his fellow-creatures, the
flower of the manhood of the two nations, were irrevocably
doomed to perish by a horrible and agonizing death.

Against this most deplorable and disgraceful war between
two great combined and Christian nations, Mr. Richard and
his distinguished friend Frederic Passy, the Secretary of the
League of Peace in France, worked with an enthusiasm
worthy of all praise, but alas! the current was too strong,
the popular frenzy was roused, and all their efforts failed to
calm the troubled waters, or to avert the impending storm,
but it is due to their labours to refer to them.

On the 16th July, immediately on the alarm of War
Mr. Richard, addressed to his colleague in Paris, Mr. Passy,
a letter suggesting whether it would not be possible to find
some efficient means for protesting against the War, and the
suggestion was followed up by the despatch of a stirring
appeal to the French Emperor and the King of Prussia, on
behalf of the Friends of Peace in France, which solemnly
invoked their statesmanship, and if that failed, their
humanity, and finally their Christianity, to

"Bid the avenging sword return into its scabbard."

These and other kindred efforts failing, Mr. Richard
wisely resolved to direct his efforts in another direction, to

circumscribe the area of the War, and to secure for England a position and a policy of an honourable and benevolent neutrality in the terrible struggle, and on August 1st he delivered in Parliament a forcible speech on this subject. Throughout that great crisis, Mr. Richard steadfastly and energetically laboured in Parliament and out of it, in this direction, and as the fierce struggle proceeded, with its succession of overwhelming victories for Germany over France, there were not wanting in England, and the other neutral Powers in Europe, strong advocates for intervention, to save the tottering dynasty of Napoleon fast hurrying to its downfall ; and, on the other hand, there was imminent danger to Belgium, lest her neutrality, guaranteed by England, should, by the conflicts raging on her frontiers, and the desire of France to secure her alliance, thereby become imperilled.

To counteract these sinister influences actively at work in England, and to prevent Great Britain being drawn into that terrible whirlpool of blood, Mr. Richard laboured incessantly by the Press and the platform. By the former, publications were issued broadcast, and reproduced in the public journals, on Belgian Neutrality, Non-Intervention, and the Lessons of the War, and by the latter agency he addressed important meetings in London, Stroud, Liverpool, and at the Free Trade Hall, Manchester.

One of the evil effects of this War, as of every European War in the past, was to raise in the minds of the military classes in Parliament, encouraged by the selfish clamour of the War vested interests outside, a panic cry for

## INCREASED ARMAMENTS.

Mr. Richard, not only from his place in Parliament, but in other directions, opposed and condemned the proposals of the Government, as he had done a few months previously, for the Government demanded at the close of the Session of 1870, an additional vote of £2,000,000 to enable · them to increase the army by 20,000 men for

I

the purpose of defending the threatened neutrality of Belgium.

During the recess, the War fever, and groundless panic fears, increased in volume and intensity, and schemes of the wildest character were advocated for the national defence. Such for instance, as universal compulsory military service, the creation of enormous reserve forces, and even of gigantic fortifications for London and of the coast line. Happily Mr. Gladstone's Government refused to listen to any of these absurd projects, and contented itself with a moderate scheme for army re-organization and reform, at a cost of £2,886,700, and the abolition of the purchase system at a cost of £8,000,000. The latter, a valuable reform, though obtained at a heavy outlay, for in the first place it not only substituted promotion by favouritism, for promotion by merit, but its tendency has been to lessen the influence and power of the aristocratic classes for military expenditure and military adventures.

Against, however, the vote of nearly three millions for otherwise securing the efficiency of the army, Mr. Richard resolutely worked, and he did his utmost to induce the electors to urge on their representatives to resist what he termed " *this reckless waste of the public money.*"

In Parliament he was ably supported by many well-known advocates for retrenchment, led by Mr. Peter Rylands, whose untiring efforts for securing a reduction in military expenditure must ever entitle him to honourable mention, and on the 23rd March, 1871, Mr. Richard delivered an effective speech in the House of Commons, on this subject.

Happily for England, and for the other Neutral Powers in Europe, no less for the belligerents, France and Germany, the policy of non-intervention, not an isolated policy, but one of benevolent neutrality, was consistently adopted throughout that Great War, benevolent in two directions, the one towards mitigating the horrors, and relieving the sufferings of its myriads of victims, (and nobly did England do her duty in that direction), and the other, a benevolent neutrality, pursued by the British Government to terminate by mediation and friendly negotiation that terrible strife, and few men worked harder and achieved more in this matter than Mr. Richard.

But we gladly turn from this deplorable and disastrous conflict, the arbitrament of the sword between two great civilised and Christian nations, to what must always be considered as a more humane, more statesmanlike, and more Christian method of settling International disputes, as witnessed by the two foremost Christian nations in the world, Great Britain, and the United States of America, in

## THE ALABAMA ARBITRATION,

for the settlement of several long-standing differences between England and America, for it was one of the most remarkable and successful instances of the practical value of International Arbitration history has yet recorded, and considering the active and valuable part played by Mr. Richard in that great transaction, an historic reference to it may be useful.

Into the unfortunate circumstances, the escape of the Alabama and other privateers, out of which arose this miserable quarrel, it is unnecessary to enter, as they were fully dealt with previously, but one fact should not be forgotten, which certainly reflects great credit on the candour of that distinguished statesman, Lord Russell, who, as Foreign Minister of the Crown, was responsible for the escape of the Alabama from Liverpool, and it is this, that when public opinion was inclined to fix the heavy responsibility for that culpable negligence on others, Lord Russell frankly declared:—

" That the Alabama ought to have been detained during the four days in which I was waiting for the opinion of the Law Officers. But I think that the fault was not that of the Commissioners of Customs ; *it was my fault as Secretary of State for Foreign Affairs*, of an error of judgment."

This admission is very honourable to the noble lord, and considering the very grave consequences to which his want of foresight and energy threatened to involve Great Britain, it ought surely to have inclined him, in an especial manner, to look favourably upon any honourable means that might be proposed for the settlement, by conciliation and justice, with the United States of so serious a quarrel. But instead of that, what was the course he pursued? On the 23rd October, 1863, the United States Ambassador, Mr. Adams, intimated that his Government was willing to submit the dispute to "any fair and equitable form of reference."

Unhappily, Lord Russell allowed this friendly suggestion to remain unnoticed for nearly two years, and then rejected it in the most haughty and peremptory spirit, in a despatch to Mr. Adams, dated August 30, 1865 in which he declared that "Her Majesty's Government are the sole guardians of their own honour."

For some years after this refusal of Lord Russell to accept the proposition of Arbitration, the question remained in abeyance, and it was not until the beginning of the year 1868, that it was re-opened by the appointment of Mr. Reverdy-Johnson as Minister for the United States, for the express purpose of renewing negociations with the British Government, and with this object in view Mr. Richard pressed on the attention of the Cabinet the importance of securing a speedy and satisfactory settlement of the vexed questions in dispute, and he drafted a Memorial on the subject to Ministers in support of their reference to an *Arbitral Process*, and a deputation was organised by him for its presentation to Lord Stanley, Secretary of State for Foreign Affairs, and its prayer was supported by the presence of Edward Baines, M.P., Sir Francis Crossley, M.P., George Hadfield, M.P., and other gentlemen.

Lord Stanley, (of whom it may be said, that few Foreign Ministers of England have better deserved the honourable title, nor more faithfully fulfilled the character of a Minister of Peace,) cordially approved of the Memorial, and expressed opinions decidedly favourable to the pursuance of a pacific Foreign policy, which could not fail to have been full of encouragement to Mr. Richard and his colleagues; in fact, Lord Stanley was the first Minister of the Crown who accepted the proposition of Arbitration, and, but for his retirement from Office at that juncture, in consequence of the defeat of the Conservative Government, his Lordship would no doubt, have quickly and effectually settled the controversy with America.

On the accession of Mr. Gladstone to power in 1868, for the first time as Prime Minister of England, Mr. Richard determined not to let the matter slide, and opened a correspondence with Lord Clarendon, who had succeeded Lord Stanley as Foreign Minister, and also with the American Ambassador, Mr. Reverdy-Johnson, both of whom were favourably disposed to the principle and practice of Arbitration in International Affairs, recommending the insertion in any Treaty between England and America for the Settlement of the Alabama and other claims, an Arbitration Clause, in case of difficulty arising out of its terms or provisions, and both Lord Clarendon and Mr. Johnson approved of the recommendation, and assured Mr. Richard that it was so provided in the Convention between the two Governments.

Unfortunately, the death of Lord Clarendon, and the subsequent rejection by the United States Senate of the Clarendon-Johnson Convention, which led to the recall of the American Minister Mr. Reverdy-Johnson, suspended for a while the negotiations for the pacific settlement of the Anglo-American difficulties ; but Mr. Richard refused to believe that there was no other way out of the difficulty than by war, and he cherished the hope for a renewal of the negotiations which would ultimately bring to a successful issue this international controversy. This hope was soon happily realised, for the successor of the lamented Lord Clarendon, Lord Granville, animated by the same faith in, and regard for, the pacific principles of his predecessor, lost no time, on his accession to Office, in making known to the Government of the United States the earnest desire of Her Majesty's Ministers to make another attempt to arrive at a *modus vivendi* for the satisfactory solution of the difficulties in dispute, and with this view he proposed the appointment of a Joint High Commission, to meet either in London or Washington, in order to lay a basis of negotiation, and this proposal was promptly and cordially accepted by the Government of the United States.

In the first place the Joint High Commission, consisting of the Earl de Grey and Ripon (now the Marquis of Ripon); Sir Stafford H. Northcote, (the late Lord Iddesleigh); Sir Edward Thornton; Sir John Macdonald, and Mr. Montague Bernard, representing England and Canada; and Mr. Hamilton Fish, Mr. Robert Cumming Schenck, Mr. Samuel Nelson, Mr. Ebenezer R. Hoar, and Mr. George H. Williams, representing the United States, assembled at Washington, and drew up the Treaty of Washington, which will ever form an important epoch in the history of International relations.

According to this Treaty the Alabama Claims were referred to a Court of Arbitration, composed of five members, one nominated by the United States, Mr. Charles Francis Adams; one by England, Chief Justice Cockburn; one by the President of the Swiss Confederation, M. Jacques Stæmpfli; one by the King of Italy, Count Frederick Sclopis; and one by the Emperor of Brazil, Viscount D'Itajubá.

This Tribunal met at Geneva to decide, whether in the *Alabama* case, England did or did not fulfil her duties as a Neutral Power, and the result was that the Tribunal arrived at a decision adverse to England, and assessed at £3,100,000 sterling the damages to be paid by her to the United States.

By the same Treaty of Washington it was agreed that the Canadian Fishery question should be referred to a Commission of three members, one appointed by England, one by the United States, and one by Austria.

The last question for settlement under the Treaty, the San Juan Boundary difference, was referred for settlement to the Emperor of Germany.

The success attending this Anglo-American Arbitration, based upon the Treaty of Washington, was not a triumph of one Government in particular, for it was a result due as much to the labours of the present Earl of Derby, as Lords Clarendon and Granville, as much to the services of the late Lord Iddesleigh as to the Marquis of Ripon, and as much to the co-operation of the late Lord Beaconsfield as of Mr. Gladstone.

Such a triumph of reason and of justice over the arbitrament of blood and carnage, is a triumph to the great credit of Great Britain and America, one which both may, without respect to faction or party, rejoice over.

Mr. Richard hailed this result, for which he laboured so vigorously for many years, with unqualified satisfaction, for he justly observed that in the first place it permanently settled grave differences which, unsettled, were full of peril to the friendly relations of England and America, and especially because it laid the foundation of a precedent, which he believed would not be without its influence on the policy of the other Nations of the world.

In the Session of 1871 was introduced the Burials Bill, the object of which was to throw open the parish churchyards to Dissenters, with the right of religious service of their Ministers. This was cordially supported by Mr. Richard for many years, both in and out of Parliament, and on its introduction for a second time into the House of Commons in the Session of 1871, by Mr. Osborne Morgan, the author of the Bill, Mr. Richard on March 1st, delivered an effective speech, in which he appealed for the two classes of persons for whom the Bill sought relief: those who were absolutely denied all rights of Christian burial in the parochial churchyards, those

Christians who disapprove of baptism, to whom no religious
service is granted; and to another and larger class, the Nonconformists, who were forbidden to have their dead buried in
the churchyards by their own Ministers, with their own form
of religious service.   He pointed out in considerable detail
the objections raised to this Measure of relief, which he
termed as chimerical, and hallucinations, and concluded as
follows :—

" The tie which binds so many millions of the people of this
country to your Church is for various reasons, very much loosened.
But there is one tie, which nearly all men feel more or less.   The
staunchest dissenter, the most inveterate Radical, is not wholly
insensible to the halo of veneration and sacredness which gathers
around the old churchyard where
                  ' The rude forefathers of the hamlet sleep,'
and among them their own forefathers."

In the same Session, Mr.  Richard also addressed the
House in support of the Parochial Councils Bill, introduced
by Viscount Sandon, and of the Ballot Bill, introduced
by Mr. Forster, and on May 9th he delivered a great
speech on the question of Disestablishment of the English
Church, which was brought before the House by his esteemed
friend Mr. Edward Miall, the member for Bradford, who
submitted the following resolution :—

" That it is expedient at the earliest practicable period to apply
the policy initiated by the disestablishment of the Irish Church
by the Act of 1869, to the other Churches established by law in
the United Kingdom."

The speech of Mr. Richard, as an eye-witness wrote, was
admirably arranged, full of apt illustrations and details
eloquently and forcibly delivered; it was a speech that
should make Welshmen proud of their countryman.

The Session of 1872, was an active one for Mr. Richard,
for he took a prominent and useful part in Debate on
several important questions upon which he was deeply
interested.

On the 21st of February, on the introduction by Mr.

Chambers of the Bill to legalise marriage with the deceased wife's sister, Mr. Richard cordially supported the measure for which he said, on one side are reason, justice, and the interests of morality, and on the other side prejudice and sentiment, and in conclusion said :—

"Believing as he did that the prohibition they were anxious to remove, had no warrant in any law of nature or of God ; that it was not sustained by the opinion of the best and most religious portion of the people of this country ; that it inflicted cruel hardship upon a most honourable and worthy class of people, and especially that it was productive of great misery and social evil to the lower classes of the community ; without hesitation, and with the utmost confidence, he would give his vote in favour of the Bill." (Cheers.)

It is a remarkable fact that few if any legislative measures introduced into Parliament have passed through such a chequered career. From 1866 to 1875 it was introduced by Mr. Thomas Chambers (now Sir Thomas) on seven occasions, on three of which the Bill received the approval either on a second or a third reading of the House of Commons, and on the remaining four occasions was rejected. From 1866 to 1889 it has been introduced into the House of Lords by Lords Houghton, Dalhousie, Monson, and the Duke of St. Albans, on eight occasions ; but in spite of being supported by the Princes of the Royal Blood, it has failed to secure a majority in its favour, and until the Government of the day take it in hand, and stake their existence upon it, there is no hope of the Bill passing into law.

On the 5th August the Nonconformists renewed their attack with redoubled vehemence on the Elementary Education Act of Mr. Forster, when Mr. George Dixon hurled a vote of censure on the policy of the Government embodied in a series of six resolutions, two of which complained of the failure of the Act to secure the election of School Boards and compulsory attendance, two of the resolutions to the operation of the 25th section, and the remaining two resolutions censured the use of public money for denominational teaching.

To Mr. Richard devolved the task of grappling with the last two resolutions, and he availed himself of the opportunity to make a vigorous onslaught on Mr. Forster for the partiality he had shown to the denominational schools, as instanced by his appointment of inspectors ; and he warned the Government against breaking up the Liberal party " by alienating and disgusting one of the largest sections of that party which had been faithful to it through all its changing fortunes."

On a division the resolutions of Mr. Dixon were negatived by a majority of 261.

On the 8th March Mr. Osborne Morgan moved a resolution of censure on the appointment of Mr. Homersham Cox, as judge of the Mid-Wales County Court Circuit, which was supported by a speech from Mr. Richard, who strongly urged the appointment of men for such positions, capable of speaking the Welsh and English languages; and the Government in effect accepted the recommendation.

On April 4th Mr. Richard. seconded the amendment of Mr. Vernon Harcourt, (now Sir William) on going into Committee of Ways and Means in favour of Retrenchment which was as follows :—

" That in the opinion of this House, the national expenditure is capable of further reduction without danger to the safety and good government of the country ; and that it is desirable that such expenditure should be reduced accordingly, in order that the taxation of the people and the public debt may be diminished in a larger measure than is proposed in the said resolutions."

In support of this amendment Mr. Richard said that he believed the national expenditure was capable of considerable reduction without danger to the safety and good government of the country. Expenditure, he said, must depend upon policy, and England having wisely adopted a policy of non-intervention, which was now loyally accepted by the leaders of all parties in this country, he considered it should be followed by a diminution of the present enormous armaments.

On April 19th he seconded the motion for an address

to the Crown on the subject of the persecution of the Jews in Roumania and Servia, moved by Sir Francis Goldsmid, which he stigmatized as a disgrace to the civilisation of the 19th century; and the Government giving an assurance that the subject would be diplomatically dealt with, the motion was withdrawn.

Mr. Richard also spoke in this Session on the Scotch Education Bill, the Occasional Sermons Bill, the Mines Regulation Bill, and on the second reading of the Military Forces Localisation Bill, brought in by Mr. Cardwell as a Government Measure, he, on the 15th July, spoke in opposition to it, on the ground, firstly, that it would involve a large expenditure of public money upon an experiment; secondly, that it would cover the country with a web of military institutions, and thus convert England into a military nation; and, lastly, because these Military Centres would exercise an injurious influence on public morality.

## NONCONFORMIST CONFERENCE AT MANCHESTER.

In consequence of the continued and determined resistance of the Vice-President of the Council on Education, Mr. Forster, to all reasonable demands of the Nonconformists, made by Mr. Richard, Mr. Dixon, and Mr Miall in Parliament, to amend or qualify the Elementary Education Act, it was resolved to hold an imposing demonstration in Manchester; and the Committee of the Liberation Society of that city summoned delegates from all parts of the country not simply with the view to confront the Educational policy of Mr. Forster, but also with the express view of considering the relation that constituent bodies, which they represented, should hereafter bear towards the Government of Mr. Gladstone and the Liberal party generally.

The position taken up by Mr. Richard and his colleagues, prior to the passing into law of Mr. Forster's Measure, and which they gave frequent expression to, during the Sessions of 1870 and 1871, by resolutions and speeches which we have already referred to, was this :—That the State cannot undertake the work of Religious Teaching in Church or School without violating the rights of conscience, on the one hand, and doing despite to the dignity of Truth on the other hand ; and it is to be regretted that all their efforts were unavailing to persuade or compel the Government to yield to their just demands.

Subsequently, however, owing to the operation of the Elementary Education Act ; to the unfavourable results of the cumulative vote ; to the intensely sectarian proceedings of many of the School Boards throughout the country, and to the official bias of the Educational Department in London, under the influence of Mr. Forster, all this conclusively brought conviction to the minds of Nonconformists that there can be only one basis of National Education, consistent with equal justice to all religious parties, namely, to confine the authority of the State to secular teaching, and to assign religious teaching exclusively to the voluntary efforts of the religious bodies.

It was with these strong convictions, and smarting under a deep sense of injustice, that on January 24th, 1872, the Nonconformists of England and Wales took the field, marshalled under tried and experienced leaders, opening the campaign in the Free Trade Hall at Manchester by a demonstration such as seldom, if ever, has been witnessed on that historic battle-ground of Freedom ; and so great was the enthusiasm, and so vast were the numbers assembled from all parts of the kingdom, that this capacious building was unable to contain them, and they were compelled to hold an overflow meeting in the next largest hall in the city.

At the Free Trade Hall assembly Mr. Richard presided, supported by Jacob Bright, M.P., Alfred Illingworth, M.P.,

Evan Matthew Richards, M.P., and the leading Nonconformists from all parts of the country, amongst whom was
Mr. Joseph Chamberlain, at that time comparatively un-
distinguished in the political world.

It was a grand and imposing spectacle, when Mr. Richard
rising to address that vast assemblage, and to open the proceedings of that important National Convention, the audience
rose *en masse*, and welcomed him with rounds of vociferous
cheering, and for some minutes he was unable to proceed,
so great was the enthusiasm displayed.

The speech of Mr. Richard on this great occasion was
one of the finest oratorical efforts which he ever made on
this question of religious toleration ; and his clear and
deliberate diction, his masterly arrangement of facts, and
the calm delivery of telling points rivetted the earnest attention of his audience ; and when he grappled with his Titanic
opponent, and fairly tore his policy into shreds, the enthusiasm of the audience knew no bounds. It was a grand
speech, worthy of the occasion and of the cause of religious
freedom.

During the Conference which followed, he read a paper
on "The Political Relations of the Nonconformists to the
Liberal Party," which was an able and historical *resumé* of
the relations of Nonconformists to successive Liberal
Governments from the Revolution of 1688 down to the
present day, and he vividly described the long-suffering
attitude of the Nonconformists during these two centuries
of struggles for religious liberty ; and he concluded with
this eloquent peroration :—

"I think I have shown that there are abundant proofs along
the whole line of our history, that we have not been unreasonable in our demands, or importunate in our expectations ; and
we are still prepared to exercise forbearance towards our ancient
Liberal allies. But we believe that there are certain great principles—principles which go down to the very foundation of all
civil, religious, and intellectual freedom—for the maintenance
and defence of which we mean to stand—(cheers)—and we do
this, not as Nonconformists, but as Englishmen, believing as we

do from the bottom of our hearts that the principles we advocate are those which will tend most hereafter, as it is acknowledged they have tended most heretofore, to establish the liberties of our country upon sure and firm foundations. We are willing to exercise patience, to make reasonable concessions ; but to adopt a course which will involve the sacrifice, or the surrender, or the serious compromise of those vital principles, for the sake of any man, or any party, is what we cannot, what we ought not, what we must not, what we dare not, and by God's help what we will not do."

At the conclusion of this thrilling address which occupied an hour in delivery, the whole audience rose and waved a round of enthusiastic cheering.

-------

## INTERNATIONAL ARBITRATION.

We now approach a memorable epoch in the public career of Mr. Richard, which not only witnessed one of the greatest Parliamentary triumphs of modern times, which not only lifted into the domain of practical politics the great principle of International Arbitration, and gave a powerful *impetus* to its practical adoption in national differences, but it placed Mr. Richard in the front rank of the Parliament of England as an orator and legislator, and secured for him a world-wide reputation worthy of his great gifts and high character, and worthy too, of the splendid cause that he had for upwards of forty years so nobly championed.

Not that Mr. Richard was the first and only pioneer in this great crusade against war, and in the advocacy of International Arbitration. For distinguished, and devoted, and noble a champion as Mr. Richard was in this holy enterprise, he was the very last of men to be unmindful of the noble army of heroic workers who had preceded him, or who were contemporaneous with him, in his great labour, and to whom he ever and anon delighted to refer to, as those to whom the Cause of Peace owed an imperishable claim of gratitude and honor, and even without whom, he was wont to declare, the progress and triumphs of the present generation would never have been achieved.

It may be said of the progress of the movement for the promotion of International Arbitration, that from the commencement of the present century there has been quietly growing up among thoughtful men in Christendom a profound conviction that wars are capable of being largely diminished, if not absolutely prevented, and they have arrived at the conclusion that friendly arbitration between nations, accompanied by attempts to arrive at a general agreement for the settlement of a definite code of International law, and the establishment of an International Tribunal, would go far to render armed collisions between nations impossible.

Accordingly, Mr. Cobden, always a cordial colleague of the friends of peace, introduced into the British Parliament, June 12th, 1849, the following Motion :—

"That an humble address be presented to Her Majesty, praying that she will be graciously pleased to direct her principal Secretary of State for Foreign Affairs to enter into communications with Foreign Powers inviting them to concur in Treaties binding the respective parties, in the event of any future misunderstanding which cannot be arranged by amicable negotiation, to refer the matter in dispute to the decision of Arbitrators."

That motion, as it has been before stated, was unsuccessful, yet there is no doubt that the agitation carried forward in its behalf in England, as well as the important debate in Parliament, exercised an incalculable amount of good, by awakening a great public interest in the question, and thereby largely contributed to the insertion in the Treaty, negotiated at the Congress which met at Paris in 1856, at the close of the Russian War, the following clause providing for a resort to Arbitration in International disputes :—

"The Plenipotentiaries do not hesitate to express, in the name of their Governments, the wish that States between which any serious misunderstanding may arise, should, before appealing to arms, have recourse, as far as circumstances might allow, to the good offices of a friendly power."

Since that date, 1856, the subject of International Arbitration has continued to receive increased attention, not confined to an advance of opinion, but by its practical adoption in many International difficulties, so that it may be said, Arbitration has become the rule, and War the exception for the settlement of national quarrels.

Therefore Mr. Richard, urged on the one hand, by its necessity, and encouraged on the other hand by its feasibility, deemed it advisable to submit the question to the House of Commons, by the following practical resolution:—

" That an humble address be presented to Her Majesty, praying that she will be graciously pleased to direct her principal Secretary of State of Foreign Affairs, to enter into communication with Foreign Powers, with a view to the further improvement of International Law, and to the establishment of a permanent system of International Arbitration."

This notice of Motion was placed by Mr. Richard on the Notice Book of the House of Commons on 11th August, 1871, for submission to Parliament early the following Session, and from that date until July 8, 1873, a period of nearly two years, great and strenuous efforts were put forth by him, assisted by many others, fellow-labourers with him in the Cause, to secure its ultimate triumph ; and amongst those who by pulpit and platform, by memorial and petition, and various other agencies, may be mentioned, Henry Vincent, William Stokes, Revs. G. W. Humphrey, G. W. Conder, Dr. Stock, J. H. Pattison, Samuel Roberts, E. Jacob, and Mr. A. B. Hayward, Mr. Thomas Snape, and the writer of this *Memorique*, and the latter, early in the incipient stages of the Movement, under the direction of Mr. Richard, organised large and successful Conferences and Public Meetings at Manchester, Leeds, Darlington, Newcastle, Bristol, Birmingham, Dublin, and many other important centres, where Mr. Richard delivered great and often impressive speeches on the question of the hour, most of which were published and widely circulated, and exercised a potent influence on the public mind.

In addition to those whose names are mentioned above, closely identified with Mr. Richard in the Movement, and whose services he gratefully and highly acknowledged, must not be omitted that noble champion of peace in the Midlands, Mr. Arthur O'Neill, of Birmingham.

ARTHUR G. O'NEILL.

Mr. O'Neill has done yeoman's service in this great cause; he has nobly fought and suffered in many a struggle for humanity, for freedom, and for Peace, and he has not lived nor laboured in vain, for he has been spared to witness many triumphs, and deserves well to wear on his brow the laurels of victory.

K

He was associated, forty years ago, in the first international movement, under the leadership of Mr. Cobden, and when Mr. Richard determined to raise once more in Parliament the question, Mr. O'Neill threw himself with all the enthusiasm of his early youth, into the fray, and heroically laboured to secure its ultimate triumph.

The day had now arrived, Tuesday, July 8th, when Mr. Richard was expected to bring forward in Parliament this great question of International Arbitration, and it was with feelings of interest and anxiety that the author of this *Memorique*, in company with several active supporters of the cause, proceeded to the House of Commons to be present at the great debate on this important subject.

At 9 o'clock, the evening sitting, the Speaker, beckoning in the direction of the benches below the gangway, called upon Mr. Richard to move his resolution.

Mr. Richard, (who sat at the end of the third bench, the lamented Richard Cobden's favourite seat, and the very spot from which twenty-four years previously he had moved a similar resolution, but with a different result,) on rising was received with a cheer. He proceeded slowly, and in measured language, to assure the House with unaffected sincerity of his own unfitness for the task before him, and made a happy allusion to the Apostle of Peace, his illustrious predecessor in the work of International Arbitration. Reference was made to the numerous petitions presented, especially those from the various religious bodies, and the Church of England, emphasizing in particular the fact that 1,038,000 of the working classes had appealed, by their signatures, in favour of the motion. The cost of the combined armies in Europe was then grappled with, giving the astounding total of 550 millions per annum; next the compulsory military service in the various European countries, driving into exile, or forcing into its despotic thraldom, the flower of the manhood of the peoples; and then the bankrupt state of European nations—specially Austria, Italy, Turkey, and

Spain—reeling beneath this colossal burden, was alluded to. In approaching the main question of the Resolution, he stated that experience had approved the practicability of the principle, and in proof of this he cited a large number of instances, such as the Portendic claims arising out of the blockade of the Moorish coast by France in 1845; the Anglo-Brazilian difficulty in 1863; the difficulty between Turkey and Greece in 1868; and lest a hostile critic might have been ready to exclaim that these were cases which had reference only to trivial matters, the answer was aptly fore-stalled:—

"Perhaps it may be said in reference to the cases of success-ful arbitration I have cited that they referred to comparatively small matters. My answer is, that they could not possibly refer to smaller matters than those which have often led to long, bloody, and desolating wars between nations. (Loud cheers.) They were not smaller matters, for instance, than the question whether the cupola of a particular church at Jerusalem should be repaired by Greek or Latin monks, and yet that was the quarrel which, through the infinite unwisdom of some of the great Powers, led to a war which cost Europe, according to Mr. Kinglake, a million of human lives and some four or five hundred millions of money."

As was to be expected, a just and eloquent eulogium was passed on the Geneva Arbitration, which was wel-comed by general cheering on both sides of the House, and a deserved tribute was tendered, with a depth of feeling that could not be concealed, to the chief actors in that great transaction, making honourable mention of Lord Granville, and not omitting a just meed of praise to Mr. Disraeli and the "leading journal," for the judicial calmness they had dis-played during those delicate negotiations. Throughout this masterly speech, Henry Richard spoke with great power and earnestness; the House, which was better attended than was expected, listened attentively, and it was evident the speech had made a real impression. After having spoken for upwards of an hour, he concluded, amid loud and general cheering from both sides of the House.

When the Prime Minister rose to reply, it was evident
he was fatigued, and unequal to a great effort, but his speech
was nevertheless admirable in its tone and temper, full of
noble sentiments, and most cordial in his estimation of the
object in view, in fact the speech of a "Great Peace
Minister." He felt, however, the time had not yet arrived
for giving effect to the resolution, and urged its withdrawal.

Sir Wilfrid Lawson followed the Premier, and during his
speech a consultation took place of the prominent supporters
of the Resolution, and it was eventually resolved not to
prolong the debate, and accordingly at the conclusion of Sir
Wilfrid's speech, Henry Richard rose, and after thanking
the Prime Minister for his eminently friendly speech, he
announced his intention to ask the judgment of the House
upon the question.

During the time that the division was being proceeded
with great interest was manifested, and when the teller
advanced to the bar, and the clerk handed to Henry Richard
the figures, the House broke out into general cheering, which
was again renewed when, with more than usual animation,
the hon. member for Merthyr announced the numbers of
Ayes, 98, Noes, 88, majority *ten* for the Resolution.

This great triumph achieved by Mr. Richard in Parliament,
it is not too much to say, astonished both friends and foes
alike, for it was an unexpected victory, and deeply gratifying,
and no man was more gratified than the Prime Minister
himself, Mr. Gladstone.

Throughout Europe and the World, wherever civilisation, justice and humanity held sway in the minds o
men, echoed and re-echoed a voice of exultation, and
the enlightened press of Europe, broke forth, even from
the most influential journals, in one approving chorus of
congratulation, not only of the British Parliament, that first
in the history of Nations had acclaimed the principle of International Arbitration, but also of the Orator, who by his
impressive and convincing speech, had swayed that august

Assembly to a declaration in favour of practical action to secure its general adoption in Europe.

From all parts of Europe and America Mr. Richard received a noble reward for his splendid victory, for he was the happy recipient of letters of high commendation from Statesmen, and philanthropists, and also of valuable addresses from numerous public bodies, and Associations of Peace rejoicing at his auspicious success, amongst which may be mentioned Charles Sumner, Senator of the United States, Auguste Visschers, member of Belgian Parliament, Van Eck, member of the Dutch Parliament, G. Biancheri, President of the Italian Chamber of Deputies, M. Larroque, the French economist, Emile de Lavelèye, of Liege, Frederic Passy, President of the Peace Society of France, Jean Dollfus, Mayor of Mulhouse, B. Castiglia, member of the Italian Parliament, General Garibaldi, Aurelio Saffo ; also from the general League of Peace for the Netherlands, the Peace Society of France, the Universal Peace Union of America, the Italian Peace Society, the American Peace Society of Boston, the League of Peace and Liberty, and in addition numerous addresses from Associations of Working Men in Italy and other countries, largely and influentially signed.

Cheered by these and many other manifestations of cordial congratulations and sincere sympathy, from devoted friends and allies in all parts of Europe and America, Mr. Richard determined not to rest on his oars, or to be lulled into repose on his laurels by this unexpected triumph, but on the contrary, accepting it with commendable gratitude and pride as the first important victory in a great struggle, and as he believed a forerunner of equally glorious achievements in the future, he resolved to buckle on his armour afresh, and with that dauntless courage which ever distinguished him to march forward into other lands, and there to stimulate by his presence, example, and spirit, others into similar action.

Mr. Richard practically opened his Continental Campaign

by taking part in an International Conference held at Brussels in October, 1873, presided over by M. Auguste Visschers, and attended by men of the highest reputation in international law and other kindred subjects, amongst whom may be mentioned David Dudley Field, of New York, Emile de Lavelèye, Rollin Jacquemym, Montague Bernard, Professor Sheldon Amos, Signor Pierrantoni, Sir Travers Twiss, Frederic Passy, and last, but not least, Henry Richard, who on his entering the Hall was loudly cheered, in honour of his Parliamentary triumph.

Towards the close of the Conference, an interesting incident occurred when Professor Pierrantoni proposed the presentation of an address to Henry Richard for the zeal, devotion, and ability, with which he had supported, for so many years, the cause of International Peace, which was cordially approved, and was ordered to be prepared by Emile de Lavelèye and signed by the President, Auguste Visschers on behalf of the Congress. One of the good results of Mr. Richard's visit to Brussels was the interest it excited in the Belgium Parliament and the encouragement it gave to the Belgian Deputies to push forward a proposal in their Parliament, similar in form and aim to the resolution carried in the English Legislature.

M. Couvreur, one of the members for the City of Brussels, whom Mr. Richard had long known, promised to raise the question, and on the 19th January, 1874, he submitted a resolution on the subject which was supported by M. Thonissen, M. Le Hardy de Beaulieu, and others ; and at the close of the debate the Minister for Foreign Affairs, M. D' Aspremont-Lynden, accepted on behalf of the Government the proposition, and when put to the vote out of 83 members, 81 voted for it.

This success in the Belgian Chamber of Deputies, was quickly followed by a greater success in the Senate, where the subject was introduced by the Baron De Roodenbeke, and the Baron d'Anethan, and supported by the

Government, and finally adopted without a single dissentient voice.

From Belgium Mr. Richard proceeded into Holland, where he received a most hearty welcome from the Dutch Peace Society, who invited him in the first place to address a Public Assembly at the Hague, presided over by Van Eck, one of the members of the Dutch Parliament, and subsequently entertained him at a banquet, both of which assemblies were largely and influentially attended. At the banquet, Herr Van Eck and Herr Bredius announced their intention to bring the question of Arbitration before the Dutch Legislature at the earliest opportunity, and on the 12th of October they redeemed their pledge by placing upon the table of the House a notice of Motion.

The discussion on this Motion took place on the 27th November, and after two days' debate and able speeches by the proposers of the resolution, Herr Van Eck and Herr Bredius, the Minister for Foreign Affairs declared on behalf of the Government a willingness to co-operate, but not to take the initiative, and therefore would not oppose the Motion, and this qualified approval no doubt resulted in a favourable division, the Resolution being carried by 35 to 30 votes.

Leaving the Hague, Mr. Richard proceeded to Berlin, where he found that the two Houses of Parliament, the Reischrath for Prussia and the Reichstag for Germany, were adjourned, but he availed himself of the presence in the capital of several eminent men, such as Dr. Lasker, Dr. Löewe, Dr. Engel, and others, and from one and all he received cordial welcome and sympathy. The state of feeling arising out of the late War with France was felt to be an obstacle for any Parliamentary action, although many, if not all, of the distinguished men who met Mr. Richard were strongly in favour of his mission, and of the policy he advocated.

From Berlin he journeyed to Dresden and Prague, where

he remained a few days, and interested many public men in the question ; and thence to Vienna, where he met with many earnest friends of the cause, who shared heartily his views : Dr. Neumann, a member of the Upper House, Count Kinsky, Baron de Kübeck, member of the Chamber, Baron Hye, and these latter two, the one in the Upper, and the other in the Lower House, gave notice of their intention to introduce a Bill, or Resolution, on the subject of Arbitration.

At Buda-Pesth, the capital of Hungary, Mr. Richard interviewed the eminent statesman, Herr Francis Deak, also several members of the Hungarian Ministry, and thus both in Austria and Hungary, he received assurances that the question in some form would be submitted in their respective Parliaments, and ultimately to the Delegations, whose special functions embrace the foreign relations of the Empire.

Of all the important countries visited by Mr. Richard, few, if any, displayed so much zeal and enthusiasm, or offered him such distinguished honour; in fact, wherever he went among the famous cities of Italy, men of great eminence and influence greeted him with marked cordiality. At Venice a banquet was given in his honour, presided over by Chevalier Ruffini, and an address was presented to him by the working men of the city, resonant with powerful appeals for the overthrow of war, and hearty congratulations and good wishes.

From Venice he hurried on to Rome, in order to be present, and as he observed, in some sense to share in the great Parliamentary triumph achieved by Signor Mancini, who on the 24th November, 1873, submitted a resolution on the subject in a great and statesman-like speech, which was received with prolonged cheers, and he was followed by Signor Visconti-Venosta, the Minister for Foreign Affairs, with a speech of emphatic approval, and, on Signor Biancheri, the President of the Chamber, putting the resolution to the vote, the whole Chamber of Deputies rose, as one man, to express their unanimous sanction.

Three days after this memorable scene, a great political banquet was given in Rome to Mr. Richard, attended by Senators, Deputies, Members of the University and of the Municipality, besides several distinguished foreigners. On this occasion Mr. Richard, inspired by the event of the 24th, which he had witnessed, and the distinguished company around him, delivered an oration worthy of the cause, the occasion, and of his oratorical renown.

Before leaving Rome Mr. Richard formed the acquaintance of Professors Pierrantoni and Sbarbaro, the former an eminent professor of international and constitutional law at Naples, and the latter a devoted and disinterested friend of peace residing at Modena, and whose friendship he greatly valued; and having finished his work in the capital, he visited Florence and Milan, and at the latter, he was welcomed by an enthusiastic demonstration and banquet, which was of a highly flattering nature, considering the rank and influence present, Senators, Deputies, Jurists, besides the Syndic of the City, Members of the City Council, and representatives of various public bodies, and in reference to which the *Courier* of Milan remarked :—

" It was in fact, the first occasion for many years on which we have seen men belonging to political parties of discordant views conversing familiarly, and shaking hands in a friendly manner.'

At Turin, the last important city of Italy visited, Mr. Richard's special object was, as he writes :

"To have the gratification of forming the personal acquaintance of the illustrious Count Sclopis, the President of the Tribunal at Geneva, whose name is imperishably associated with an event which will be regarded hereafter as forming a great landmark in the history of civilisation,"

and he was rejoiced to find how entirely devoted this distinguished son of Italy was to the cause of international peace.

The last of the brilliant series of international fraternisations for the purpose of doing homage to the great principle of Arbitration, and to its distinguished advocate, Mr. Richard, took place at Paris, presided over by M. Renouard, Member of the Institute of France, and in proposing the health of the guest of the evening, Frederic Passy delivered a remarkable speech.

This campaign of Mr. Richard, for the purpose of stirring into action the leading men in the chief countries in Europe, with the view of bringing public opinion to bear on their Governments, and thus securing the concurrence of other nations to the principle of Arbitration, was undoubtedly crowned with success far beyond his anticipations. Wherever he went during this three months' important mission, it was his good fortune to find the deepest interest kindled by the success of his efforts in the British Parliament, and soon after his return to England, at a soirée given in his honour at the Cannon Street Hotel, presided over by Mr. Mundella, M.P., and influentially attended, we find he thus refers to this remarkable tour :—

" No one could have been more surprised than he was himself to find that his feeble voice, which had been raised in the House of Commons in favour of justice, reason, and humanity, had awakened so great a feeling as had been found to be the case. Everywhere he had gone he had been received with open arms, as the friend and Apostle of Peace. * * * He greatly rejoiced that working men in various countries were taking up this question, for, whoever else might gain by War, they at least were sure to suffer. The blood and bones of working men had covered every battlefield of Europe. Others carried off the spoils, the titles, the honours, the emoluments of War ; but everywhere and always the working men came in for the main share of its sufferings—they and their families. * * * He had come back to England with the strongest conviction that there was diffused throughout society, in all parts of the Continent, an intense abhorrence of the War system, and a longing for deliverance. * * *"

## THE NEW PARLIAMENT, 1874.

In the beginning of the year 1874, a political crisis arose that during the session of 1873, on more than one occasion, threatened either a dissolution or the resignation of Ministers, partly consequent on the persistent opposition of the Non-conformist supporters of the Government to the educational policy of Mr. Forster, and partly the result of the defeat of Mr. Gladstone's Measure for University Education and Reform in Ireland.

Suddenly, without warning from any political storm signal, and it may be said somewhat precipitately, the Prime Minister, with the sanction of the Crown, on the eve of the re-assembling of the fifth Session, dissolved Parliament and issued a stirring and remarkable address, to what was practically to the electors of the United Kingdom, for a renewal, on behalf of his Administration, of the trust and confidence of the nation.

In this crisis, Mr. Richard lost no time on behalf of the Peace Party, in the issuing of a Manifesto to the electors throughout the Kingdom, which was both retrospective and prospective, in the former, referring with pride to the successful effort of the late Government, in for ever setting at rest the complicated difficulties with the United States, and the moral support given to the International Arbitration resolution; and prospectively, the burdens and extravagance of large military establishments, and the expediency of disarmament, and of more economical modes of settling national disputes than by the sword.

In addition to this direct appeal to the electors everywhere, Mr. Richard and his friends prepared and widely circulated numerous election papers and placards containing valuable facts and statistics; and by these and other agencies endeavoured to keep before the public eye the importance of sending men to Parliament willing advocates of peace, retrenchment and reform.

The electoral contest was short, sharp, and decisive. At Merthyr-Tydvil Mr. Richard was returned after a strong struggle at the head of the poll, and whilst many of his friends and supporters were equally fortunate, yet others whose services he greatly appreciated were unfortunate; but to his mind the greatest disaster of all, disastrous as he believed to the cause of international peace, was the overwhelming defeat of the Liberal chief, Mr. Gladstone, in his position as Prime Minister of England.

The first important speech delivered by Mr. Richard after his election to the Twenty-first Parliament of the reign of Her Majesty Queen Victoria, was on the 4th May, 1874, upon the following amendment moved by Sir Wilfrid Lawson to the resolution of Mr. Hanbury on affairs in the West African Settlements of the Crown :—

"That this House is of opinion, that in the interests of civilisation and commerce, it is desirable to withdraw from all equivocal and entangling engagements with the tribes inhabiting the Gold Coast."

Mr. Richard supported this amendment, declaring that the Ashantee War was not a just or necessary war, that it might have been avoided, and that it arose from a contemptuous disregard of notorious and acknowledged rights of King Coffee Calcali, and he strongly condemned the character of the military operations and the useless expenditure of men and money, and considered that the results of the war were not triumphs of civilisation, but of barbarism and brute force.

In the course of the debate, which involved a criticism of the policy of both Liberal and Tory Governments consequent upon the Ashantee War, speeches were delivered by Mr. Roebuck, Mr. Knatchbull-Hugessen, Mr. Mc Arthur, the Marquis of Hartington, Mr. Disraeli, and others, and on a division the amendment was rejected by 311 against 75 votes.

The next subject which claimed the attention of Mr. Richard referred to an alteration of Mr. Forster's Elementary Education Measure, and in conjunction with Mr. Samuel Morley, Sir Thomas Bazley, and other Nonconformists, Mr. Richard brought in a Bill for that object.

On the 10th June he moved that the Bill be read a second time and spoke at some length, and at the onset reviewed the history of the question, and the reasons that had compelled the Nonconformists to oppose, in 1870 and subsequently, Mr. Forster's Measure since it had passed into law, and to obtain an amendment of the obnoxious provisions, as they considered them, contained in the 25th Clause of the Act. The object of this Bill was to remove from the Education Act this clause, which Mr. Richard described as a stumbling-block, and a rock of offence, infusing bitterness and discord into School Boards, and placing a serious obstacle to the harmonious working of the Act for promoting the education of the people. The rejection of the Bill was moved by Mr. Saul Isaac, the member for Nottingham, who was supported in debate by Mr. Forster on behalf of the late Government, and Viscount Sandon, on behalf of the Government in power, and on a division the Bill was rejected by 373 against 128 votes.

The advance of the Ritualistic practices in the Church of England, and the indifference, and even defiance, shewn by the High Church Party to Episcopal authority, led to the introduction of a Measure, based upon the recommendations of the Ritual Commission, of 1867. This Measure was introduced, in the first instance, into the House of Lords, by the Archbishop of Canterbury, on April 20th, the object of which was to bring the practices of the clergy more under control of the congregations, and confer on the Episcopacy increased power to check those practices, deemed inconsistent with the ritual of the Church of England, and its third reading passed the Lords on June 25th.

The conduct of the Measure in the House of Commons was entrusted to Mr. Russell Gurney, and the debate thereon shewed considerable difference of opinion upon the Ministerial and Opposition Benches, Mr. Gathorne Hardy and Mr. Gladstone strongly opposing it, whilst Sir William Harcourt and Mr. Disraeli supported it. Upon the amendment of Mr. Hall, the Member for the City of Oxford, to defer proceeding with the Bill, Mr. Richard addressed the House,

July 15th, and, at the close of an interesting speech, said, that he believed the Church of England reformers were on the wrong tack in endeavouring to reform a great spiritual body by the coarse machinery of law, and that there was only one way by which it could disembarrass itself, to cut asunder the fetters which binds the Church to the State, in one word, " Disestablishment."

This Measure, after many vicissitudes in both Houses of Parliament, passed its third reading, and became law 3rd of August.

Mr. Richard also took part in the debate on the Government Measure for the amendment of the Endowed Schools Act, which was brought into Parliament by Viscount Sandon, and finally carried, but which he opposed ; also he supported in debate Mr. Osborne Morgan's proposal, recommending appointments to the County Courts in Wales of Judges conversant with the Welsh language.

During 1874, in addition to his Parliamentary and other labours, Mr. Richard addressed two important Meetings on Peace and Arbitration, the one at Birmingham, and the other at Liverpool. The former was the first Annual Meeting of the Midland Arbitration Union, and was presided over by Mr. George Dixon, M.P., who was supported by Mr. George Palmer, Reading, Mr. J. S. Wright, Rev. C. H. Collyns, who with the Chairman, delivered admirable speeches on the question, and afterwards Mr. Richard followed with an eloquent speech, passing in review in graphic language, his recent mission to the Capitals of Europe, which, as Mr. O'Neill remarked :—

" Was listened to with deep interest, for it reminded those present of the glowing narratives of the Missionaries of former ages, when they described how wonderfully God had opened their way among the tribes and nations."

The Meeting at Liverpool was under the auspices of the Peace Society of that city, (whose Secretary at that time was the indefatigable and earnest worker, the lamented Mr. A. B. Hayward), and was presided over by its President, the Rev. Hugh Stowell Brown, whose massive and trenchant eloquence, whether in the the pulpit or on the platform, in support of the Cause, should long and gratefully be cherished by the friends of Peace.

In September 1874 Mr. Richard attended two important

## CONGRESSES AT GENEVA,

the first, in order of time, being the Institute of International Law (Institut Droit), founded in 1873 at Ghent, by M. Rollin Jacquemyn, its object in the main being to secure a uniformity in the Laws of Nations so far as they affect private rights, and the relations of international commerce, property and civil procedure; and the second Congress, the Association for the Reform and Codification of the Laws of Nations, founded at Brussels in 1873 by Dr. Miles and David Dudley Field of New York, its aims being, as its title implies, a Consolidation of the Laws of Nations, not confined to private but also public international law, with a view to the establishment of a general code, administered by a Central Tribunal.

The Institut Droit was presided over by Signor Mancini of Rome, and was attended by a considerable number of very eminent Jurists, and Mr. Richard, and the writer of this *Memorique* attended, not as members taking part in the deliberations, (as the Institut is exclusively judicial,) but as visitors interested in the discussion of all questions bearing on international law, whether public or private.

The Association for the Reform and Codification of the Laws of Nations, assembled immediately after the former closed its labours, in the historical Hall, now called the Salle d'Alabama, where met in 1871-2 the members of the Geneva Tribunal for the settlement of the Anglo-American difficulties, and was presided over by David Dudley Field, of New York, the founder of the Association. At this Congress, on the third day of its session, Mr. Richard read a most interesting paper entitled, "The Gradual Triumph of Law over Brute Force," a masterly production, which may be summarised in his own words:—

"We have seen how, in course of time, the domain of law has been continually enlarging, and banishing brute force further back in an ever-widening circle. First, individuals have laid aside their arms, and submitted their differences to judicial reference. Then the feudal barons, with their large following of clients and vassals, acknowledged a similar jurisdiction, and were merged into one compact community. Then separate tribes of the same nation became merged into one. Then distinct nationalities, although aliens to each other in race, language, and religion, obeyed the same powerful law of assimilation. But if this tendency to bring larger and still larger communities of men under the authority and protection of general law is thus clearly traceable in all history, is there any harm, is it not, indeed, a clear duty, to employ all practicable means to facilitate and hasten this consummation as respects the great nations of Europe and the world?"

At the close of this Congress, and in order to meet the wishes of the friends of peace in Geneva, a large public meeting was held in the Hall of Reformation, under the presidency of David D. Field, at which Mr. Richard delivered in English a forcible speech followed by a magnificent oration by Le Pere Hyacinthe of Paris, who rejoiced that the work of peace and goodwill among men, commenced by the ecclesiastics, had now been taken up by Jurists, learned men, and philanthropists, and his fervent prayer was that they would be able to reach the goal.

In the Session of Parliament of 1875, the Burials Bill was introduced by Mr. Osborne Morgan, and Mr. Richard, on behalf of the Nonconformists, claimed the attention of the House in stating their grievances, for which the Bill was designed to remove. The debate was prolonged, and joined in by leading men on both sides, including Mr. Gladstone, Mr. Forster, Mr. Bright, and on a division it was rejected by 248 against 234 votes.

The Bishopric of St. Alban's Bill, introduced by the Government, encountered on its second reading, May 11th, the opposition of Mr. Richard, on the ground that a continuance of politico-ecclesiastic State officials is not to the advantage of either Church or State, and he moved its rejection, but on a division he was defeated by 273 against 61 votes.

In addition to these two speeches in the Session of 1875, Mr. Richard addressed several important questions to the Government, of which the principal were, South African affairs, India in her relations with Burmah, and the bombardment of Carthagena.

In the month of September, 1875, Mr. Richard attended the Third Annual Congress of the Association for the Reform and Codification of the Laws of Nations, held at the Hague, which was largely and influentially supported, and amongst whom were, several of the members of the Dutch Ministry, and the proceedings awakened much interest in Holland, the Queen receiving its members as guests at the Royal Palace, and a generous and unbounded hospitality was displayed by the Government to the members of the Association.

The President of the Congress was David Dudley Field, of New York, assisted by Sir Travers Twiss as Vice-President. The programme of the Congress was confined to subjects under the head of Private and Public International Law, the sub-divisions of which were numerous; but the chief interest centred in the important questions of international arbitration and disarmament, and on the former Mr Richard gave an interesting address, in which he showed there were limits to its exercise, and that it was not an infallible panacea for all international disputes.

Dr. Miles, of Boston, U.S.A., presented a paper on an International Tribunal, Dr. Jencken, of London, on Disarmament, and Professor Birbeck, on Non-intervention; and upon these various phases of the peace question, interesting discussions followed, and the result was the adoption of two resolutions, the one on International Arbitration, which referred in cordial terms to the action of

L

several Legislatures in acclaiming the principle, and of its adoption by several States; and the second resolution which deplored the enormous and ever-increasing Armaments, and dwelt upon their disastrous results, and urged the Governments to effect a mutual reduction of them. Both these resolutions were drafted by Mr. Richard, and proposed by him at the Congress, and were adopted.

## PARLIAMENTARY EFFORTS.

In the Session of 1876, a determined but unsuccessful effort was made by a small but courageous minority against the persistent policy of extravagantly increasing the national Armaments during a period of profound peace. During the two years that Lord Beaconsfield's Government had been in office the military expenditure had increased £2,300,000, and with the prospect of further increase, Mr. Richard, assisted by Sir Wilfrid Lawson, Mr. Pease, Mr. Rylands, and Mr. Jacob Bright, took the opportunity when the Estimates were submitted, to raise a protest by the following amendment :—

"That, in the opinion of this House, the interests of the Nation do not demand an increased expenditure in the land forces."

This motion was made by Sir Wilfrid Lawson in one of his happiest speeches, which was seconded by Mr. Richard, who did not hesitate to charge the military class with the condition of affairs, not in England alone, but in the Councils and Parliaments of Europe generally, where their influence is directed to keep up the fatal system of rivalry in Armaments, and creating a burden too heavy to be borne.

On a division the motion was rejected by a majority of 192 votes against 63. Defeated by a majority, said Mr. Richard, closely connected, either personally or by family relations with some of the Services, into whose hands these enormous sums are poured in increasing proportions year by year.

Again, on May 15th, Mr. Richard raised his voice in the House of Commons, on behalf of Economy, by supporting the resolution of Mr. Rylands, against any increase in the income tax; and in doing so, he justly observed how both parties in the House were tarred with the same brush, and he twitted the Liberal Party with their professions for Retrenchment, which they scatter to the winds when called upon to put them to the test. He compared the clamours of the Services for increased expenditure, to the daughter of the horse-leech, whose cry continually was "Give, Give;" and that however much is given, it was like pouring water into a sieve, for the country had nothing to show for it, which he proved by stating that from 1856 to 1875, a period of twenty years, 550 millions sterling had been spent on defence, and still the military authorities declare England is defenceless.

Towards the end of June he brought before Parliament the state of our relations with China, and submitted the following motion, in an interesting speech :—

"That, having regard to the unsatisfactory nature of our relations with China, and to the desirability of placing those relations on a permanently satisfactory footing, the House is of opinion that the existing Treaty between the two countries should be so revised as to promote the interests of legitimate commerce, and to secure the just rights of the Chinese Government and people."

This Resolution was supported by Mr. Mark Stewart, Sir George Campbell, Sir George Balfour, and Sir Charles Dilke, and on behalf of the Government, Mr. Bourke, approving of the general object in view, and promising steps should be taken in the direction indicated, the Resolution was withdrawn.

In the same Session, the Government of Lord Beaconsfield brought in a Bill to make further provision for Elementary Education, and on June 19th, during the debate on the second reading, Mr. Richard addressed the House, on

behalf of the Nonconformists, who were decidedly opposed
to the Measure, on the ground that it would promote not
national, but sectarian education ; in fact, a continuance of
the system of giving religious instruction in schools supported
by public money, and he gave notice of his intention to
raise this question by a distinct protest on going into Committee, and accordingly on July 10th, he moved the following amendment :—

"That, in the opinion of this House, the principle of universal
compulsion in education cannot be applied without great injustice
unless provision be made for placing Public Elementary Schools
under public management."

and after a prolonged debate, it was rejected on a division
by a majority of 218 votes.

Throughout the discussions in Committee on this Measure,
Mr. Richard frequently took part, sometimes supporting and
at other times opposing the propositions of the Government,
and, on the third reading, on August 5th, dissatisfied with
the results, he recorded his emphatic protest against it as the
worst Bill, the most unjust, the most reactionary, and the
most tyrannical in spirit that had been brought before
Parliament, since Lord Bolingbroke proposed his Schism Bill,
in the reign of Queen Anne ; for its object was to put the
education of the people into the hands of the Church of
England by discouraging and suppressing all kinds of education. He was supported in debate in this final resistance to
the Measure, by Mr. Cowen and Mr. Burt, but on a division
the Bill was carried by 119 to 46 votes.

At the close of the Session, which had been an
active and an anxious one for Mr. Richard, he left
England to attend the Conference, held in September,
at Bremen, on International Law, at which he met many
representatives to the Conference from Germany, France,
Austria, Denmark, Norway, and Sweden, and on most of the
subjects considered, he gave the weight of his knowledge and
experience, and on the question of the principles of Inter-

national Law which ought to govern the intercourse of Christian with non-Christian peoples, introduced by Dr, Thompson, of Berlin, he spoke at some length in support of the recommendations proposed. The subject of International Maritime Law was introduced by Professor Sheldon Amos, and four propositions submitted in favour of the reforms indicated by the Congress at Paris in 1856, and Mr. Richard supported this view, and after an interesting discussion, the Conference decided to defer their further consideration until the following year.

## THE CONGREGATIONAL UNION.

In May 1877, Mr. Richard was elected to the honourable position of Chairman of the Congregational Union for England and Wales, in succession to Dr. Aveling, which he accepted with considerable reluctance, partly owing to the distractions arising out of the Eastern Question, and to the heavy task, amid all his anxieties, to prepare an inaugural address worthy of the occasion.

Conscious however that it was an imperious call to public duty, he did not shrink, however great the sense of weariness might be, from obeying the summons and grappling with the heavy task imposed upon him, of preparing and delivering the Address from the Chair, and nobly did he discharge it.

The subject he chose, or rather the title which he gave to it was, " The Relations of the Civil and Spiritual Powers in various countries in Europe," and it proved a masterly survey of the ecclesiastical condition of Europe, dealing successively with the relations of Church and State in France, Germany, Italy, Austria, Belgium, and Switzerland, and he shewed the character and vastness of the conflict the Nonconformists were engaged in, and pointed out the teaching lessons to be derived therefrom, reversing the injunction of the Great Apostle, "Let no man join together what God had put asunder," and he closed with a forcible description of the evils inseparable from the alliance of religion with the State, and of the great blessings that would flow from its emancipation.

Valuable as in many respects, and able without exception as was this instructive address, and greatly as it interested and impressed that large religious gathering, there were, as it was natural to expect in such a highly intellectual assembly, those who did not agree in every particular, and this divergence of opinion displayed itself at the close of the sitting, when Dr. Dale introduced the Eastern Question, and submitted a resolution of sympathy with the course recommended by Mr. Gladstone, of Coercion against Turkey.

The subsequent speakers, Dr. Allon, Dr. Raleigh, Rev. J. G. Rogers, Rev. Newman Hall, and Dr. White, were unanimous in condemning the withdrawal, or the modification of any of the famous Resolutions proposed by Mr. Gladstone, and they strongly supported giving practical effect to the decisions unanimously arrived at by the Representatives of the Powers, in order to compel Turkey to carry out the mandate of Europe.

As Chairman of the Assembly, Mr. Richard was placed in a trying position, for, as the Apostle of Peace, he could have no sympathy with force, or the potential exercise of force, even though it was against oppression and for freedom, and his courage on this occasion was as admirable as his diplomacy, to extricate the Congregational Union from an awkward dilemma, for, in closing the discussion he gave a cordial concurrence to the resolution of Dr. Dale, which expressed high appreciation of the signal services rendered by Mr. Gladstone to humanity and freedom, and he rejoiced in its firm declaration against the material or moral support of England being exercised on behalf of Turkey, for it showed how great was the change of opinion amongst those who supported the Crimean War and the policy which led to it, and he hoped that those who were so widely wrong in 1854, when they so heartily advocated war on behalf of Turkey and against Russia, would not go to the other extreme, and advocate the reverse policy in 1877 of war against Turkey, and on behalf of Russia.

On a second occasion during his Chairmanship of the Congregational Union, Mr. Richard eloquently addressed that influential body at its Annual Autumnal Meeting held at Leicester, 16th October, on the subject dear to his heart, and chose for his subject "The application of Christianity to Politics," which was a comprehensive survey of the results of the relationship of the Church with the State, and of Religion with Education, and he dealt also with the Slavery question, the conduct of States towards Aboriginal Tribes, and non-Christian nations, and lastly War, and on this latter subject he dwelt upon the moral, the physical, the economic, and the Christian view in a most able and exhaustive manner.

At the concluding Session of the Union, the following resolution expressive of grateful appreciation of Mr. Richard's services, and for his powerful addresses, was proposed in a highly eulogistic speech by Dr. Allon, and supported in an equally flattering manner by Mr. Byles and Mr. Grimwade:—

"That the Assembly hereby cordially thanks Henry Richard, Esq., M.P., for the efficient manner in which he has conducted the business of the Union during his year of office, and for the useful and powerful addresses which he has delivered from the chair. The Assembly desires also to recognise the great service Mr. Richard has rendered to the cause of religious equality as a Member of Parliament, and to pray that his health and life may be long maintained, that he may render yet further services in the ecclesiastical controversies of his day."

During his visit to Leicester, the Working Men's Peace Association presented him with an illuminated address, expressive of their admiration of the services he had rendered to the cause of Peace, and accompanying the deputation were several of the ministers and aldermen, besides numerous representatives of the working men of the town ; and in reply to the address and speeches delivered, Mr. Richard observed that few things had given him more pleasure than the formation of the Working Men's Peace Association, whose efforts for the promotion of Peace had been conducted with great earnestness and prudence, and he considered that there was no class in the community that had stronger grounds for action, as the burden of War invariably fell upon them.

With the exception of two questions addressed to the Under Secretary of State for Foreign Affairs on the expedition to Yunnam, and the persecution of Christians in Armenia, Mr. Richard took no part in the debate during the Session of 1877, and on the prorogation of Parliament, he attended the Annual Congress of the Association for the Reform and Codification of the Laws of Nations, held at Antwerp from the 31st August to 4th September, under the presidency of the ex-Chancellor of Ireland, Lord O'Hagan, and on this occasion he presented a paper on " The Obligation of Treaties," an admirable summary, and favourable criticism of which, appeared in the *Times.*

A similar paper was read by Dr. Thompson, of Berlin, entitled " Treaties as Matter of the Law of Nations," and an interesting discussion followed on both papers, at the close of which Mr. Richard moved a resolution, seconded by Professor Sheldon Amos, in favour of the insertion of an Arbitration Clause in all future International Treaties, which was unanimously adopted.

## THE EASTERN QUESTION.

In 1875, for the fifth time over a period of 100 years, the troublous affairs in the East once more disturbed the general peace of Europe, and in an endeavour to form a correct

judgment of the character and the history of the complications, and which have been continued down to the present
time, there are two leading facts which must not be over-
looked, and they are these.

Prior to the Crimean War, the Christian populations
of the Turkish Provinces in Europe were recognised by the
Treaty of Adrianople of 1829, and confirmed by the Treaty
of Unkiar-Skelessi of 1832, as being under the protec-
torate of Russia; but the Treaty of Paris 1856, which
followed the Crimean War, changed this, and imposed upon
the Great Powers the obligation which had previously been
claimed and exercised by Russia.

From the year 1856 to 1875, when the insurrection broke
out in Bosnia and Herzegovina, there had been constant
and repeated complaints in regard to the rapacity, injustice,
and brutality of the Turkish Government, or its officials, and
time after time remonstrances had been made by our own,
and other Governments, but to no avail.

In the autumn of 1873, a memorial was presented to the
Austrian Government by a number of the inhabitants of
Bosnia, praying, among other things,

" That an impartial Commission, composed partly of Christian
subjects of the Sultan, should be sent from Constantinople, for
the purpose of inquiry into the state of Christians in Bosnia; and
that this Commission should carry on its labours with the support of the signatory Powers to the Treaty of Paris."

Earl Granville was Foreign Secretary at the above date,
and he wrote to Sir H. Elliott, asking for further information. In the spring of 1874 Mr. Disraeli's Government
came into power, and the matter thus passed into other
hands; but one thing is certain, the needed reforms were
not carried out, and in the summer of 1875 the population
of Bosnia, and also of Herzegovina, broke out into insurrection.

On the 31st January, 1876, Count Andrassy, the Prime
Minister for Austria, anxious for a pacific solution, submitted
to the Great Powers the famous document known by the

" Andrassy Note," which summarised the wrongs under which the Christian population of Turkey suffered, and which suggested five proposals.

" 1. Reforms were essential in the direction of full religious liberty to the Christians. 2. The system of tax-farming to cease. 3. The direct taxes raised to be applied to the use of the Provinces. 4. The establishment of provincial Councils. 5. To secure the execution of reforms, the re-organization of the police."

The " Andrassy Note " was accepted by Russia, Germany, Austria, and Great Britain; but the weakness of the "Andrassy Note" was the omission of any real guarantee from the Porte for the carrying out of these reforms, and the result was, that the insurgents declared they would not accept such conditions.

On the 11th May, 1876, the Emperor of Russia arrived in Berlin to confer with the Emperors of Germany and Austria in favour of more stringent measures for the pacification of the East, than those indicated in the "Andrassy Note ; " and the result of those Conferences was the issue of the celebrated " Berlin Memorandum," which was drawn up on the basis of the reforms indicated in the " Andrassy Note."

The declarations of the " Berlin Memorandum " insisted on a suspension of the insurrection for two months, during which time negotiations should proceed; and, if the armistice should expire without a pacific result, the Great Powers should come to an agreement with a view to prevent the insurrection from spreading.

Lord Derby refused to support the "Berlin Memorandum," because England had not been consulted, and that its demands were unreasonable ; and this declaration was followed up by the despatch of the English Fleet to Besika Bay, not, as it was alleged, for the purpose of protecting Turkey against external aggression or internal dismemberment, but, in the event of the breaking out of a sanguinary civil war at Constantinople, to protect British subjects, and foreigners in general, from what was apprehended would be a general massacre. This refusal of England, and the demonstration of its Fleet, led practically to the withdrawal of the "Berlin Memorandum;" and, despairing of a pacific solution, the Servians and Montenegrins (incited, no doubt, by Russian Panslavists, and supported by Russian gold and Russian officers), soon afterwards declared war against Turkey, which banished all hopes of peace in the East being maintained.

Towards the end of April the insurrection, fomented by foreign emissaries, spread to Bulgaria; but it was characterised by such barbarous atrocities that naturally aroused a storm of public indignation in England against Turkey, and a strong demand was made that England should separate herself from a nation which perpetrated such cruelties; that a stop should be put to Turkish rule in Bulgaria, Bosnia, and Herzegovina; a demand which compelled the Porte to take vigorous measures to stamp out the rebellion.

Mr. Richard and the friends of Peace were placed in a difficult position, for on the one side they had to contend with the traditional policy of England to maintain what was euphemiously called the integrity and independence of the Ottoman Empire in Europe, allied with which was the jealousy and hatred of Russia, and on the other side was the outburst of indignation against Turkey for the hideous outrages perpetrated by the Moslems upon the Slav and Christian population in various parts of her Empire, which called forth throughout Europe angry protests, and a demand for armed intervention against the Government of the Porte.

Between the horns of this dilemma, both tending or pointing in the direction of war, the Scylla, of hatred to Russia, and the Charybdis, of hostility to Turkey, Mr. Richard endeavoured to hold an even keel, and in such a peculiar crisis his calm judgment, and his courage for consistency did not forsake him throughout, though tried as it must have been, even to a hair's breadth, whilst his energy of resource, and marvellous activity and zeal was seldom, if ever, so conspicuously displayed.

The first prominent action taken by Mr. Richard at this early stage of the crisis was in reference to the important Deputation of the 14th July, 1876, to present a Memorial to the Minister for Foreign Affairs, Earl Derby, for although the originators and promoters of the Deputation hailed from Birmingham, yet Mr. Richard welcomed the proposal, and prepared the way for its adoption, for it expressed the earnest hope that the Government would observe a policy of strict neutrality, except where it may be able to interpose its friendly offices to mitigate the horrors, and to hasten the close of the conflict then raging in the European provinces of Turkey.

This Memorial, drafted by Mr. Richard, was largely and influentially signed, and was supported in its presentation by Mr. Bright, Mr. Chamberlain, and upwards of 40 Members of Parliament, and 250 representative men from all parts of the country, and in reply to this Memorial and the speeches delivered, nothing could have been more excellent in manner, or more re-assuring in tone, than Lord Derby's speech, as to the views and policy of the Government, and which were clearly set forth in the following terms :—

" The policy of Her Majesty's Government will be a policy of strict neutrality, except where it may be able to interpose its friendly offices to hasten the close of the war. * * *

" We have done what was in our power to prevent this war breaking out. In that we failed. We shall now do what is in our power to keep it within certain limits * * * We shall not intervene, we shall do our utmost, if necessary, to discourage others from intervening.

" If an opportunity of mediation should offer itself, we shall gladly avail ourselves of it ; while we retain, as we are bound to do, our own freedom, and our own independence of action and of judgment, we attach quite as much importance as those others with whom we have acted to that general understanding among the great European States, which is the best and surest guarantee of peace."

These declarations of the Foreign Minister were received

with genuine satisfaction, and produced a salutary and tranquillising effect, not only in this country, but throughout all Europe.

Upon the first symptoms of alarm and danger at the course events in the East were taking, especially directed against Russia, Mr. Richard re-published a pamphlet, which has been previously referred to, on the History and Origin of the War with Russia in 1853-4, that thus, as he stated in the preface:—

" By throwing light on the causes of that War, an opportunity should be afforded to the young generation that has come into political life since those days, to judge for themselves what really was the nature and amount of those Russian demands in 1853-4, which were swollen to such portentous dimensions by the jealousies and fears of the moment,"

for he feared that attempts were being made in 1876 to reproduce the same state of feeling towards Russia, which hurried England into that disastrous conflict in 1853.

This succinct and remarkably able pamphlet had, as it deserved, an extensive circulation. Copies were sent to the members of both Houses of Parliament, to editors of the Press, and public men throughout the country; and its value and usefulness at that critical time was considerable, for it helped with other circumstances to awaken in the public mind a consciousness of the great blunder of the Crimean War.

At this juncture, whilst danger of war on behalf of Turkey was lessening, there was steadily rising a tide of furious indignation, stirred by the infamous and execrable horrors in Bulgaria, not confined to an armed intervention against Turkey, but a clamour, loud and deep for a war of vengeance and of extermination " bag and baggage " of the unspeakable Turk from the soil of Europe.

Against this war of vengeance, as a punishment for the cruel crimes committed by England's former ally, Turkey, Mr. Richard vigorously and justly denounced, equally as he had in 1853, that in fighting for the Turks we were fighting the

battle of freedom, justice, and civilization, for he considered
such a war would drive Mahomedan fanaticism to desperation,
and "scenes would be enacted throughout Europe and Asia,
wherever the Ottoman dominions extend, which would be
an imitation on a large scale of the very worst of the iniquities
at which the world is now so loudly expressing its indignation."

To stem this rolling wave of popular fury, Mr. Richard
issued a powerful appeal, bearing his signature alone,
a masterly review of the deplorable result of the Crimean
War, which he summed up by the declaration of the *Times*,
"that never was so great an effort made for so worthless an
object;" and he earnestly exhorted his countrymen to make
their voices heard, that on no pretext whatever should
England again enter into partnership with Mahomedan
fanaticism.

The next important step undertaken by Mr. Richard, in
conjunction with some of the foremost men of the day, was
the formation of the Eastern Question Association, which
may be described as the outcome of the influential deputation to the Foreign Minister, Earl Derby, previously referred
to; as its inception dates from that event, and was the
direct result of the important declarations of the Noble Lord,
in reply to the Memorial presented on that occasion.

It would be impossible to over-estimate the great value
of this important and diplomatic move at this critical
moment; for, looking back on the stirring events of that
day, there can be but one opinion, that by virtue of its
eminently influential and representative character, and its
vigorous action, it decided for England the great issues of
peace or war in the East, and that issue was *Peace*. For
what at that supreme crisis was the attitude, what the
policy, of the Government of Lord Beaconsfield? For
many weary months, in fact from the day of the outbreak
of the insurrection in Herzegovina, through all that dark
and dismal period of the reign of terror, and the orgies of

blood and carnage in Bulgaria, the responsible members of the Government in both Houses of Parliament, and their official organs in the press, steadily and stubbornly withheld — whether from High State reasons of diplomatic reticence, or some hidden and settled design to bamboozle the country into war, it is difficult to say—all information, all despatches, and all declarations of opinion or policy, from the ear and eye of the Representatives of the people.

Moreover, it was obvious from the important speech delivered by the Secretary of State for Foreign Affairs, Earl of Derby, to the Deputation at the Foreign Office on the 14th July, and reading between the lines, that within the Councils of the Crown, there had been and still remained two policies, and probably two powerful factions ; the one favouring a benevolent neutrality, a dignified policy of non-intervention, and the other gravitating and drifting towards an armed intervention in the East ; whether for Turkey or against Turkey, whether for Russia or against Russia, was not clear, but an armed intervention in the name, for the interests, the honour, and the prestige of the British Flag, which were in no manner or degree in peril.

To meet therefore this emergency, to sustain and strengthen in the Councils of the Crown the Ministers of Peace who were firmly resolved on England's neutrality, and to counteract and withstand the Ministers of War, who were determined on England's active intervention in the East, was the one aim of the friends of peace and non-intervention, and by marshalling their widely-scattered forces, Members of both Houses of Parliament, the Clergy of all denominations, Mayors and Magistrates, members of the Universities and other public bodies and representatives of the people, and uniting them in one compact and powerful National Union, to stimulate and arouse such an overwhelming volume of public opinion that no Minister, or Parliament, or Cabal, dare to resist.

This Eastern Question Association was launched into existence by, it is no exaggeration to say, the most remarkable and powerful demonstrations ever witnessed in this country held at St. James's Hall the 8th December 1876, and was presided over in the forenoon by the Duke of Westminster, K.G., and in the evening by the Earl of Shaftesbury, K.G., and at the former Mr. Richard was amongst the many speakers, and at the latter Mr. Gladstone delivered a great speech, worthy of his great oratorical powers.

Many and varied were the operations of the Eastern Question Association, established for the purpose of watching events in the East, for giving expression to public opinion, and spreading useful information, and as effective and telling in their restraining and constraining influence upon the policy of the Government; and perhaps the most influential were the rapid succession of publications compiled by able and well-known writers, bearing on the many-sided aspects of the complicated Eastern Question, and covering the wide domain of the government of the Porte in its Asiatic and European Dominions.

The first of these useful and striking issues from the press was from the pen of Mr. Richard, on the "Evidences of Turkish Misrule," in which, as the *South Wales Daily News* wrote :—

"The degeneracy, the brutalism, and the foul immoralities of the Turk, and the life-long suffering of the subject races under his sway, are painted in terribly lurid but faithful colours. Mr. Richard has rendered valuable service to humanity, and to the cause of civil and religious freedom before now ; but civilisation itself is indebted to him for bringing into one compact whole such an array of evidence from historians, travellers, diplomatists, statesmen and Government officials, who were witnesses of what they describe, in proof of the incurable and deadly misrule of Turkey."

Whilst these efforts, happily successful efforts, were being put forth by Mr. Richard and others, to prevent England drifting into war, for or against Turkey, events of great significance were marching apace in the East, to which reference may suitably be made.

At the close of the year 1876, in consequence of the victories of the Turkish arms in Servia and Montenegro, the Russian Ambassador Ignatieff, presented an ultimatum to the Porte, demanding an immediate armistice, with a view to a Conference for the restoration of peace, and this proposal was finally accepted by the Sultan, and the Great European Powers.

The Conference assembled on the 23rd November, 1876, under the presidency of Safvet Pasha, the Turkish Minister for Foreign Affairs, and the Great Powers of Europe were represented by Germany, Austria, France, Great Britain, Italy, and Russia, who declared they were actuated by a sincere wish to arrive at a solution of the great Eastern Question satisfactory to Europe, and to the disaffected Provinces of Turkey.

After much deliberation and negotiation, the result of which showed considerable harmony on the part of the representatives of the Great Powers, it was resolved by the Conference that Turkey should be advised to carry out great concessions in the direction of internal reforms throughout the whole of her Empire, as the only means whereby its dismemberment could be averted, and the general peace of Europe maintained.

Unfortunately for Turkey these wise recommendations of the Conference were received by the Ministers of the Sultan with disfavour and resistance; and unfortunately, too, for the peace of Europe, the Governments of Great Britain, Germany, France and Austria, and others represented at the Conference, failed in their endeavours to induce Turkey to carry out the recommendations of the Constantinople Conference.

In consequence of this refusal by Turkey to adopt these measures of reform, and in consequence of the widespread disturbance and atrocious outrages perpetrated in many of the Turkish Provinces, the Czar declared to the Notables at Moscow his intention to act independently, and without the

M

approval of any of the Great Powers, Russia declared war against Turkey, and on the 24th of April, 1877, her armies advanced simultaneously into Asiatic and European Turkey.

It is unnecessary, however, to refer at length to the dismal record of those military events which characterised this War; the gathering of the Russian Armies in Europe and Asia, their advance from Bessarabia across the Danube into Bulgaria; and from Alexandropol into Armenia, a great military drama, in which scenes full of thrilling and painful incidents pass before us, sometimes quickly, sometimes slowly, but always exhibiting a ghastly spectacle of mangled humanity, a war of races and creeds developed in all its horror and repulsiveness.

On the last day of the year 1877 Turkey, in a despatch of great moderation, anxious to avoid a further effusion of blood, appealed to the Mediation of England, and to the honour of England her Government appealed to Russia, whether enough had not been achieved by the armies of both Empires to satisfy all questions of Military honour.

This appeal was at first unsuccessful; Russia refused on the ground that she would receive overtures only direct from her vanquished foes, but the appeal of England was not to be denied, backed by the voice of Europe, and by the movement of the British Fleet to the Dardanelles, was firmly pressed, and Russia slowly and sullenly gave way, by consenting to an armistice, and the preliminaries for Peace were accordingly signed at Adrianople on the 18th January, 1878.

In the little village of San Stefano, the plenipotentiary for Turkey, Safvet Pasha, and for Russia, General Ignatieff, surrounded with all the pomp and triumphs of a victorious army, deliberated for many anxious weeks over the exacting terms dictated by the Conqueror.

The conditions contained in this Treaty of San Stefano, signed on the 3rd March, 1878, sent a shudder through Europe, and evoked such a storm of indignation from the public press and the public voice, that no Cabinet or Government could for a moment withstand.

Against these exorbitant demands, Europe and the Government of England vehemently protested, despatch succeeded despatch, courier after courier followed one another in quick succession to St. Petersburg, the British Fleet was ordered to move into the Dardanelles, the Indian troops were summoned to Europe, the Parliament voted six millions to prepare for an emergency, and for a time a great crisis arose which seriously threatened to involve England and Russia into a tremendous War.

Throughout this prolonged crisis, it must be acknowledged, that the Statesmen of both Nations did their utmost by their diplomatic skill, their forbearance and patience, to secure a pacific settlement, honourable alike to England and Russia, and satisfactory to Turkey and the provinces under her sway.

Happily, at this serious junction of affairs, Russia was represented by a diplomatist of conspicuous merit, Count Schouvaloff, who with a great devotion to his country and the Government from which he was accredited, combined in a remarkable degree a spirit of conciliation, of moderation, of wisdom in counsel, and of energy in action, which largely helped to secure a solution of the delicate and difficult causes in dispute.

Finally, after three months of anxious negotiation, and subtle diplomacy, Russia yielded to the will of Europe by consenting to an European Congress to be held at Berlin, to which the Treaty of San Stefano should be unreservedly submitted for consideration and revision by all the Great European Powers.

In the month of June this important Congress assembled at Berlin, under the presidency of the Chancellor of the German Empire, Prince Bismarck : a great assembly of the leading Statesmen of Europe, Prince Gortchakoff for Russia, Count Andrassy for Austria, Count Corti for Italy, M. Wad-

dington for France, Caratheodori Pasha for Turkey, and
last, but not least, the venerable and astute Lord Beaconsfield, as the representative for Great Britain.

For several weeks this Congress of the Ambassadors of
the Great European Powers, deliberated earnestly and
anxiously on all the supremely important questions submitted to them for the pacification of the East, embracing among many others, the defining of the boundaries of
Bulgaria, Roumelia, Servia, and Montenegro ; the administration of Bosnia and Herzegovina, by Austria ; the recognition of the sovereign independence of Servia and Roumania;
the granting of complete political, civil, and religious liberty
to the populations of every one of the Balkan States ; and
the readjustment of the Turkish Empire on assured foundations.

To the honour of the eminent Statesmen assembled at
that Congress, a sincere and resolute determination was
apparent to achieve a peaceful issue, and complete harmony
prevailed on the many difficult and conflicting high matters
of State policy submitted to them for consideration and
decision.

This great international compact, the Treaty of Berlin,
may be truly called a great historical landmark, for it trans-
formed an Empire, removed long-standing causes of discontent, pacified provinces torn by dissention and misrule,
placed barriers between rival forms of bigotry, stopped many
avenues of foreign intrigue, abridged the Power of a Despotic
Empire, and gave peace to Europe, which, let us hope, no
Government or Ruler will attempt to disturb.

Before leaving this subject reference should be made to the

## DEPUTATION TO THE BERLIN CONGRESS,

consisting of Mr. Richard, Leone Levi, and Frederic Passy,
for the purpose of bringing before the Representatives of
Europe there assembled, the subject of International
Arbitration.

The deputation reached Berlin 1st July, and their first step was to forward to each of the Plenipotentiaries the Memorial to the Congress which was signed, in addition to the members of the deputation, by Signor Mancini for Italy, Aug. Couvreur for Belgium, D. Van Eck for Holland, Adolf Franck for France, and others, and the prayer of this Memorial set forth the many evidences of the practicability and progress of Arbitration for terminating in a pacific manner the differences between nations, and asked the Congress to reaffirm the great principle, which was declared in the Treaty of Paris in 1856.

In response to this petition, the deputation were honoured with invitations for a personal interview, with the British Ambassador at Berlin, Lord Odo Russell, the Plenipotentiary for Italy, Count Corti, the Secretary of State for Foreign Affairs for Germany, Baron de Bülow, and also M. Bücher, one of the official representatives of the Congress, and the result of these conferences were eminently satisfactory, in the direction of sympathy and approval with the principle and practice of international arbitration, but to quote Count Corti,·

" He feared that even if the Congress entertained the question, the plenipotentiaries would not be brought to accept the proposal of a clause binding the Congress to Arbitration, as that might be thought inconsistent with the independence of Governments;"

but he made this important admission :—

" The present Congress is really a Court of Arbitration. We find England and Austria on one side, and Russia on the other, and the other Powers, Germany, France, and Italy are *Arbitrators*, who have to adjust their conflicting claims, and bring them into harmony."

In addition to the important Conference with the plenipotentiaries referred to, written communications were received from Lord Beaconsfield, Count Schouvaloff, Ambassador for Russia, Count Haymerle, Ambassador for Austria, Count de Saint-Vallier, Ambassador for France, and also the Marquis of Salisbury, Ambassador for England and the latter, conveyed, what was in effect the decision of the Congress, in the following terms :—

" It has several times been laid down by the President, and has been accepted by the Representatives of the Powers, that no subject not arising directly out of the Provisions of the Treaty of San Stefano, can be entertained by the Congress."

Against this inflexible decision, notwithstanding efforts made, there was no concession, but the deputation were gratified however in finding subsequently, that their labours were not altogether in vain, inasmuch as by the 63rd Article of the Treaty of Berlin it was declared :—

"That the Treaty of Paris of 1856, as well as the Treaty of London of 1871, are maintained in all such of their provisions as are not abrogated or modified by any of the stipulations in the Treaty of Berlin."

Truly, as Mr. Richard wrote on his return from this Mission :—

"We venture to hope that by bringing the question of Arbitration before so many of the leading Statesmen of Europe, and by means of the press, before the world, we have done something to sow seed which may hereafter bring fruit."

---

## PARLIAMENTARY EFFORTS.

On the Meeting of Parliament in 1878, the Eastern Question was early the subject of serious consideration.

On January 28, the Chancellor of the Exchequer, Sir Stafford Northcote, in view of the assembling at Berlin of a Congress on Eastern Affairs, and to give strength, as he believed, to the position of the plenipotentiaries for England, proposed the following resolution :—

"That a sum not exceeding £6,000,000 be granted to Her Majesty, beyond the ordinary grants of Parliament, towards defraying the expenses which may be incurred during the year ending on the 31st March 1878, in increasing the efficiency of the Naval and Military Services, at the present crisis of the War between Russia and Turkey."

This proposal was opposed by the whole force of the Liberal Party, by an amendment, moved by Mr. Forster, to the effect, that the conditions of England's neutrality not having been infringed by either Russia or Turkey, there was no justification for deviating from a policy of neutrality and peace, and no reason for voting unnecessary supplies, and a great debate followed, lasting up to the 11th February, in which most, if not all the foremost orators, and statesmen of the House took part, Mr. Cross, Mr. Bright, Marquis of Hartington, Mr. Hardy, Mr. Gladstone, Mr. Cowen, and Sir Wilfrid Lawson, and it was during this debate, that Mr. Richard, on 8th February, the day following the ordering of the British Fleet to pass the Dardanelles, for the protection of the lives and properties of British subjects at Constanti-nople, delivered a speech, in which he condemned the appointment of Mr. Layard to the post of Ambassador at Constantinople, and also, the "great swelling words" of Lord Beaconsfield, as tending to excite the nation, and to breed resentment abroad, and especially that whilst the Government declared it was not for War, that members of the Cabinet made warlike speeches, and on the eve of the assembling of a Conference for Peace, despatched the Fleet to Constanti-nople, and demanded a vote of six million sterling.

Again, on April 9th, Mr. Richard took part in the debate which followed the declaration of the Government to call out the Reserves in the eventuality of war with Russia, not, as Mr. Richard said, for the defence of British interests, or the balance of power, or the freedom of Europe, but from a blind, unreasoning hatred and fear of Russia. He ridiculed these "fits of terror," and shewed their tendency in the past against France, United States and other countries; and as regards Russia, he considered England had no commission from God or man to inflict chastisement upon her for her wrong-doings, or for her aggressions, and that England should not apply one standard to herself, and another to the rest of the nations of the world.

On Feb. 12th, Mr. Leatham raised the question of the traffic in Church Livings, and moved a resolution to prevent the evasion of the law, and to check abuses in the sale of livings in private patronage ; and in the course of the debate Mr. Richard addressed the House in its support, in which he wondered that a scandal so flagrant should have been permitted to exist so long, for by the canons of 1693, every clergyman, before his admission to his living, is required to take an oath declaring that he has not committed simony in any form whatever, and yet, in face of this, it is notorious that sale and barter for the " cure of souls " continues to this day, which, he said, dishonors the Church, degrades its clergy, and brings religion into contempt.

During the progress, in Committee, of the Intermediate Education Bill, brought in by the Government, Mr. Richard opposed it, because it proposed to give public money to promote and perpetuate sectarian education.

Upon the subject of the Bishoprics' Bill, introduced by the Government, which gave an increase to the number of Bishops, Mr. Richard supported an amendment brought forward by Mr. Cowen, declaring it was undesirable to make any increase in the number of Bishops, and said he would not consent to the creation of any more of the politico-ecclesiastical officials, or of any class of men appointed by the State to perform spiritual functions ; but on a division the amendment was lost by a majority of 37, and the Bill having passed through Committee, eventually became law August 15th, 1878.

## THE AFGHAN AND ZULU WARS.

In September, 1878, Mr. Richard was alarmed at the serious complications which arose between Great Britain and Afghanistan and at the first appearance of the difficulty he drafted an appeal to the Friends of Peace throughout the country, urging them in every practicable way to protest against war.

This appeal was followed up by three important demonstrations at Bristol, Bradford, Leeds, Birmingham, and London, the former of which, held in Colston Hall, under the presidency of Mr. E. S. Robinson, Mr. Richard attended, and delivered a speech of earnest protest against the war, in which he ably reviewed the whole question, and in spite of much tumult and organised rowdyism, the resolutions in favour of peace were carried by an overwhelming majority. .

In addition to these active efforts, public meetings, and memorials to the Government, Mr. Richard wrote a series of letters on the Afghan question, addressed to the *Christian World*, which were afterwards published in a pamphlet form, and widely distributed; an historic survey, and masterly statement of facts, that proved of great interest and value for the right appreciation by the public mind, of the real causes of that deplorable quarrel.

In the same year, 1878, and nigh at the same period o time of the declaration of War against Afghanistan, England was engaged in a similar enterprise in South Africa, which Mr. Richard by pen and voice vigorously opposed, for he considered the complications, and the War which followed, were the direct result of the spirited foreign policy of Lord Beaconsfield's Government.

It bore its own bitter fruits ; the disaster at Isandula, the death of the youthful Napoleon, pierced by the assegais of a people who had never done him, or threatened to do him any harm, the terrible sacrifice of human life, estimated at upwards of 20,000 Zulus and its consequent results, the reign of terror and of blood in Zululand—these and many other sickening details brand that war, as the most inglorious war waged by the arms of England.

## ELIHU BURRITT.

In March 1879 passed away in his home at New Britain Connecticut, Mr. Elihu Burritt, a name honoured and beloved in his own and many lands, for his life-long service to the cause of international peace ; and few if any felt more

ELIHU BURRITT.

keenly his death than his attached friend and colleague Mr. Richard, and justly so, as they were over many years, and in many memorable conflicts, brothers in arms,

> " For on many a well foughten field,
>   They held together in their chivalry."

In the columns of the *Herald of Peace*, Mr. Richard wrote

a just and well-deserved tribute to the memory, the labours, and the great services of his departed friend, and conspicuous amongst those varied and important services were his efforts in connection with the Congresses of Paris, Frankfort, and Brussels from 1848 to 1850 ; his peace Missions to many Continental Countries ; his labours for a scheme of Ocean Penny Postage, and in the Anti-Slavery Cause ; and above all, by his unceasing advocacy by the press in many languages, and by the public voice in many countries, to secure the abolition of War.

Two passages from Mr. Richard's *in memoriam*, just referred to, may be appropriately given here, as the right estimate of a noble life :

" His was a life consecrated to works of benevolence with a devoted and disinterested spirit, and it is impossible to doubt that the good seed sown broadcast by him, for so many years, and in so many lands, will be found after many days."

And again, in concluding his interesting sketch :

" He was a man of rare faculties, inspired in an eminent degree with the enthusiasm of humanity, who devoted his powers, his acquirements, and in fact all that he had, to the service of truth and justice, and the highest forms of Christian charity, with a simplicity, and completeness of purpose which have been rarely equalled."

---

## PARLIAMENTARY EFFORTS AND DISARMAMENT.

During the Session of 1879, upon the second reading of the Bill brought into the House February 26, by Mr. Monk, called the Consecration of Churchyards Act, (1867), Amendment Bill, to provide for Nonconformists, in the rural parishes, the same means of burial as had been provided for them in the towns, Mr. Richard opposed it, on the ground that its object was to introduce into Churchyards a distinction between consecrated and unconsecrated ground,

which he considered would be an offensive distinction, and
lead to much irritation and animosity.   The result of this
debate was unfavourable to the Bill, and on a division it
was defeated by a majority of thirty-one votes.

The subject of Economy in the National Expenditure, was
brought before Parliament early in the same Session, by
Mr. Rylands, who moved a series of resolutions, which in
effect, declared regret at the increased National Expenditure,
that it was unnecessary, that it tended to pauperism and
crime, and that therefore, immediate steps should be taken to
relieve the taxpayer.   An important debate followed, in
which the leaders and finance authorities on both sides of
the House took part, and Mr. Richard, being of opinion that
expenditure depends on policy, and not policy on expenditure, availed himself of the opportunity to assail what was
termed the spirited Foreign policy of the Government, which
he considered meant a policy of aggression, of bluster and
blood.

At the close of the Session, a Bill for promoting University Education in Ireland, was brought into Parliament
by the O'Connor Don, and elaborately discussed at adjourn-
ments, from May 15 to June 25, and on the latter date, Mr.
Richard addressed the House in opposition to the Measure,
as he objected to one of the proposals to endow a Roman
Catholic University, out of the funds accruing from the
revenues of the disestablished Church of Ireland.   At the
close of the debate, Mr. Assheton Cross, on behalf of the
Government, unable to accept the Bill of the O'Connor Don,
announced his intention to introduce a similar measure on
June 30.   Lord Cairns redeemed this promise, and, in spite
of opposition by the Roman Catholic party, it passed into
law.

In addition to these efforts of Mr. Richard in the Session of
1879, he closely followed the state of affairs in South Africa,
and in India, and addressed important questions to Government on these and other matters of foreign policy.

The subject of a general, proportionate, and simultaneous disarmament closely occupied the attention of Mr. Richard during the years 1879 and 1880, and involved him in much labour and anxiety; and it may be interesting to notice, before we refer in detail to the effort he made in Parliament in the Session of 1880, the origin and progress of this agitation.

This special movement of 1879-80 had its origin in the Paris Congress of 1878, for the ruinous system of armed rivalry amongst the Governments of Europe, produced alarm and dismay in all minds, and a cry was raised, in various parts of Europe, to reverse this disastrous system, and to demand that the Governments should concert together for this object.

At this Peace Congress at Paris in 1878, amongst the eminent representatives present were: Austria, Dr. Stürm; France, M. Garnier; Holland, D. Van Eck; Belgium, M. Couvreur; Italy, Marquis Pepoli; Germany, Baron von Holtzendorf; and England, Henry Richard: and the following were the resolutions submitted on the subject of Disarmament:

"No. 10. That an International Commission, composed of representatives of each nation, be appointed to secure a reduction of the armaments of each nation.

"No. 11. That the Governments of civilized peoples should open as soon as possible negotiations to arrive at a proportional and simultaneous disarmament in each country."

These propositions claimed the attention of the Congress with more than ordinary interest, the discussions upon them showed much enthusiasm, and they were unanimously adopted. The members of this Commission to carry them out, represented the principal countries in Europe, and their action, as it was to be expected, led to active efforts being put forth, as the following statement will show.

The first parliament in Europe, where the question was raised, after this Congress, was the Reichstag at Berlin, on which occasion the devoted and distinguished friend of peace, Jean Dollfus, deputy from Alsace, delivered a remarkable speech, condemnatory of the enormous military budget, the withdrawal from labour of millions of men, and especially, by the perfection of weapons, the murderous character of modern wars, which he described as a terrible curse to humanity.

This appeal, delivered in the Reichstag at Berlin, was followed in March by a practical proposal submitted by Herr von Bühler, an earnest and sincere friend of peace, who presented the following resolution :

" To request the Prince Chancellor of the Empire, to bring about the convening of a Congress of the various States of Europe, for the purpose of introducing an effective and general reduction, and disarmament of the armies to about half of their present average strength, when on a peace footing, such reduction for the present, to last for the term of 10 to 15 years."

This proposal of Herr von Bühler, was supported by only twelve members, but, undaunted by this defeat, he addressed to Prince Bismarck a letter, enclosing the resolution, in which he reminded him of their meeting on the battlefield of Gravelotte, and of the determination he made there, to prevent a repetition of the horrors of that war. To this communication Bismarck courteously replied, to the effect, that only after reconciling our neighbours to their views, could Germany undertake the responsibility of such projects.

These earnest protests against the enormous armaments in Europe, made in the Parliament of Germany, by Jean Dollfus and Herr von Bühler, though unavailing, exerted an influence in other countries.

In Austria, a movement was set on foot in its favour, and a Committee was appointed, consisting of Dr. Stürm, Dr. Füchs, Dr. Fishoff, and several members of the Reichsrath, and the result, as it was stated, the Government signified a willingness to take the initiative, if it was possible, to arrive at an understanding amongst the other Great Powers.

In Italy, a strong movement was made. Meetings were held at Milan and Naples ; at the latter a Conference was held in October, 1879, attended by Signor Ricciardi, Professor Sbarbaro, and Baron Von Holtzendorf, of Germany, and a Memorial was adopted in its favour, to the Government.

In England, Mr. Richard gave considerable *impetus* to the Movement, for Disarmament had taken such strong hold on leading men of enlightenment in Europe, by bringing the question before the International Conference that met in London on the 11th August, convened by the Association for the Reform of the Law of Nations, consisting of repre-sentatives from England, Belgium, Holland, France, and Sweden, presided over successively by the Lord Mayor of London, Sir Robert Phillimore, and Lord O'Hagan. The title of the paper which Mr. Richard read was "International Reduction of Armaments," a comprehensive statement of facts embracing its numerical, financial, moral, and political bearings ; and, at its close, an important debate followed, participated in by Mr. Stollmeyer, of Trinidad, Mr. Atkinson, of Hull, Frederick Passy, of Paris, Prof. Leone Levi, and H. W. Freeland, of London, but, owing to some differences of opinion in regard to the resolution submitted, the subject was referred to a Committee to report upon another year.

In October, 1879, Mr. Richard attended a meeting at Warrington in support of his Parliamentary motion for dis-armament, and he was supported by Mr. Rylands, M.P., and Mr. McMinnies, the candidate for the borough, when he spoke at some length on the subject of the military condition of Europe, condemning in vigorous language the prolific waste of revenues wrung from the toiling millions, and the tyrannous conscription, which leads to the expatriation of the young manhood of the Continent; and at the close of his address, which was loudly cheered, a resolution was adopted of earnest protest against the war system, and of cordial support of Mr. Richard's Motion for disarmament.

In November, 1879, an important Conference, attended by influential men from all parts of South Wales, was held in the Guildhall, Swansea, in favour of International

Disarmament, which Mr. Richard addressed at considerable length, and earnestly invoked the help of his countrymen in the arduous work he had undertaken; believing that if the British Parliament adopted his resolution in favour of Disarmament, other European nations would gladly follow its example.

At the opening of the year 1880, it may be said, Europe was agitated on the subject of Disarmament, and a general conviction seemed to prevail, that some efforts should be made to put an end to the insane rivalry of military preparations.

On January 26th, 1880, a definite proposal was made in the Austrian Reichsrath by MM. Füchs and Keilsberg, as follows:—

" The Chamber of Deputies expresses the wish that the Imperial and Royal Governments will consider the idea of a general, proportionate, and simultaneous army reduction, which will not alter the respective strength of the different States."

The forcible speech of Dr. Füchs made a great impression, and was supported by the votes of forty-nine Members, amongst whom in addition to the proposers, to their honour may be mentioned, Dr. Beer, Dr. Roser, M. Bareuther, Baron Kübeck and Dr. Stürm, and it was a gratifying fact that the Minister of War, subsequently declared, that he gladly hailed the proposal, and that he regarded it as eminently practical.

Encouraged by these efforts in Germany, Italy, Austria, and Hungary, Mr. Richard finally resolved with the full concurrence of his numerous friends, to submit a resolution to Parliament, in favour of promoting a gradual Disarmament in Europe, and accordingly he issued a circular letter to his supporters in this country which, after reciting the manifest reasons for his action, suggested four methods, for influencing members of the Legislature in favour of a question,

" The importance of which cannot surely be surpassed by any question that can claim the attention of Parliament."

To stimulate activity and to arouse public attention to the subject, Mr. Richard attended and took a prominent part in several Conferences and public meetings, the most important of which was a demonstration in the St. George's Hall, Liverpool, under the presidency of Mr. William Rathbone, one of the members for that city, which was preceded by a Conference, presided over by Mr. Hugh Mason, the member for Ashton-under-Lyne, and both these assemblages were largely and influentially attended, and great unanimity, in fact enthusiasm prevailed.

On the 15th of June, the date balloted for, and by the marked special favour of the Leader of the House, Mr. Gladstone, Mr. Richard brought forward his resolution which was as follows :—

"That an humble address be presented to Her Majesty, praying that she will be graciously pleased to instruct Her Principal Secretary of State for Foreign Affairs to enter into communications with other Powers, with a view to bring about a mutual and simultaneous reduction of European armaments."

The speech of Mr. Richard on this occasion was one of his happiest efforts, and there was no part of his speech more effective than the passage at its close :—

" I venture in conclusion to make a very earnest and respectful appeal to the right hon. gentleman at the head of Her Majesty's Government, that he will not turn aside from this great question. The task to which I invite him is not unworthy, even of his transcendent abilities. It is not unworthy of his high character, as I estimate it, as the passionate friend of justice and humanity. He has already won many laurels by great deeds of practical statesmanship ; and a greater than any of them awaits his hand. No greener wreath ever surrounded any man's brow, than that which will encircle his, if only he will consent to grapple with this high argument, and bring the nations of Europe into general concert to reduce their armaments. This would at once liberate great masses of capital, which would help to establish the cause of Peace on solid and sure foundations. I cannot but believe that he would be welcomed in such a proposal by the Governments themselves, for they cannot but view with alarm the increase of those armaments. Above all, he would earn the grateful benediction of millions of people now groaning under taxation, the result of this baneful system of militarism." (Cheers.)

N

This resolution of Mr. Richard's was seconded by Mr. Baxter, member for Dundee, and was supported by Colonel Burnaby, who said that as a military man he had the greatest horror of war, at the close of which Mr. Gladstone rose who delivered a magnificent speech, which Mr. Richard described as one of the most eloquent expositions of the policy of peace he had ever listened to, and at the close he made an earnest appeal to Mr. Richard not to push his motion to a divison.

Referring to this appeal of the Prime Minister, and the closing incident of the debate, the *Herald of Peace* in a leading article thus wrote :

" Mr. Richard was naturally placed in considerable perplexity by such an appeal. It is possible he might have carried his motion, as he did in 1873, but it would have been against the will, and, it may be, to the considerable embarrassment of the Prime Minister. And yet he was unwilling that the discussion should close without some formal expression of Parliament. From this predicament he was relieved by Mr. John Bright, who undoubtedly, next to Mr. Gladstone, is the most important and influential member of the Government. Mr. Bright, after Mr. Gladstone's speech, beckoned Mr. Richard to him, and placed in his hand a resolution which he had proposed, and said, " If you will accept this instead of your own, I think Mr. Gladstone would let it pass." And as it really recognised the principle of his motion, in the form of a resolution, instead of an address to the Crown, Mr. Richard gladly accepted the suggestion. And as, according to the rules of the House, he could not move it himself, he put it in the hands of his friend, Mr. Leonard Courtney, and it was carried by a unanimous vote of the House, and amid general cheering.

---

## THE WAR IN THE TRANSVAAL.

At the beginning of the year, January, 1881, Mr. Richard introduced a Deputation to the Colonial Minister, (Lord Kimberley), consisting of some twenty-five Members of Parliament and other gentlemen, upon the condition of affairs in the Transvaal, and he presented a Memorial, which was drafted and signed by him, as Secretary of the Peace

Society, which declared that the annexation of the Transvaal was secured by fraud, and advised that England should renounce this act of aggression, and stop without delay any further bloodshed, by a restoration of the independence of the Boers.

This Memorial was followed up by two others forwarded to the Prime Minister by Mr. Richard, one from Holland signed by D. Van Eck, the president of the Dutch Peace Society, and the other from the Flemish inhabitants of Belgium, also entrusted to Mr. Richard for presentation to the Government.

This war in the Transvaal mainly arose from the interference of the English Government in the affairs of the Boers in 1877, and in sending Sir Theophilus Shepstone to investigate, and to advise the Boers in regard to their frontier disputes.

Sir Theophilus Shepstone took with him a small escort of mounted police, but the Boers knew that the entire armed power of England was at his back, though they did not know that he held a Commission in his pocket, which was to be the deathblow to their Independence.

Sir Theophilus Shepstone arrived in Pretoria in January, 1877, and in April, *in direct defiance of the wishes of the people, he issued a proclamation, coolly annexing a territory as large as France*, containing a population of 40,000 whites and 250,000 blacks.

The President and the Volksraad protested against the deed, and a deputation was sent to England to plead for justice for their country, and when Lord Carnarvon told them that their people desired and even demanded annexation they were astounded, and denied it.

The deputation thereupon returned to South Africa, and organised an agitation against annexation, and, to counteract it, Sir Theophilus Shepstone issued a proclamation to imprison, fine, and punish all opponents, and when the deputies held a meeting at Pretoria, to plead for the restoration of their independence, the representative of England directed cannon upon the Assembly, and he called up troops to overawe them.

In spite of this, however, the memorials poured in signed by *6,591 enfranchised men against*, and only *587 enfranchised men for the annexation*.

From the date of the annexation, in April, 1877, till 1880, the Boers contented themselves with peaceable protests and petitions, to induce the English Government to restore them their independence; for they had read the speeches of Mr. Gladstone, where he said "that the annexation of the Transvaal was dishonorable, and should be repudiated," and throughout the Transvaal it was felt that if Mr. Gladstone came into power, the hour of their deliverance was at hand.

Unfortunately, high as the hopes of the Boers had been raised, the more bitter was their disappointment when they found that the advent of Mr. Gladstone to power did not bring them nearer the goal of independence, for which they were prepared to sacrifice their lives, and the war followed as an inevitable consequence.

Happily, by many efforts of kindred associations, by large public demonstrations at Birmingham, Leeds, and other places, and Memorials from various parts of England, the Government of Mr. Gladstone were induced to reverse the policy of their predecessors, and to adopt pacific methods, conciliation and negotiation for a settlement of the dispute.

They were not dismayed either by the disaster at Majuba Hill, though it added greatly to their difficulties; and it must ever remain an honourable and dignified act, that when the cry of vengeance was raised, they resisted that cry, and refused to continue the war, but bravely persevered in the negotiations for peace, even in the face of defeat, and finally succeeded in concluding a preliminary Convention with the Transvaal Government, which was ratified by the House of Commons in July, 1881, by a majority of 105, which, far from being a humiliation to England, reflects upon her the highest renown, and especially on the statesmanship of the Prime Minister of England, W. E. Gladstone, who in noble language declared :—

"That the honour of England does not require the putting down of the rebellion first, in order afterwards to negotiate with the Boers. * * * *

"The honour of the English nation demands that without further bloodshed to expiate the wrong committed in 1877, she should recognise the independence of the Transvaal, and proclaim her wish to live in friendship with a brave people, which has proved itself worthy to be the pioneers of civilisation against the despotisms of Africa."

## PARLIAMENTARY AND OTHER EFFORTS.

During the Session of 1881, Mr. Richard brought before Parliament the subject of British Representatives abroad, and on the 29th April he submitted the following motion :

"That the power claimed and exercised by the representatives of this country, in various parts of the world, to contract engagements, annex territories, and make war, in the name of the nation, without authority from the Central Government, is opposed to the principles of the British Constitution, is at variance with recognised rules of international Law, and is fraught with danger to the honour and true interests of the country."

The Prime Minister (Mr. Gladstone), whilst sympathising with the aim and spirit of the resolution, pointed out the difficulties to carry it out in such an Empire as ours, and considered that the first step required was a reform of the Central Authority itself, and that the most potent influence for restraining the aggressive action referred to, was by mutual influence exercised on the Crown, the Government, and Parliament. Sir George Campbell, Mr. Rylands, and Mr. Lyulph Stanley supported the resolution, and on a division Mr. Richard ran the Government close, being 72 against and 64 for, a narrow majority of 8.

At the close of the Parliamentary session of 1881, Mr.

Richard attended the ninth annual Conference of the Association for the Reform and Codification of the Laws of
Nations held at Cologne, 18th and 19th August, and at one
of the sittings, under the presidency of Sir Travers Twiss,
he read a paper on "The Recent Progress of Arbitration,"
in which he dealt firstly with the objections raised against
its application, and then proceeded to present the cases of
Arbitration from 1871 to 1881, of which he enumerated
fourteen instances, which supplied ground for encouragement
and hope.

On Mr. Richard's return to England, he attended and took
part in an important Conference of the Friends of Peace for
the Northern Counties, under the presidency of Canon
Jackson, (a truly Christian prelate of the Church of England,)
held at Leeds in November 1881, for the purpose of considering firstly, the anti-Christian nature and tendency of
War ; secondly, the best means of solving international
difficulties without resort to War ; and thirdly, the enormous
evils of standing armies.

Papers were read by Dr. Spence Watson on the anti-
Christian nature and tendency of war ; by the Rev. Thomas
Green, on the duties of Christian Ministers, and peoples in
relation to war ; and by Mr. Edward Butler on the enormous
evils of Military establishments and Standing Armies, and at
the close, the writer of each paper proposed a resolution in
accordance with the subject ; and on the first resolution,
proposed by Dr. Spence Watson, and seconded by Mr.
Arthur Pease, M.P., which declared that war is un-Christian,
a hindrance to the Gospel, and that the principles of Christian
morality are as binding on nations as upon individuals, Mr.
Richard addressed the Conference in its support.

A public demonstration was held in the evening, in the
Albert Hall, at which Mr. Alderman Tatham presided, and
again Mr. Richard was to the fore, and delivered a rousing
speech in support of the following resolution :—

" That the enormous armaments maintained in Europe are a

discredit to civilisation, a danger to liberty and peace, as well as an intolerable drain upon the resources of the industrial classes ; and in the judgment of this Meeting, statesmen are called upon to make a persistent effort to arrest this tremendous evil."

During the year 1881 Mr. Richard also addressed a Town Hall Meeting at Reading, on the "War System of Europe," presided over by Mr. George Palmer, the member for the Borough; also at Leicester on October 6th on "International Armaments, or, International Arbitration," presided over by the Mayor, Mr. Alderman Bennett, and the opportunity was taken by the Workmen's Peace Society of the town, to present him with an address of welcome, which recounted, in gratifying terms, his labours for Peace and goodwill among nations, and his consistent support of the principles of civil and religious liberty.

During the Session of 1880, Mr. Richard took part in the debate on the Opium question, introduced by Mr. J. W. Pease, to put a stop to the India-China traffic in Opium, and against the raising of the revenues for the Indian Exchequer thereby.

On 30th June, the second reading of the Sunday-closing Bill for Wales, was brought into Parliament by Mr. John Roberts, and Mr. Richard seconded the motion, and in so-doing he referred to the favourable operation by an array of figures of the Forbes Mackenzie Act for Scotland, from 1852 to 1880, and of the Irish Sunday-closing Act, since it was passed in 1878, and he claimed a similar Act for Wales, especially on the ground of the great preponderance and the strong manifestations of Public opinion in its favour, and because the Bill proposed to deal with a great evil that was corrupting the people, and exercising disastrous influence upon their highest interests.

The Government not opposing the Measure, it was read a second time, and finally passed into law.

For many months after the General Election of 1880, the House of Commons was the scene of stormy debates and strange episodes, on the subject of admission, either by oath or affirmation, of Mr. Bradlaugh, and it was not until the 1st

July that the vexed question was finally settled, by the Government introducing a resolution, which was proposed by Mr. Gladstone, to the following effect :—

" That every person returned as a Member of this House, who may claim to be a person for the time being by the Law permitted to make a solemn affirmation or declaration instead of taking an Oath, shall henceforth be permitted, without question, to make and subscribe a solemn affirmation in the form prescribed by the Parliamentary Oath's Act 1866, as altered by the Promissory Oath's Act 1868, subject to any liability by statute."

Mr. Richard, as the spokesman of the Nonconformists in the House supported the resolution, mainly on the ground that it was in the direction of civil liberty, of the abolition of all those religious tests which operated against the various sections of the Nonconformist and Roman Catholic body for so many generations, and he earnestly appealed, from the beneficial influences that have resulted from these Acts of Toleration, to extend still more the privileges of the Constitution as the best means to secure the stability of the State, and to increase four-fold the prosperity of the Church of England.

During the progress of the Burials Bill in Committee Mr. Richard frequently spoke, and ere the close of the Session he had the satisfaction of seeing placed on the Statute Book, a Measure, that both in and out of Parliament he had for many years manfully struggled for.

Besides the debates referred to, in which Mr. Richard took part, he addressed questions to the Government on the Wars against the Basutos, and the Ashantees ; questions also on religious liberty in the Channel Islands, upon the relations of the Ruler of Berar with India, and on the subject of the Sovereignty of the Solomon Islands.

---

## THE EGYPTIAN WAR.

Few if any recent events in the public career of Mr.

Richard involved him in so much anxiety and labour as the disastrous and deplorable intervention of England in the internal affairs of Egypt, and its consequent and inevitable result of insurrection and war; for, in the first place, it was a sad departure from the policy of non-intervention in Foreign States, and an equally sad departure, by a Liberal Administration, of the vaunted policy of peace as opposed to a spirited foreign policy, by which it had so largely succeeded in raising itself to power in 1880.

This trouble in Egypt was originally brought about by the direct intervention of England and France in 1875 in the internal affairs of Egypt, mainly with a view of regulating its finances, in the interests of the bondholders.

Up to the year 1862 Egypt never borrowed money, but in that year the Khedive, Said Pasha, contracted the first debt, against the advice and entreaties of his Minister, who warned him that such a policy would be its ruin.

Ismail Pasha, who succeeded Said Pasha, was an extravagant and oppressive Khedive, and to meet his claims he threw himself into the hands of European speculators, who lent him money at a ruinous rate of interest, and in a few years he contracted a debt of £90,000,000, of which only £45,000,000 was received by the Egyptian Treasury, the remaining £45,000,000 being absorbed by the Financier. The gross revenue of Egypt of £8,500,000 was raised by every sort of oppressive taxation on the people, and of this sum £5,700,000 went to pay the interest contracted on the loans.

Ismail Pasha's financial difficulties pressed heavy upon him and in 1875, at his earnest request, the Government of Mr. Disraeli despatched Mr. Stephen Cave to examine into, and report on Egyptian finances, and he was compelled to acknowledge that Egypt was in a desperate strait, that she suffered from the ignorance, dishonesty, and extravagance of the Pashas, bringing her to the verge of ruin; and he recommended that England should send out a financier, who should act as the Khedive's Chancellor of the Exchequer, and accordingly Mr. Disraeli appointed Mr. Rivers Wilson, and, on his recall, Mr. Goshen, and with him M. Joubert for France, representing the Bondholders, and the result of their joint mission was to recommend to their respective Governments the appointment of English and French Controllers, and the Marquis of Salisbury, as Secretary of State for Foreign Affairs, gave his consent to the establishment of the Dual Control, from which sprang all the subsequent complications

·Thus it was that England and France took the direct responsibility of dictating the internal government of Egypt, a policy that has been full of serious consequences to England and Egypt alike, for, in June, 1879, in consequence of the action of the Khedive in dismissing his Ministers, and with them the two Controllers, England and France, supported by the other European Powers, obtained the sanction of the Sultan of Turkey to despatch their diplomatic representatives to the Khedive, calling upon him to . abdicate in favour of his nephew, Prince Tewfik, and a few days afterwards the Sultan signed his Irade, deposing Ismail Pasha.

For two years tranquility reigned in Egypt, the financial difficulties were arranged, and the appointment of English and French Controllers with the rank of Ministers gave a guarantee that the new law would be respected, but alas ! this dream of settled progress and tranquility was rudely shaken, for, on 1st February, 1881, a Military Insurrection broke out in Cairo, led by Arabi, an officer in the Egyptian army, which steadily extended itself over the whole country.

The result of this insurrection was the formation of a powerful National Party in Egypt with a declared policy, based on a strong hostility to the Dual Control, and the international engagements of Egypt with Foreign Powers, and the cry was raised, " Egypt for the Egyptians ! "

England and France were now alarmed, for Arabi, formerly a Colonel of the 4th Regiment of Infantry, had rapidly advanced to the position of Minister of War, and was practically master of the situation, and they resolved to support the authority of the Khedive, and on the plea of protecting life and property at Alexandria, ordered two Ironclads to anchor in the Bay. The presence of the allied Fleet increased rather than allayed the danger to the Europeans in the City, for on June 11th a serious riot broke out, the Consul General of England was dragged from his carriage, and many English and French subjects were killed.

At this juncture, Arabi Pasha was in command of the army and fortifications before Alexandria, and the English Admiral Beauchamp-Seymour, in view of the preparations going on to defend the city, sent an ultimatum to the Khedive for its surrender within three days, failing which to open a bombardment.

To this threat no answer was received, and the British Fleet, consisting of 8 ironclads and 5 gunboats, took up their position in Line of Battle, whilst the French Fleet, acting on orders from Paris, withdrew to Port Said.

At seven o'clock in the morning of 11th July, the bombardment commenced, and lasted two days, resulting in the destruction or surrender of the principal Forts, and towards the close of the second day, Arabi abandoned the whole line of fortifications, and retreated, leaving the city of Alexandria to the mob. Then followed the general outbreak of anarchy in the city, the prison doors were thrown open, many parts of the city were set on fire, and for two days the work of devastation continued, during which upwards of 2,000 Europeans perished, and a vast amount of property was destroyed.

The bombardment of Alexandria was followed by the occupation of the city by the Blue Jackets and Marines, and by a Declaration of War against the *de facto* Government of Egypt, which was practically ratified by Parliament on the 27th July, 1882.

On the 22nd August Sir Garnet Wolseley, accompanied
by Sir John Adye, Sir Archibald Wilson, Generals Graham
and Drury Lowe, and the Duke of Connaught, landed at
Port Said, in command of 40,000 troops of all ranks, and
on the 24th and 28th delivered battle successfully with the
Egyptian army respectively at Tel-el-Mahuta and Kassassin,
and finally at Tel-el-Kebir, where Arabi sustaining an overwhelming defeat, fled to Cairo, and upon the arrival there
of the advanced guard of the British forces, he quietly
surrendered himself a prisoner to the Government of
England.

Mr. Richard, several weeks prior to the outbreak of hostilities, issued a strong protest against any armed intervention
of England in Egypt, whether for the right-of-way through the
Suez Canal, or the protection of the Bondholders, on the
ground that in the first place the Suez Canal was not in danger,
and that it was a departure from the policy of non-intervention accepted by the Government of England whether Liberal
or Tory, and especially, that the blood and treasure of
England should not be expended in protecting the pecuniary
interests of any body of investors or speculators.

On June 29, he followed up this manifesto by an important question which he addressed to the Prime Minister,
whether, before employing the military forces of the Crown
to maintain in Egypt the rights of the Sultan, of the Khedive,
and of the foreign bondholders, an· opportunity would be
given to Parliament to consider the subject, but the Government declined to give any pledge, and claimed the right to
act on their own responsibility.

On July 11, immediately on the receipt of the intelligence
of the bombardment by the British Fleet of Alexandria, Mr.
Richard again questioned the Government, whether there
was not an understanding among the Powers represented at
the Constantinople Conference, that no separate action
should be taken by any one Power, pending its deliberations,
and, whether the bombardment of Alexandria was not a

violation of this understanding, to which the Prime Minister replied that there was a general understanding, subject to exceptional circumstances, and that this bombardment must be included under that head.

The following day, owing to the unsatisfactory replies given by the Government to the numerous questions addressed to them, the adjournment of the debate was moved by Mr. Gourley, and seconded by Sir Wilfrid Lawson, who denounced the "cowardly, cruel, and criminal act" of the bombardment of Alexandria, and Mr. Richard supported this heavy indictment, and expressed his

"grief and humiliation at the course taken by the Government in whose wisdom, moderation and justice he had been accustomed to repose the most absolute confidence."

In the same Session of 1882, Mr. Richard opposed the Charter which had been conceded by the British Government to the North Borneo Company, and in March he supported the following resolution of Mr. Gorst in favour of its cancellation :—

"That an humble address be presented to Her Majesty, praying that she will be graciously pleased to revoke or alter so much of the Charter as gives an implied sanction to the maintenance of Slavery under the Protection of the British Flag."

In the course of his speech, Mr. Richard condemned the Charter, not only because it sanctioned the institution of Slavery, but also for the annexation it recognised, which involved serious National responsibilities, and he was supported in this view by Mr. Rylands, Dr. Cameron, and Sir George Campbell, but on a division the resolution was rejected by 125 to 62 votes.

In addition to the debates on the North Borneo Charter, the Cemeteries Bill, and the Egyptian War, Mr. Richard addressed important questions to the Government on South African affairs, Church Patronage, Burials Act, and the employment of Indian Troops in Egypt, and Welsh Intermediate Education.

At the Annual Congress of the Association for the Reform

of the Law of Nations, held at Liverpool in August 1882, and presided over by Lord O'Hagan, Mr. Richard presented a paper on the subject of " The Necessity for an Authoritative Code of International Law," and referred at the onset to the Supreme Court of the United States of America, which adjudicates in all matters of dispute between the States and the Union, and quoted Chancellor Kent, John Stuart Mill, and Emile de Lavelèye in evidence of its immense value to civilization and humanity. In Europe, he showed that International Law is variable and ambiguous, and deficient in sanction, and he referred to the progress in International Maritime Law from the *Il Consolato del Mare*, established in the fourteenth century, down to the Declaration at Paris in 1856, also to the frequency with which Governments have recourse of late years to arbitration, and he believed that they marked distinct advances towards the ultimate goal of the triumph of law over war.

---

## THE EGYPTIAN WAR.—*(Continued)*.

England was now at war with the *de facto* Government in Egypt, and the next step in this bloody drama, was to move Parliament for supplies for the war, and accordingly on the 24th July Mr. Gladstone proposed as follows :—

"That a sum not exceeding £3,300,000 be granted to Her Majesty, beyond the ordinary grants of Parliament, towards defraying the expenses which may be incurred during the year ending on the 31st March, 1883, in strengthening Her Majesty's forces in the Mediterranean."

The debate on this Motion was continued *de die in diem* to late on Friday night, the 27th, and during the four nights' debate most of the ablest speakers took part, in general approval of the policy of the Government, but there were exceptions, notably Sir Wilfrid Lawson, O'Connor Power, and Mr. Richard ; the latter, speaking on the second night, delivered a forcible speech, in which he traced the history of this Egyptian embroglio from 1875 to 1880, during the administration of Lord Beaconsfield, and he deeply regretted that, on the accession of Mr. Gladstone to office, the political and financial inheritance from Egypt was not absolutely repudiated, as it might, and ought to have been. He minutely referred to the course of events from 1880 to the outbreak of hostilities in 1882, and which gradually drifted and dragged England into War, and bitterly censured the barbaric bombardment of Alexandria, which precipitated the War, and he concluded in the following eloquent language :—

"No language can adequately express the disappointment, surprise, and pain with which I see the nation led into this miserable embroglio in Egypt by statesmen whom I have so deeply honoured and so implicitly trusted as I have the Prime Minister and Lord Granville. I have not been accustomed to use flattering words towards the right hon. gentleman at the head of the Government, because I should not have regarded myself as of sufficient importance to make any tribute from me of much value to him. But now that I am obliged to dissent from his policy, I may be permitted to say that I have yielded to no man living in intense admiration of his transcendent abilities, and profound veneration for his character. The name and fame of men like him form a part of the common inheritance of the Liberal Party, and indeed of the nation at large, and not the least painful misgiving I feel at the present moment is lest these unhappy events should cast a shadow on the close of a great and illustrious career. (Cheers.) I cannot vote for this money, which to me is nothing else than blood money, and as it is only by refusing to support the vote that I can put on record my practical protest against proceedings which in my conscience I believe to be as impolitic as they are immoral, and which open before us a future full of ominous and perilous possibilities, I am determined to record my vote against this proposal, even if I have to walk into the lobby alone. (Cheers.)"

Ominous indeed were those last words, which were almost fulfilled, for if we except eleven Irish members, he was followed into the lobby of the Noes by only eight English and Scotch members, (one of whom was a Conservative, the Hon. Percy Wyndham), whose names are worthy to be filed— Thomas Burt, Jesse Collings, Alfred Illingworth, Sir Wilfrid

Lawson, Samuel Storey, Sir David Wedderburn, and T. C. Thompson.

But where were the rest, and who were they, and wherefore did they go astray ?

The question is important, and for this reason, that their desertion from the ranks of the Peace party in Parliament, at this critical moment, was, it is believed, the accelerating cause of the great Leader of the Liberal Party plunging into that most cruel and cowardly war ; therefore, had they remained as firm and resolute as Mr. Richard, their champion ; had they followed the sagacious counsels of the Great Tribune, Mr. Bright, when, (having resigned his high position in the Government of the Queen,) he uttered these memorable words :—

"I asked my calm judgment, and my conscience, what was the path I ought to take. They pointed it out to me, as I think, with an unerring finger, and I am endeavouring to follow it;"

had these influential members of the Peace Party in Parliament acted, spoken and voted as their distinguished leaders, there is no doubt whatever that this Egyptian War from 1882 to 1889, with all its accumulated horrors of human carnage in Egypt, and the Soudan, and all its great uncertainties in the dim and distant future, would never, so far as the intervention of England is concerned, have taken place.

At the opening of the session of 1883, Mr. Richard renewed his opposition to the War, and on the 16th February, he delivered a speech in the debate on the Address, in support of Sir Wilfrid Lawson's amendment, which was as follows:—

"That this House humbly expresses its opinion that no sufficient reason has been shown for the employment of British forces in re-constituting the Government of Egypt and re-organizing its affairs, under the authority of the Khedive."

In consequence of a mis-direction by the Speaker, this question was not put, and therefore on March 2nd, Sir Wilfrid Lawson took advantage of the motion on going into Committee, " That the Speaker now leave the chair," to bring it to an issue by submitting an amendment of a similar character :—

"That this House regrets that it should be called upon to place increased burdens upon the people, in consequence of the late military operations in Egypt."

This was seconded by Sir George Campbell, and supported by Mr. Labouchere and Mr. Illingworth, and on a division, 24 voted for and 94 against it; and again it is worthy of mention that Mr. Richard was under the painful necessity of entering the lobby unaccompanied by his colleagues and friends.

For a third time during the Session of 1883, Mr. Richard withstood the proposals of the Government, and it is satisfactory to find, that he was supported by those who had on former occasions, unfortunately abandoned him in opposing the military policy of the Government.

On this occasion, the 13th April, the Government announced a message from Her Majesty, proposing to Parliament that, in consideration of the "signal services" rendered by Admiral Seymour, in the barbaric bombardment of the ancient and renowned city and port of Alexandria, and also of the "signal services" rendered by General Sir Garnet Wolseley, in the "glorious achievement," won by the highly-disciplined British forces, supported by all "the resources of civilisation," over the wretchedly-disciplined Egyptian soldiers of Arabi, at Tel-el-Kebir, that independent of conferring upon these two principal actors, in this bloody drama, the distinguished honour of a Peerage, that they and their successors for two generations, should receive from the Crown a pension of two thousand sovereigns per annum.

The consideration of this proposal was fixed for the 19th April, and it was introduced by a strong speech in its support by the Prime Minister, and in the course of the debate, Mr. Richard addressed the House, and strongly opposed it, for he considered that to lavish distinctions and pensions upon fighting men, was a custom that might be

O

more honoured in the breach than in the observance, and that it was unwise and un-Christian to stimulate the military spirit, by a recognition of martial deeds in such an inglorious war, but his opposition was unavailing, as the recommendations of the Crown were carried by a large majority.

From this date of English intervention in Egypt, the events which followed are written large, in letters of blood, on the pages of history.

In September 1883, Hicks Pasha, (a retired Indian officer in the service of the Khedive,) at the head of an army of 11,000 Egyptian troops, was ordered by the Government at Cairo to advance, in order to suppress the rebellion, in the Equatorial Provinces of the Soudan, and to protect or relieve in Kordofan, Sennar, and El Obeid from the forces of the Mahdi ; but alas ! this ill-fated expedition, after suffering for two months every conceivable privation under a tropical sun, was surrounded by the fanatical hosts of the Prophet, overwhelmed, and utterly annihilated.

This was followed by as great a catastrophe in the Eastern Soudan, where Baker Pasha and his scratched army of 3,500 men, in an attempt to relieve Tokar and Sinkat, were completely crushed and massacred by the forces of Osman Digna, and in that disaster perished several English officers, Morice Bey, Leslie, Forrester, Walker, Carroll, and other Englishmen.

To retrieve these disasters, the Government of England, yielding to public clamour and party exigencies, were forced to despatch, in March, 1884, a formidable expedition under the command of General Graham, which, landing at Suakim, moved forward to encounter the undisciplined hosts of a brave people, "struggling to be free," and fought murderous battles at El Teb, Tamai, and Tamanieb, which resulted in terrible slaughter, not less than 5,000 of the brave Soudanese being slain ; and, satisfied with these avenging defeats of the lieutenant of the Mahdi, Osman Digna, General Graham and the British forces returned to England.

Against those horrible massacres, Mr. Richard felt it to be

his duty, and well he might, to make an emphatic and indignant protest, in the first place by addressing a Memorial to the Prime Minister, Mr. Gladstone, against any further sanguinary expeditions to the Soudan, and especially against entrusting any longer the issues of peace or war to the naval and military officers in the East; but the reply of the Premier, being considered a defence of this policy, Mr. Richard resolved to raise his voice in Parliament, in earnest condemnation of this dreadful work, and he was manfully assisted by the voice and vote of Sir Wilfrid Lawson and others.

The opportunity was taken of the Saturday sitting, March 15th, in order to vote the Supplementary Estimates, to submit the following resolution :—

"That the necessity for the great loss of British and Arab life, occasioned by the military operations in the Soudan, have not been made apparent."

This resolution was moved by Mr. Labouchere, who attacked in justly bitter terms the policy of "rescue and retire ;" and Mr. Richard, in seconding it, described it as a protest against the horrible butcheries in the Soudan, and because he had from the first regarded our presence in Egypt as a calamity and a crime.

For six hours the debate was continued by prominent men on both sides of the House : Lord Randolph Churchill and Mr. Cowen, Mr. John Morley and Mr. Bourke; and it was evident a strong alliance was formed of Tory and Radical against the policy of the Government, the former from motives of policy, and the latter from motives of humanity; and when the division took place the Government narrowly escaped defeat, the numbers being 111 against, and 94 in favour of the resolution, which led Sir William Harcourt to exclaim, *sotto voce*, "So their dirty trick has not succeeded."

The division list showed that Mr. Richard was supported by the united vote of the Tory and Irish party, and that

with the exception of Sir Wilfrid Lawson, Mr. Passmore
Edwards, and Mr. Illingworth, not one member of the influential members of the Peace Party in Parliament, voted
with him in the lobby; in fact, their names are to be found
on the side of the Government, as voting in favour of these
ruthless massacres in Egypt.

Prior to the Meeting of Parliament in 1885, Mr. Richard
attended and took part in a Peace Conference and Public
Demonstration at Darlington, presided over by Sir J. W.
Pease, supported by the following Members of Parliament :
Sir Henry Havelock, Theodore Fry, Arthur Pease, and Isaac
Wilson. At the former, he read a paper on the work of the
Peace Society, its history, constitution, and its operations
from 1816 to the present time, and pointed out the necessity
for a wider organization, more abundant pecuniary means,
to enable them "to spread through the earth the good
tidings of great joy."

At the Public Meeting in the evening, held in the Central
Hall, at which the Mayor, J. B. Hodgkin, presided, Mr.
Richard spoke chiefly on the armed condition of Europe,
but the chief interest of the meeting centred in the speech
of Sir J. W. Pease, who vindicated his conduct in Parliament from the attacks of the Press, in abstaining from voting
"with his hon. friend Mr. Richard," on the various occasions
during the years 1882-3 and 4, that the latter had opposed
the policy of the Government in Egypt, and divided the
House on the question of Peace or War.

The following month Mr. Richard visited Liverpool, and
took part in an important Public Meeting, presided over by
Mr. W. P. Lockhart, to protest against the continuance of
the War.

The next painful episode, in this miserable Egyptian
embroglio, was the capture of Khartoum by the Mahdi,
and the cruel massacre which followed, including the
death of the chivalrous General Gordon.

The news of this sad event reached England on the eve of

the assembling of Parliament in February 1885, exactly 12 months from the date of his acceptance of the heroic mission, to proceed to Khartoum, for the purpose of devising measures to protect the 11,000 men, women and children from massacre, at the hands of the Mahdi's advancing hosts. The history of this ill-fated mission is one of the most tragic events of British intervention in Egypt, and it is generally believed that his difficulties, and sad fate must be attributed, not to the action of the British Government in sending him, (though their inaction in devising measures for his relief, until it was too late, was universally condemned,) but rather, to the supplemental appointment conferred upon him by the Khedive, with the sanction of the Cabinet in England, as Lieutenant Governor of the Soudan, which considerably enlarged the scope, and increased the responsibilities of his mission.

As early as January 1885, before the sad news of poor Gordon's death had reached England, Mr. Richard issued a manifesto to the friends of peace and non-intervention, strongly deprecating the despatching of another military expedition to the Soudan, either for the purpose of rescuing Gordon, or resisting the advance of the Mahdi's forces, and on the assembling of Parliament in February, he supported the vote of censure on the policy of the Government.

The stirring intelligence of the ignominious fate of the ill-fated defender of Khartoum, and of its capture by the Mahdi had just reached London, and the public indignation was roused, which forced the Opposition in Parliament to give expression to, and accordingly, Sir Stafford Northcote, submitted an amendment to the address from the Crown, which was virtually a vote of censure, to the effect that in view of the great sacrifices of life and treasure in Egypt, measures should be taken to assure a good and stable government in the Soudan. To this amendment Mr. John Morley moved a more sweeping one, regretting the employment of the armed forces of England against the Mahdi, and

Lord George Hamilton, moved a more drastic one still, which declared that, as the Government had failed in their policy, or unable to indicate a clearly defined policy in the Soudan, that the confidence of the House of Commons, and of the Nation in her Majesty's Ministers is not justified.

A prolonged and acrimonious debate followed, which continued from 24th February to 28th February, and on the fourth night of the debate, Mr. Richard addressed the House in one of his impressive and telling speeches, and as it was the last occasion, in Parliament, that he assailed the policy that led to, and promoted this unhappy Egyptian war, a reference to that speech may be of interest.

He commenced by asking who was responsible for this grave national crisis, and in answering this question he said, that whilst all those who promoted, who instigated, and who sanctioned England's unhappy armed intervention in Egypt were responsible, yet that the heaviest measure of guilt was at the door of the Conservative party, firstly, because the miserable complications sprang from the course they took when in Power ; and secondly, because they had since done their utmost in Opposition, to push the Government further and further, into the policy of aggression and war.   He then proceeded, with a severe earnestness of language and manner, to trace the various events, that eventually culminated in those disasters in the Soudan ; and he considered that the fountain and origin of all the mischief was the policy of the Marquis of Salisbury, when at the Foreign Office from 1878 to 1880, in establishing the Dual Control, and in the deposition of Ismail Pasha ; and, turning to the Ministerial Bench, he severely condemned the Ministry in Power, for sending the British Fleet into Egyptian waters, and the British forces into Egypt, and especially the invasion of the Soudan, and lastly, the mission of General Gordon to Khartoum.   In conclusion, he solemnly appealed to the Government not to sanction any further aggressive policy, no war for revenge or prestige, no smashing of the Mahdi, no conquest of the

Soudan, no attempt to impose Egyptian rule in the Soudan, no countenance to any insane projects, to occupy and govern the vast regions of Africa.

He refused to vote for the amendment of Sir Stafford Northcote, on the ground that it recognised indefinite and serious responsibilities of England in the Soudan, which he could not admit, and declared his intention to vote for the amendment of Mr. John Morley, as he considered it pointed to the only true and safe policy, the withdrawal, at the earliest practicable opportunity, of British troops from Egypt and the Soudan.

The result of this memorable debate and division was as follows: For Sir Stafford Northcote's amendment 288, against 302 ; for John Morley's amendment, 112 for, 455 against ; for Lord George Hamilton's, 277 for, 299 against ; and a glance at the division list showed, that the first and last were on distinct party lines, and that the Government narrowly escaped, by a majority of 14, censure and defeat.

In the same session of 1883 Mr. Richard introduced the Cemeteries Bill, the object of which was to secure an alteration in the law with respect to burials, and it proposed to relieve Burial Boards from the obligation of dividing cemeteries into consecrated and unconsecrated ground, also from the necessity of building two chapels, and the raising of fees to meet those requirements.

The Government, believing that the Measure would remove existing religious difficulties, gave their support, under certain limitations, to its second reading, but owing to the factious opposition of Mr. Beresford-Hope and Mr. O'Donnell, the debate was prolonged to the hour of adjournment, and in spite of a majority in its favour, the Bill was eventually withdrawn. It was re-introduced by Mr. Richard in the session of 1884, but in consequence of the renewed opposition of the "no surrender" party of the Church of England, led by Mr. Beresford-Hope, notwithstanding a

majority of 22 in its favour, the Measure met with a similar
fate as in the preceding session.

During the Parliamentary recess of this year Mr. Richard
visited Italy, and attended the eleventh Annual Congress
of the Association for the Reform of the Law of Nations,
which was held at Milan on September 11th, on which
occasion he read a paper on the " Progress of the Principle
of International Arbitration," and at the close of the discussion which followed, a series of resolutions were unanimously adopted, expressing, with satisfaction, the increased
disposition on the part of civilized Governments to recognize
Arbitration, as a just and reasonable method for settling
international differences.

During this visit of Mr. Richard to Milan, an address
was presented to him from various Masonic Lodges throughout Italy, conveying their full sympathy with him in his
" noble propaganda in favour of peace," which they described
as the most pure and sublime manifestation of the Masonic
idea.

On his return to England he visited his constituents, as
his annual custom was, and on this occasion it proved of
more than ordinary interest, as the subjects discussed referred
mainly to the interests of the colliers, and upwards of 4,000
of the Taff Vale miners assembled in the Market Square,
Merthyr-Tydvil, under the presidency of their leader, David
Morgan.

Mr. Richard, in accordance with his usual practice, addressed this vast assemblage, first in the Welsh language,
and afterwards in English, and the interest of his speech
centred on the advocacy of a Board of Conciliation for
South Wales, similar to those established in the Midlands
and the North of England, under the respective Arbitrators,
Mr. Rupert Kettle and Mr. David Dale, for the settlement
of all questions of difficulty, and the prevention of the social
wars between the colliers and the colliery proprietors.

In November, 1883, a Conference of ministers and laymen of various denominations was held in the Rooms of the Social Science Association, to promote mutual knowledge and sympathy between men of different churches, and at one of these Conferences, under the presidency of Dr. Martineau, Mr. Richard delivered an instructive address on "The Duties of England as a Christian Nation towards the Non-Christian Races of the World." At the onset, he referred in terms of high commendation to those who were sowing the seeds of Civilization and Christianity in foreign lands, but feared there was danger of their invoking, in their zeal for their mission, the arm of flesh to facilitate their labours, and thus degrade and dishonour a great and holy cause, and he rejoiced that eminent Divines, such as Dr. Jeremy, of Cambridge, and Dr. Pusey, of Oxford, had rebuked these indiscretions.

On the subject of the Duties of Christian Nations to the Non-Christian Races, he referred to the oppression and misery which followed the conquests of the Spaniards in Mexico, Paraguay, and Peru, the Portuguese in Brazil, the Dutch in South Africa, and England in India, China, Japan, Burmah, and elsewhere, for he considered their action was in utter disregard of the cardinal principles of Christian faith and practice, and he strongly inculcated a fuller recognition by Missionaries abroad, of the precepts of the Christian religion, to influence and govern men by moral power, and thus win them to submission and confidence, by kindness and love.

In March 1885 a danger arose of an armed collision between

## ENGLAND AND RUSSIA,

arising out of the delimitation of the Afghan boundary, and the facts are as follows.

In 1882 the Russian Government proposed, with a view to prevent disturbances on the borders of Afghanistan, that the frontier lines should be definitely laid down, and it was mutually agreed that an Anglo-Russian Commission should be appointed, but pending their arrival on the debatable ground, the Military forces of the two rival States massed their Troops, the Afghans advanced northwards from Bala-Murgab to Pendjeh, and the Russians advanced southwards from Sarracks to Pul-i-Khatum, and an inevitable collision took place, which resulted in the defeat of the Afghans, and a lamentable loss of life.

At this alarming intelligence reaching England, and the imminence of war arising therefrom, Mr. Richard addressed a question to the Government, whether England and Russia being parties to the declaration of Paris of 1856, it did not afford just and sufficient ground for invoking the good offices of some friendly power, to which Mr. Gladstone replied in the affirmative, and that as diplomatic negotiations were proceeding on the "late regrettable incident," it would be premature to permit a discussion.

In consequence however of the gravity of the crisis, Mr. Richard prepared a memorial to the Prime Minister, signed by John Bright, Samuel Morley, James Bryce, and upwards of eighty members of Parliament, emphasizing the recommendation of the 16th protocol of the Treaty of Paris ; and he also issued an appeal, addressed to his fellow countrymen, in which he forcibly set forth the facts of the dispute, the great calamities of a war, that the dispute being a question of boundary, was eminently suitable for reference to an Arbitral *process.*

These efforts were not wholly unavailing, as on May 4th, the Prime Minister was able to announce to Parliament, that England and Russia had agreed to refer to the judgment of the Sovereign of a Friendly State, any difference which may be found to exist, with a view to the settlement of the dispute, in a mode consistent with the honour of both States.

## PARLIAMENTARY EFFORTS.

In the beginning of the Session of 1886, the Under Secretary of State for India, Sir Ughtred Kay-Shuttleworth, moved a resolution declaring that the revenues of India shall be applied, to defray the expenses of the military operations against Burmah, to which an amendment was moved by Mr. William Hunter, as follows :—

" That this House is of opinion that it would be unjust to defray the expenses of the military operations in the Kingdom of Ava out of the revenues of India."

Mr. Richard, in seconding the amendment, said, that the summary annexation of that Kingdom was an act of high-handed violence for which there was no adequate justification, and he referred to the three principal motives for this annexation—the massacres and cruelties perpetrated by the King, Theebaw, upon his own relatives to protect himself against rival claimants to the throne ; his entering into communication with the French and Italian Governments, without the sanction of England, and his quarrel with the Bombay and Burmah Trading Company ; and he maintained that England had no right to tax the people of India for this war, as they had no part or lot in the complications which led to the conflict, and annexation which followed.

The amendment was supported by admirable speeches from Mr. McIver and Dr. Clark, but on a division it was rejected by 297 votes to 82, a majority in favour of the War of 215.

On March 9th, the question of Disestablishment of the Church of England in Wales, was brought before Parliament by Mr. L. L. Dilwyn, who submitted the following resolution :—

" That as the Church of England in Wales, has failed to fulfil its professed object, as a means of promoting the religious interests of the Welsh people and ministers, to only a small minority of the population, that its continuance as an established Church in the Principality, is an anomaly, and an injustice, which ought no longer to exist."

Mr. Richard seconded this resolution in an able speech,

and contended that the Church of England in Wales is not, and never has been, the Church of Wales, that it has failed to win the love and loyalty of the people, and has never discharged its own professed functions as the religious instructor of the people; but, on the contrary, it has been employed as an instrument for the extinction of the Welsh language, and the suppression of Welsh nationality; and he gave an interesting *resumé* over a period of 300 years in support of this contention. He referred in high terms of the Welsh people as intelligent, religious, moral, and orderly a people as can be found in any quarter of the globe, and he considered that the Christian civilization of Wales was, beyond all doubt, mainly due to the Nonconformists, and concluded with an eloquent appeal to the justice and generosity of Englishmen to liberate the Welsh people from what they feel to be an anomaly that ought to be swept away, and that they would thus gain a thousandfold by the gratitude and loyalty of his countrymen. To this resolution Mr. Albert Grey moved an amendment, substituting in effect disestablishment for the introduction of such reforms as will enable it to adapt itself more efficiently to the religious needs and wishes of the Welsh people, and, on the division, the amendment was carried by 241 to 229 votes.

## NATIONAL ENGAGEMENTS

On the 19th March, 1886, Mr. Richard brought before Parliament a question, as he considered, of great national importance, that the power of making war, the annexation of territory, and the negotiation of Treaties, should, in their final sanction, be transferred from the Crown to the representatives of the people, and the resolution he moved was as follows :—

" That in the opinion of this House, it is not just or expedient to embark in war contract engagements involving grave responsibilities for the nation, without the knowledge and consent of Parliament."

In moving this resolution he observed, that whilst England is proud of being considered a self-governing nation, and her people sensitive against any tax or obligation being imposed without the authority of Parliament, yet on a question of far higher importance, involving far-reaching issues—the control of her Foreign Policy—she is absolutely helpless. He showed by a reference to numerous precedents from the writings of such historians as Freeman, Mayne, and Hallam, that our ancestors were extremely jealous against entrusting these formidable powers, now exercised by the Crown, to an irresponsible Executive. He passed in review the wars of the present generation—the first Afghan and Burmah wars ; the Syrian, Scinde, Chinese, Persian, Japan, South African, and Egyptian wars, and showed that there was ample time and opportunity, in each of them, to discuss their necessity, and to consult the nation beforehand. On the subject of Treaties, he stated they were 37 in number, binding Great Britain to onerous obligations in all parts of the world, in the ratification of which Parliament had had no voice; whereas in most foreign countries—such, for instance, as the United States and France—Treaties were only binding after being approved by their Legislatures. He condemned the mania England had shown in the past for annexation of territory, which he described as "an insatiable earth hunger," and that her possessions amounted to one-fifth of the surface of the globe. In conclusion, he declared that he had lost all faith in Governments, who were delivered over to a rampant militarism, which was the curse of Europe, and that his only hope was in the democracies throughout Europe, to lift up their voices and show their determination no longer to suffer it, but that they should make the Governments to understand that they, the people, did not desire fighting, and that if there is to be any bloodshed—

> " Let the men who make the quarrels,
>   Be the only men to fight."

## ARBITRATION CONFERENCE IN LONDON.

In July, 1887, Mr. Richard attended the thirteenth Annual Meeting of the Association for the Reform of the Law of Nations, which, being held in the Guildhall, London, under the authority and approval of the Lord Mayor, attracted an unusual number of influential men—Mr. Justice Butt, Sir Travers Twiss, Sir Walter Phillimore, Professors Leone Levi, D. D. Field, (New York,) and many others.

On the first day of the Conference, Mr. Justice Butt delivered an admirable address on the subject of International Arbitration, and spoke hopefully and favourably, remarking :—

" It was impossible to conceive any question of more universal interest, more closely touching the happiness of the human race. * * * The goal might be distant, but he refused to believe it was unattainable. Each step on the way, each international dispute settled by peaceful means, was a step in the right direction, and one which might save an incalculable amount of human misery and suffering."

The first paper read at the Conference was by Sir Travers Twiss, on " International Conventions for the Neutralization of Territory, and their Application to the Suez Canal," and Mr. Richard followed on the subject of International Arbitration, which he introduced by a reference to the military and financial condition of Europe, which he summed up as follows: The number of men in the armies of Europe on the peace footing, 3,041,054 ; and on the war footing, including second class reserves, 17,000,000 ; the annual cost by direct taxation on the people, £158,428,740, and including the indirect losses, first, the withdrawal of so many millions of able-bodied men from productive industry, and the loss of interest on the prodigious capital invested in preparations for war, as estimated by competent statisticians, amounted to £500,000,000 per annum, to Europe alone. He stated that the aggregate national debts of Europe, amounted to £4,649,286,882, on which an annual interest is paid of

£213,640,000, which shews an increase, since 1866, of £2,040,000,000, and of interest, £136,120,000.

Having referred to previous papers on this subject which he had presented to the Conferences of the Association, one at Cologne in 1881, and the other at Milan in 1883, he proceeded to give an historical recital of the various instances of successful Arbitration between States since 1883 : Between Holland and St. Domingo, arising out of the seizure of a Dutch ship—referred to the President of the French Republic; between England and Germany, arising out of claims in Fiji ; between Spain and the United States, arising out of the seizure of an American ship—referred to the Italian Minister at Washington ; between Chili and Peru, resulting from the great war—referred to an International Commission; between Russia and England, on the Pendjeh incident—referred to the King of Denmark ; and between Germany and Spain, on the dispute over the Solomon Islands—referred to the Pope of Rome.

In addition to these cases of successful Arbitration between States, he referred to the agreement arrived at the Berlin Congress, to determine differences that may arise between the 15 different states in the Congo Territory, also to the Treaty of Arbitration entered into between Columbia and Honduras, and to the creation of an International Court, for the peaceful settlement of all differences between the South American Republics.

In conclusion Mr. Richard said, and as these were the last words that emanated from his pen, that he publicly rehearsed on behalf of this great cause, to which he had dedicated his life, we quote them in full :

"We shall find, on looking back over the past, that the charges now brought against us, of being missionaries and preachers of impracticable Utopias, have been brought against others who, in former times, had faith and courage to labour for great reforms against the traditions and customs of their age, but who, nevertheless, by patient continuance in well-doing, did succeed in achieving great and lasting triumphs for civilisation and humanity. None of us are sanguine as to expect that we can accomplish all our hearts desire by a sudden *coup*. Nobody knows better· than we do, the difficulty of the object we are aiming at ; but we must be content to work on earnestly and steadfastly for the right—and most men admit that we have the right on our side—with the calm and firm conviction that even in such a world as this, the right is destined ultimately to be victorious."

The Attorney-General, Sir Richard Webster, took part in the discussion which followed the delivery of Mr. Richard's address, and heartily congratulated the Conference on having had the opportunity of listening to such an important compilation of historical facts, he strongly commended the principles which had been so forcibly advocated, and urged on all not to be satisfied with their enunciation simply, but to devote their earnest attention to their practical carrying out in an international direction.

Professor Leone Levi, Sir Wilfrid Lawson, the Hon. D. D. Field, and Frederic Passy followed, with telling and effective speeches on the same subject.

---

## THE RETIREMENT OF MR. RICHARD,

from the Secretariat of the Peace Society in May, 1885, the position, that without a single break, he had so worthily held for the lengthened period of thirty-seven years, was an event not altogether unforeseen, nor to those within the inner circle of its Executive, who had sorrowfully observed his waning strength, was it unexpected; but inevitable and regrettable as was his decision, mainly, if not entirely, because of his advancing years and failing health, it could not but be otherwise than a heavy blow to his colleagues and Committee, and a serious, nay, an irreparable loss to the interests of the Society, whose fortunes had been for nigh a generation so intimately bound up with his life and service, and whose usefulness had been, in the main, created and sustained by the versatility of his genius, the loyalty of his convictions,

and the splendid courage he had, through its many vicissitudes and conflicts so conspicuously displayed. It was
therefore with no ordinary feelings of sorrow and regret that
the friends and supporters of the Society assembled at their
annual gathering in Finsbury Chapel, the *rendezvous* for
upwards of half a century of its anniversary meetings, to
receive the sorrowful announcement from his lips, of his
resignation, which he conveyed in the following touching
words :—

"This is the last time I shall appear on the platform as the
Secretary of the Peace Society. I have been in that capacity
for thirty-seven years (cheers), and I have been engaged in the
cause of Peace for forty years. I have far outlived all the
original members of the Committee, and almost everyone of
those who were actively engaged in the cause of Peace when I
first took office, have disappeared from the scene. I should like
to explain the reason of my retirement, because the Press would
probably assign a reason of their own, which would be likely to
prove incorrect. My one reason is this : I am 73 years of
age, and although I am thankful that my bodily and mental
powers are not more impaired than they are, yet I feel that I
am not what I have been—that there are signs of declining
power, and sometimes a failing of health, which warn me that I
must not put the same strain on my powers that I have been
accustomed to, and must husband the little strength that remains
for me. I have survived four Presidents of the Society : Mr.
Charles Hindley, Mr. Joseph Sturge, Mr. Joseph Pease, and Mr.
Henry Pease, for their friend in the Chair was the third of his
honourable name, who had filled that office. I am not tired of
the work, nor am I discouraged. If God spares me I hope even
yet to be of some service in connection with the Cause. I hope
there are young men who will come forward in order to take
from my paralysed hand the flag of peace, and hold it with a
resolute arm. What I would say to them is : Don't be dismayed
by the vastness of the enterprise, or the formidable character of
the obstacles that are before them. The work you have in hand
is a good work ; you are advocating a cause which, in my
innermost convictions, I believe to be the cause of truth, reason,
justice, humanity, the cause of religion, and I would venture to
say, the cause of God. (Loud applause)."

These parting words from Mr. Richard, the great Apostle
of Peace, spoken with much emotion, "with trembling lip
and timid tones," within the walls of that Temple of Peace,
which had for the uninterrupted period of forty years,

P

resounded with his stirring and powerful eloquence, on behalf of the sacred cause of "on earth peace, and good will among men," must never be effaced from the memory of those present, who listened to them, nor from those who were absent, and have perused them on the printed page; and to the young men, and the strong men who are left to labour in this great enterprise, it is a call, loud, earnest, and deep, to come forward, and grasp the fallen banner, that banner which noble-hearted Henry Richard bore so manfully and bravely, in the storm and dust of battle, in his day and generation, and with resolute arm and unfaltering step to bear it aloft, that it may be displayed, in the name of justice, humanity, and Peace.

Excellent and well-merited was the eloquent tribute which his colleagues of the Committee of the Peace Society rendered to him on his retirement, and that found a warm response in the hearts of many thousands beside, who admired and loved him for his work's sake, his high character, and many victories, and the following passage of that tribute, deserves a place in these pages :—

"The Committee feel that the severance of a bond which has continued unbroken for such a lengthened period, cannot be otherwise than an occasion of sorrow to those who have had the privilege of associating with him in the Society's work. Their regret is intensified as they look back over the history of the Society, and recall the extent to which its progress has been influenced by Mr. Richard's indomitable patience, his resolute will, his political sagacity, and his intellectual power. But their gratitude is heightened, in equal degree, when it is remembered that during his occupancy of office, and in large measure owing to his fearless and eloquent advocacy, by pen and speech, the Society has surmounted the antagonism by which it was formerly confronted, and has gained a continually growing influence upon the national mind. Neither daunted by contumely, nor discouraged by apathy, where there should have been support, nor deterred by adverse criticism, Mr. Richard, 'by labors more abundant,' and with zeal that never flagged, has urged the adoption of International Arbitration, the mutual Reduction of Armaments by the European Powers, Non-Intervention in the affairs of other nations, and the promotion of the holy cause of Peace."

It was fitting, too, that the Sister Society in France, as it has been appropriately termed, should, by the hand of its excellent President, Frederic Passy, for many years and in many struggles the faithful friend and colleague of Mr. Richard, tender its sincere and earnest tribute, and none could have possibly been more gratifying to its recipient, none more honourable :—

"You have been for forty years, not only the foremost amongst your countrymen in the sacred crusade against war ; you have been the guide and the support of all the men of Peace throughout Europe."

The last great speech delivered by Mr. Richard in the Parliament of England, was on the 19th March, 1886, previously referred to, for during the Sessions of 1887 and 1888, conscious of his failing strength and the necessity of following the advice of his medical attendant, to avoid great mental or physical exertion, he took no part in debate, but his interest was unabated in public affairs, and his wonted zeal, especially in foreign relations, was forcibly illustrated by important questions which he addressed to the Government on the unhappy war in Burmah, and the rumoured annexation of territory on the East Coast of Africa.

For the last time he appeared on the platform of the Peace Society's Annual Meeting, in May, 1887, and delivered, what proved to be his last public utterance, outside the walls of Parliament, on the Cause so dear to his heart, and these were his closing words, worthy of being cherished by all those who desire, however feebly, to follow his noble example :—

"They must not be discouraged by the magnitude of their task in attempting to uproot a custom which has sunk deep into the traditions of the world, about which poetry and romance had thrown the halo of a false glory, and which was maintained in all countries by powerful classes, whose interests, personal, political, and pecuniary, were involved in its continuance. But I believe the powers that are for us are greater than those that are against us. Reason is for us, for war is an outrage on reason ; justice is for us, for war tramples justice under foot ; humanity is for us, for war desolates humanity, and has written its scroll within and without with mourning and lamentation Civilisation is for us, for war is the incarnation of barbarism; and, above all, religion is for us, for it is not possible that He who made of one blood all nations of men, can look with complacency upon His children engaged in butchering each other; and we have the benediction of Him whom we consider our Master and Head, and who is destined to become the King of the universe, and who has said, 'Blessed are the peacemakers, for they shall be called the children of God.'" (Applause).

At the close of the Session of 1888, his last year on earth, premonitory symptoms of ill-health appeared, arising from an affection of the heart, from which he had for some years past suffered, and he sought for rest and change. Accompanied by Mrs. Richard, whose watchful care and solicitude for him had, it is believed, prolonged considerably his valuable life, he proceeded to North Wales, on a visit to his esteemed friend, Mr. Richard Davies, the Lord-Lieutenant of Anglesey, and the former Member of Parliament for the Constituency of Anglesey, and there at his charming home at Treborth Hall, near the Menai Bridge, amid a congenial circle of political and dear friends, he passed the few remaining days on earth.

On Tuesday evening, the 21st of August, the summons came, and with his faculties unclouded and unimpaired, he passed peacefully and painlessly away, and his purified spirit, freed from the shackles of this mortality, with its mingled coil of joy and suffering, quitted its earthly tenement, as we may reverently believe, to enter that better Home above,— the glorious Rest of the Redeemed.

> " Soldier of Christ, well done !
> Rest from thy loved employ:
> The battle fought, the victory won ;
> Enter thy Master's joy."

Hutchings, Printing Works, Uxbridge, W.

# A P P E N D I X.

---

## THE NATIONAL EISTEDDFOD OF WALES,

AND THE LATE

## MR. HENRY RICHARD, M.P.

AT the Meetings of the National Eisteddfod, held at
Wrexham in September 1888, The Right Hon. W. E.
Gladstone, M.P., paid the following warm tribute of admira-
tion and respect to the memory and services of Mr.
Richard :—

" Now, this is a day of retrospect, and having spoken of
Welsh nationality, I am reminded to look towards that
inscription which you see upon a portion of your walls, and
which bears the name of Henry Richard—a name than
which there can be no better symbol of Wales. I have had
the honour of knowing him for the last 20 years, if not
more; and I have always been glad to take occasion of
saying that I regarded him, in respect of Wales—in respect
of the conduct, character, faculties, and hopes of the people
of Wales—that I regarded him as a teacher and a guide. I
have owed to him much of what I have learned about
Wales, as my experience has enlarged, and I owe a debt to
him on that account which I am ever glad to acknowledge.
But he has broader claims upon you. He has upon you
the claim of having exhibited to the world a model of
character such as any country cannot but regard as an object

of sympathy and of delight. I have seen him in Parliament
the advocate of decided opinions; the advocate of some
opinions, perhaps amongst the best he entertained, for
instance, with respect to peace, in which he had no great
number of sympathisers or followers. I · have seen him
always uniting a most determined courage and resolution in
the assertion of his principles and views with the greatest
tenderness, gentleness, and sympathy towards those who
differed from him. The fact is, though I don't wish un-
necessarily and officiously to introduce here considerations
so solemn—perhaps they are better reserved in the main for
another place—the fact is that there was in him what I may
call an inner peace, which was the secret of his outward self-
command and of his gentleness as well as of his courage.
It was impossible to see him without saying that he was not
only a professor of Christianity, but that his mind was a
sanctuary of Christian faith, of Christian hope, and of
Christian love; and all those great powers and principles
radiated forth from the centre, and let his light shine before
men, though he himself would have been the last either to
assert or to recognise that there was in him any kind or
degree of merit. I know his name will long be remembered and ever be revered among you, and I am glad
to have had the opportunity of paying to him this brief and
imperfect, but hearty and sincere, tribute of admiration and
respect."

Sir John Puleston, M.P., the President, on the 7th
September, in moving a resolution of condolence to Mrs.
Richard, said :—

" Having offered you these congratulations on the magnificent success of this Eisteddfod in Wrexham, I must next
refer to a sadder subject, and you will allow me, I am sure,
in your name and my own as Eisteddfodwyr, to ask you on
this, the last of our morning gatherings, to unite in passing
a vote of condolence and sympathy with the bereaved widow
of Mr. Henry Richard. Mr. Richard, as we all know, took

a great interest in all that concerns the Eisteddfod, and he did so because he conceived, as we all conceive, that the Eisteddfod was revived and re-established for the best interests of Wales and of the Welsh people. Mr. Richard, to whose memory so feeling a tribute was paid last Tuesday in the masterly oratory of Mr. Gladstone, was never happier than when he was ministering in one way or another to bring our old institution to the high level it has attained. He knew well the Welsh character, and he never allowed differences of politics or religion to stand between him and others in the promotion of the success of the Eisteddfod; and as a private citizen, it could be said of him that he wore the white plume of a blameless life. It would be fitting that a word of condolence and sympathy should be sent from that vast assembly to the bereaved widow, of one who occupied so large a space in the history of the Principality, and whose devotion to the cause of peace among the nations would be put by his countrymen side by side with his devotion to Wales and to the Eisteddfod. It will, I am sure, be some solace to Mrs. Richard, in these days of her affliction, to be reminded by such a resolution, as I now propose should be sent, of the fact that the memory of her devoted husband is kept green and sacred by the institution he loved so well."

Mr. Evan Morris, Chairman of the Eisteddfod Committee, seconded the resolution, and said :—

" He did not think he would be discharging his duty to that large assembly, as Chairman of the Executive Committee, if he did not avail himself, as he gladly did, of the privilege to second the vote of condolence to the widow of the late Mr. Henry Richard. He was obliged to Sir John Puleston for giving them that opportunity of placing upon record their deep sense of gratitude for the services rendered by the late Mr. Richard. He would not add a word to what Sir John Puleston had so well said, or to the touching eloquence of Mr. Gladstone on Tuesday, but he would propose that this resolution and Mr. Gladstone's impressive tribute, expressing their deep sympathy with Mrs. Richard, should be printed on vellum and sent to her " :—

"That we offer to Mrs. Henry Richard our sincere sympathy and condolence in her great bereavement ; and that we desire to convey to her, by the voice of this large gathering, the assurance that the services rendered by her late husband to the National Eisteddfod of Wales are warmly appreciated throughout the Principality, and that his memory will be cherished by the Welsh people."

# A WELSH ADDRESS TO MR. RICHARD,
## 1874.

ON the return of Mr. Richard from his Peace Mission to the various European countries in 1873, a large number of his fellow-countrymen gave him a cordial reception at a meeting held at the Cannon Street Hotel, presided over by Sir John Puleston, M.P., and which was attended by the following representative Welshmen : Mr. Osborne Morgan, M.P., Mr. Hughes, M.P., Mr. Fothergill, M.P., Mr. Morgan Lloyd, M.P., Mr. Brinley Richards, and others.

In the course of the proceedings, Mr. Stephen Evans presented, on behalf of the Welsh Nation, an address to Mr. Richard, commending his efforts to extend a more accurate knowledge of Wales and its people in England, to encourage and foster the institutions of the Principality, and to advance the cause of Peace at home and abroad.

Mr. Richard, in reply, said that he imbibed the love of Wales with his blood, and if anything could reward him for what he had done for Wales or for Peace, it was the approbation of Welshmen.

This Address was subsequently engrossed and framed, and placed in Mr. Richard's library, and was highly appreciated by him as a valuable testimony from Wales.

# FRIENDLESS AND FALLEN
## YOUNG WOMEN AND GIRLS.

## LONDON FEMALE PREVENTIVE and REFORMATORY INSTITUTION.

### SUMMARY OF THE WORK OF THE PAST YEAR.

NUMBER OF INMATES IN THE HOMES and Open-all-Night
Refuge, Jan. 1, 1888 ... ... ... ... ... ... 177
ADMITTED TO THE HOMES during 1888 ... ... ... ... 585
RE-ADMITTED temporarily during 1888 ... ... ... ... 181
ADMITTED to the Refuge during 1888 ... ... ... ... 589
RE-LODGED at the Refuge during 1888 ... ... ... ... 479
Religious Services, Bible Classes, &c., conducted in the Homes
numbered nearly ... ... ... ... ... ... ... 3,000
In the further interest of the friendless virtuous a new Home was
purchased'at 459, Holloway Road.
The following Homes are now sustained by the general funds:—

PREVENTIVE HOMES, especially for Friendless Girls    No. of
in their teens—                                      Inmates. Total.

| | No. of Inmates. | Total. |
|---|---|---|
| The Jubilee Home, 7, Parson's Green ... ... ... | 50 | |
| 195, Hampstead Road, N.W. ... .. ... ... ... | 18 | |
| 459, Holloway Road ... ... ... ... ... ... | 30 | |
| | | 98 |
| REFORMATORY HOMES— | | |
| 200, Euston Road, N.W. ... ... ... ... ... | 24 | |
| 35, Eden Grove, Holloway ... ... ... ... ... | 33 | |
| Milton House, Brompton ... ... ... ... ... | 30 | |
| The Holt-Yates Memorial Home, 5, Parson's Green ... | 30 | |
| | | 117 |
| OPEN-ALL-NIGHT REFUGE— | | |
| 37, Manchester Street, W.C. Visited every morning by Mr. Thomas, to endeavour to arrange permanent help to all new comers ... ... ... ... ... ... | 20 | |
| | | 20 |
| Total number of inmates to maintain ... | | 235 |

---

### MEALS TO BE PROVIDED FOR INMATES.
### Daily, 940.   Weekly, 6,580.   Annually, 343,100.

September 15.—The Committee are in urgent need of Funds to carry
on the Work of Mercy as above, and meet daily expenses.
*There have been nearly ONE THOUSAND applications for help this year.*

---

#### REMITTANCE OF CONTRIBUTIONS.
*Contributions will be thankfully received by the Bankers, *LLOYDS' BANK,
Limited, 72, Lombard Street, E.C., and 54, St. James's Street, S.W.;
FRANCIS NICHOLLS, Esq., (of the Committee), 14, Old Jewry Chambers,
E.C., or*

200, EUSTON ROAD, LONDON, N.W.   **EDWARD W. THOMAS,** *Secretary.*

◦ Cheques and Postal Orders should be crossed on the Bankers as above.
*Whenever possible, receipts are sent per return of post.*

# Works Published by GEORGE POTTER.

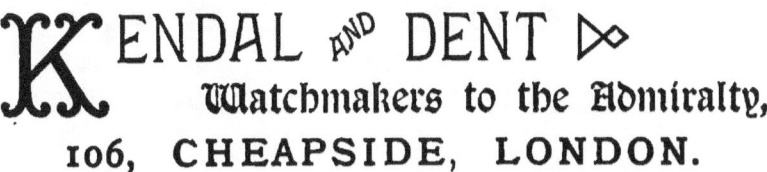

# NATARA!

## Dries up a Cold in the Head in a Few Hours.

## FOR INFLUENZA, BRONCHITIS, AND ASTHMA IT HAS NO EQUAL.

Natara is unequalled as a purifying agent; it combines in its action the absorbent and antacid properties of the most famed German Mineral Waters, with much of the strengthening properties of Iron and Quinine, whilst it exerts none of the injurious effects of these latter agents. The advantages of this Preparation are, that whilst it is simple and harmless, it is at the same time speedy and penetrating in its action; it exerts the most extraordinary curative properties in almost all forms of Chronic Diseases. The above statements are not by any means exaggerated, the effects of Natara are too obvious to need any untruthful recommendation for purposes of sale.

**The Dose recommended is 10 drops of the Natara, to a wine-glassful of ordinary water.**

In the weakness following confinements, and in all female disorders, Natara ought to be partaken of frequently, and this applies also to Chronic Bronchitis, Bronchitic Asthma, as well as to Catarrh and to Stone in the Bladder. For such complaints give the full dose, four or five times a day.

Natara exerts a strengthening effect upon both the muscular and nervous systems; for example, in cases where the Voice is failing or is altogether lost, in Palpitations of the Heart due to Weakness, especially in Hysterical Palpitations and Hysterical Weaknesses, it not only strengthens the parts affected, but it also gives tone to the entire body.

MRS. HENRY VARLEY writes:—

48, Elgin Crescent, Notting Hill, W.

DEAR SIR,—I am not a great believer in special remedies, but I am compelled to speak as I find. As long as I can remember I have been subject to severe "cold in the head," and all the miseries belonging to that disease. Nothing ever seemed to do me any good, and it always had to take its course, and leave me weak and miserable. I was persuaded to try your Natara, and as I took it at an early stage in the cold, I was perfectly surprised to find that it entirely prevented its continuance, and the next day I had no sign of a cold, though I well knew I was in for a really bad attack of catarrh. I have much pleasure in giving this testimony to its wonderful power to beat back a cold. Yours very truly,

SARAH VARLEY.

**Price 1s. and 2s. per Bottle.** *By Post, 2d. extra.*

PREPARED ONLY BY

# J. OCKENDEN,

### Chemist,

## 18, MOORFIELDS, E.C. (Opposite Moorgate Street Station.)

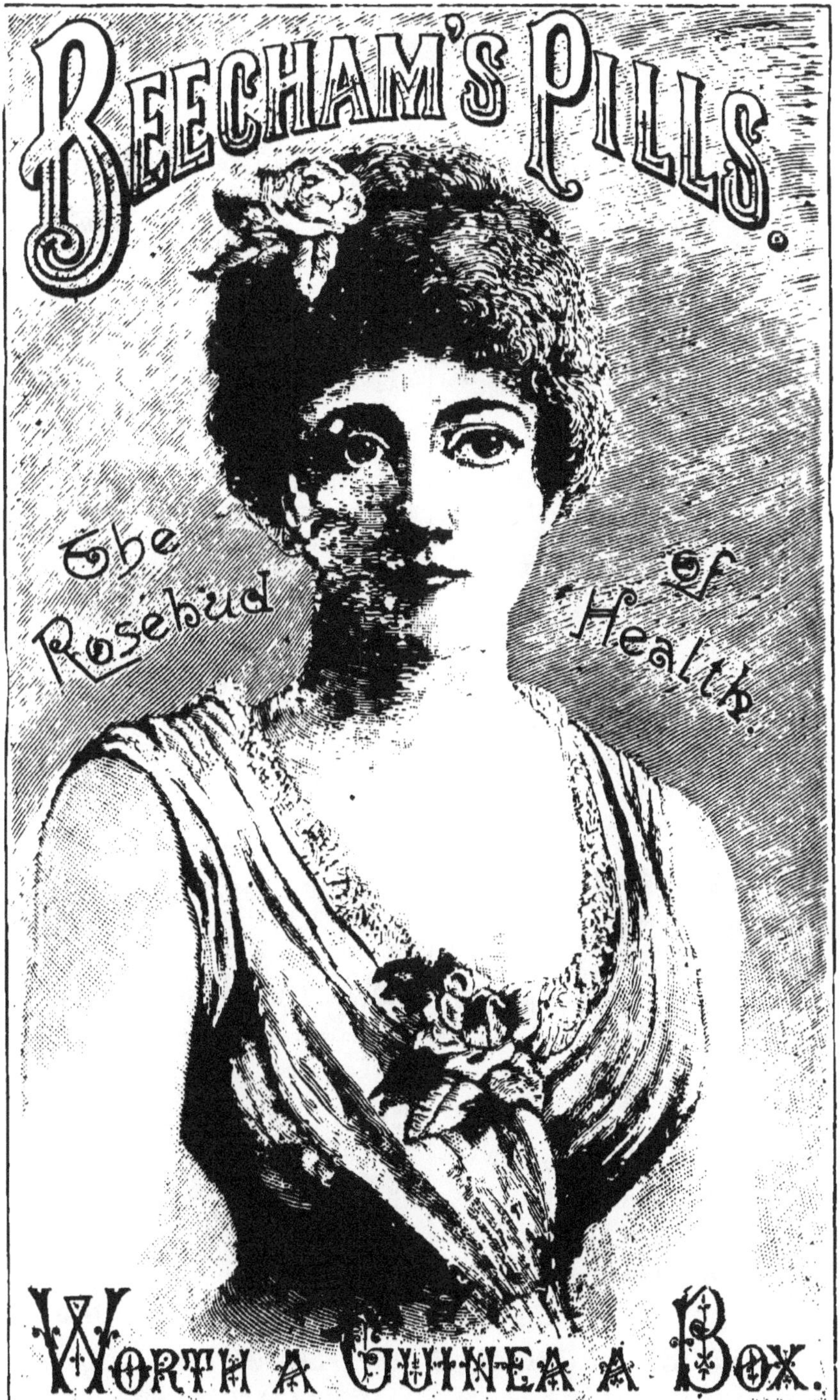
BEECHAM'S PILLS.
The Rosebud of Health.
WORTH A GUINEA A BOX.

...USTRIALS: Adventures & experiences among Curious Industries. By ALEXANDER H. JAPP, LL.D., F.R.S.E., Author of "Industrial Curiosities," "Golden Lives," &c., &c. Crown 8vo, cloth, 6s.

CONTENTS:—Quinine and its Romance—Curiosities of Canary Culture — Rice — Pearls — Amber — Common Salt — Burton Ale and Dublin Stout — Petroleum — Electric Telegraph — Railway Whistle—Historical Bedsteads—Knives and Forks—Arsenic in Industry—Famous Diamonds—Artificial Diamonds—Postage Stamps.

## IMPERIAL GERMANY: A Critical
Study of Fact and Character. By SIDNEY WHITMAN. Crown 8vo., cloth, 7s. 6d.

## MORAL ORDER AND PROGRESS:
An Analysis of Ethical Conceptions. By S. ALEXANDER, Fellow of Lincoln College, Oxford. Being a New Volume of "The English and Foreign Philosophical Library." Post 8vo., cloth, 14s.

## THE MORAL IDEAL: A Historic
Study. By JULIA WEDGWOOD. Second Edition. Demy 8vo., cloth, 9s.

## ISLAM; OR, TRUE CHRISTIANITY.
Including a Chapter on Mahomed's Place in the Church. By ERNEST DE BUNSEN. Crown 8vo., cloth, 5s.

# NEW NOVELS.

## GIRALDI; or, The Curse of Love.
(A Tale of the Sects.) By ROSS GEORGE DERING. In 2 vols. Crown 8vo., cloth, 12s.

## THE WING OF AZRAEL. By MONA
CAIRD. In 3 vols. Crown 8vo., cloth, £1 11s. 6d.

## UNCLE PIPER, OF PIPER'S HILL:
A Novel of Australian Life. By TASMA. Second Edition. Crown 8vo., cloth, 6s.

## A MODERN PALADIN. By EDWARD
JENKINS, Author of "Ginx's Baby," &c Cheap Edition. Crown 8vo., cloth, 5s.

## ULLI: The Story of a Neglected Girl.
Translated from the German of EMMA BILLER. By A. B. DAISY ROST. Crown 8vo., cloth, 5s.

# NEW BOOKS OF POETRY.

## IN MY LADY'S PRAISE. Being
Poems Old and New, written to the Honour of FANNY, LADY ARNOLD, and now Collected, for her Memory by Sir EDWIN ARNOLD M.A., K.C.I.E., C.S.I., Author of "The Light of Asia." &c., &c. Imperial 16mo., parchment, 3s. 6d.

## FLOWERS OF THE NIGHT. A New
Volume of Poems. By EMILY PFEIFFER, Author of "Gerard's Monument," "The Rhyme of the Lady of the Rock." "Under the Aspens," "Sonnets," &c. Crown 8vo., cloth, 6s.

## THE DAWN OF DEATH. By LUS-
COMBE SEARELLE, F.R.G.S., Composer of "Tone Poems," the Operas "Estrella," "Bobadil," "Isidora," &c. Crown 8vo., cloth, 4s. 6d.

## INDIA: A Descriptive Poem. Dedi-
cated by kind permission to His Excellency the Right Hon. the Earl of Lytton G.C.B., G.C.S.I., C.I.E., H.B. Majesty's Ambassador at Paris (late Viceroy and Governor-General of India), by H. B. W. GARRICK, Assistant Archæologist to the Government of India. Crown 8vo., cloth, 7s. 6d.

# THE LOTOS SERIES.

Post 8vo., bound in two styles—(1) cloth, gilt back and edges; (2) half-parchment, cloth sides, gilt top, uncut, each 3s. 6d.

*First Volume.*

## BARON MUNCHAUSEN: The Travels
and Surprising Adventures of Baron Munchausen. With Original Illustrations by ALFRED CROWQUILL.

*Second Volume.*

## THE BREITMANN BALLADS. By
CHARLES G. LELAND. Author's Copyright Edition, with a New Preface and Additional Poems.
A NEW, REVISED, and ENLARGED EDITION.

*Third Volume.*

## ESSAYS ON MEN AND BOOKS. Se-
lected from the Earlier Writings of LORD MACAULAY. With Critical Introduction and Notes by ALEXANDER H. JAPP, LL.D., F.R.S.E., Author of "Life and Writings of Thomas De Quincey," "German Life in Literature," &c. With Portraits.

101 Large-Paper Numbered Copies (only) of each Volume have been printed for sale in England, price 12s. 6d. each, net.

# LONDON: TRÜBNER & Co., LUDGATE HILL.

www.ingramcontent.com/pod-product-compliance
Lightning Source LLC
Chambersburg PA
CBHW020118030726
47498CB00006B/2159